Dramatherapy for People with Learning Disabilities

A World of Difference

of related interest

Art Therapy and Dramatherapy
Masks of the Soul
Sue Jennings and Åse Minde
ISBN 1 85302 027 3 hb
ISBN 1 85302 181 4 pb

Dramatherapy with Families, Groups and Individuals
Waiting in the Wings
Sue Jennings
ISBN 1 85302 144 X pb
ISBN 1 85302 014 1 hb

Post Traumatic Stress Disorder and Dramatherapy
Treatment and Risk Reduction
Linda Winn
Foreword by Alida Gersie
ISBN 1 85302 183 0

Storymaking in Education and Therapy
Alida Gersie and Nancy King
ISBN 1 85302 519 4 hb
ISBN 1 85302 520 8 pb

Storymaking in Bereavement
Dragons Fight in the Meadow
Alida Gersie
Foreword by Ofra Ayalon
ISBN 1 85302 176 8 pb
ISBN 1 85302 065 6 hb

Play Therapy
Where the Sky Meets the Underworld
Ann Cattanach
ISBN 1 85302 211 X

Play Therapy with Abused Children
Ann Cattanach
ISBN 1 85302 193 8 pb
ISBN 1 85302 120 2 hb

Focus on Psychodrama
The Therapeutic Aspects of Psychodrama
Peter Felix Kellerman
Foreword by Jonathan D. Moreno
ISBN 1 85302 127 X

Dramatherapy for People with Learning Disabilities

A World of Difference

Anna Chesner

Foreword by Sue Emmy Jennings

Jessica Kingsley Publishers
London and Bristol, Pennsylvania

Note

The names and some identifying details of clients described have been changed to preserve confidentiality.

First published in the United Kingdom in 1995 by
Jessica Kingsley Publishers Ltd
116 Pentonville Road
London N1 9JB, England
and
1900 Frost Road, Suite 101
Bristol, PA 19007, U S A

Copyright © 1995 Anna Chesner
Foreword copyright © 1995 Sue Emmy Jennings

Library of Congress Cataloging in Publication Data
Chesner, Anna
Dramatherapy for People with Learning Disabilities
I. Title
616.891523
ISBN 1–85302–208–x

British Library Cataloguing in Publication Data
A CIP catalogue record for this book is available from the British Library

Printed and Bound in Great Britain by
Biddles Ltd., Guildford and King's Lynn

Contents

Foreword

This is an excellent book with which to approach the Millenium. It is the first book to address the contemporary issues in the application of dramatherapy with people who have learning disabilities. In the past, authors and practitioners have addressed various aspects of creative drama which have contributed to dramatherapy, such as: developmental movement, educational drama, remedial drama, and life and social skills. Anna Chesner's thoughtful writing moves the theory and practice forward in an accessible way.

Chapter 1 introduces the reader to this focused area of practice and addresses difficult issues such as terminology, and societal attitudes. Dramatherapy process is conceptualised as a tree which grows from solid roots in the earth, to the trunk of structure and containment, which expands into branches of imagination and expression and is able to transform with the leaves of insight and change, birth and death. Chapter 2 describes the preliminary processess 'from Referral to Goal Setting' and is model of clarity with a step-by-step progression. The eight stages of the diagnostic spectogram are very helpful. Chapter 3 addresses that difficult area of work with profound learning disability and again provides basic principles and working structures. Chapter 4 acknowledges the pioneering work of Veronica Sherborne and describes a myriad of possible movement and dance work including the 'movement poem' and the 'circle dance'. Chesner rightly states that movement and self-massage are crucial for roots, grounding and trust. Chapter 5 moves on to dramatherapy and games, and provides a varied range of graded game structures. Chapter 6 is a detailed case-history of one-to-one dramatherapy with demonstrates the importance of establishing a shared language. It is well illustrated with client pictures and explains how the dramatherapist enables the client 'to find a form for the feelings', which may include fury and revenge. Chapter 7 provides a working methodology and conceptual framework for group dramatherpy which is followed by a collaboration in Chapter 8 between dramatherapy and music therapy. Chapter 9, the final chapter, breaks unique ground with a psycho-dramatic approach to dramtherapy for people with learning disabilities.

The strength of this book is in its up-to-date, 'user-friendly' mode of writing which includes dialogues, vignettes as well as client illustrations. Chesner has broken new ground in building bridges between dramatherapy and music therapy as well as dramatherapy and psychodrama. I remember how scary it felt when Åse Minde and I wrote about the relationship between art therapy and dramatherapy (Jennings and Minde 1993.) Perhaps this is the wind of change as we approach the Millenuim: a building of bridges between the arts therapies and a discovery of the fuitful and creative outcome when these professions take risks with each other. Above all, Chesner helps us to understand this 'world of difference' where energy can be harnessed in new and exciting ways, through the artistic and therapeutic process of dramatherapy.

Sue Emmy Jennings PhD
Stratford-upon-Avon

CHAPTER 1

Introduction
A World of Difference

We are approaching the end of the millenium, a point in time which stands somehow in the collective consciousness as a kind of marker in the long history of our civilisation. Society has developed and advanced in many ways over the centuries; yet our attitude towards difference highlights our continuing proximity to primitive and irrational fear. Although there have been improvements in care and in attitudes towards people with learning disabilities, this group still tends to be marginalised in our society. We are not sure how to name them, and we are not sure where to place them. Their identity as a minority group and their position within society as a whole is a cause for collective confusion and unease.

Our discomfort seems to stem from the fact of difference. The difference from our assumed norm is many faceted, and, if we look at people with learning disabilities, it is often very visible. It may manifest itself physically in terms of genetic abnormalities, sensory impairment, damage to the person sustained before, during or after birth. It may be expressed behaviourally in terms of autistic, obsessive, disturbed, confused, institutionalised or angry behaviours that are very different from what is socially expected and acceptable. It may be apparent in terms of communication skills. In a society where the spoken and written word is the currency for sophisticated communication of abstract ideas and the means by which we build relationships, we find it hard to communicate with those whose verbal skills are limited or non-existent. Difference is also expressed in terms of overall presentation and lifestyle. This is a complex area and depends on a multiplicity of factors. Clothes may have been chosen by a carer or a parent, or they may be worn with a lack of awareness of the finer points of grooming. Posture may express the low self-image accumulated and reinforced over time, or a lack of spatial awareness. Ideas that are expressed by people with learning disabilities may have their origin exclusively in the spoken word, or in television. Books, travel, and full participation in the available culture are enriching influences that may be virtually absent from the identity of some people with learning disabilities.

A particular aspect of learning disabilities that is the cause of major discomfort when faced head on is the fact that much of the difference is permanent. We are not dealing with a short term or temporary disease, or something that people can simply grow out of. While some apparent learning disability may have its roots in emotional trauma that can be worked through in therapy, most people with learning disabilities will continue to be different and learning disabled throughout their life. Their existence may be a reminder that there is suffering in the world, unfairness and perhaps bad luck. Another view of people with learning disabilities seeks to deny these uncomfortable elements and to focus exclusively on the fact of difference as 'specialness'.

Facing these factors causes discomfort. How is society to incorporate this group of people? Whilst groups of people with physical or sensory impairment are willing to identify themselves and give themselves a clearer voice and more public visibility, they are often at pains to dissociate themselves from learning disability. It is understandable that someone with purely physical limitations should wish people to know that they still expect to be treated as an intelligent human being. The outcome for people with learning disabilities, however, is that they are sometimes marginalised even within the world of disability.

Naming and Placing People with Learning Disabilities

Valerie Sinason (1992) explores the historical difficulty with naming this client group at length. Current terminology amongst professionals includes 'mental handicap', 'learning difficulties' and 'learning disabilities'. I use the term 'learning disabilities' which is the label most commonly accepted in health and social service contexts at present. I prefer it to the 'cap in hand' associations of 'handicap'. The term 'difficulties' does not for me do justice to the permanency and profundity of the problems faced by this client group. I experienced myself as having learning 'difficulties' when I struggled to learn to drive some years ago; my problem was a temporary one that I eventually surmounted. Although I choose the term 'learning disabilities' for use in this book, I am not entirely happy with that either. I notice that, when I talk to non-specialists about my work, I have to add a definition or description in order that they understand who I am talking about. There is still some confusion in the public mind between mental illness and learning disability. Perhaps this has its origin in the marginalisation of the client group, and is a problem of awareness and attitude that cannot be changed through purely semantic means.

As to the question of the place people with learning disabilities have in our society, this is reflected quite literally in the issue of where they should live. We are in the middle of a process whereby people who have lived in large institutions, for many years in some cases, are being 'resettled' into the 'community', often to live in group homes of varying sizes. Some have lived and continue to live in the family home in the community. The general trend is a move away from large institutional settings into the community, an attempt to integrate the client group with the population as a whole. Reactions from clients, families, carers and the public vary considerably. For some, the change is welcome and long awaited; for others it is seen as the loss of specialised provision, and the loss of home.

The clients I work with, and whose dramatherapy processes have provided much material for this book, are part of this historical change. I have witnessed women who have spent seventy years within a large institution finding their way back into the wider community: a community from which they were originally banished, not because of significant learning disabilities, but because of family circumstances, or unacceptably promiscuous behaviour. Over the decades, the fact of institutionalisation in itself becomes disabling. Expectations and self-image are defined within the context of the large ward and the institutional lifestyle. As part of a resettlement team I have seen such women weep with pride (and many other feelings) as they have used a telephone for the first time in preparation for the move into the community; and after the move I have seen some of these women find their voice, their assertiveness and even their mobility skills.

For these people, the move into the community at large is a blessing. In the light of such cases it is tempting to see the closure of the large residential institutions as totally positive. However, it is important to remember that these institutions have been home to many people with learning disabilities. They are a community in their own right, at best a community that caters for the specific needs of the population that lives there. They can provide a degree of autonomy and freedom that is unavailable in the community at large. Behaviours which are odd and would be seen as disturbing in the wider community can be more easily tolerated within the special community of the large residential institution. People who have been free to wander around the large institution and its grounds can find themselves isolated within a small group home in the community, unable to go out without an escort, and in effect trapped and isolated within an apparently 'normal' environment.

Without the habitual outlets for self-expression and connection with the familiar environment, clients can lose the skills that they have, and more importantly, the meaning they have in their life.

The issues are complex, and there is ongoing debate. Whatever the advantages and disadvantages of the various options, the climate is one of change, with all its attendant feelings of hope, fear, loss and disappointment. This forms the background to the examples of dramatherapy process I refer to in this book; the psychological climate that is internalised by clients and staff alike. Most of the sessions I describe have taken place within the dramatherapy studio of a large residential institution that has been in a continual process of change for the last five years. From the perspective of the institution, 'the community' is often charged with an aura of mythological significance, as people prepare to move onwards into it, or part with friends and colleagues who move on first. It may be seen as heaven on earth, a place just outside the 'hospital' gates where dreams come true and all needs are met. At the same time the institution itself may be seen as a place of security and familiarity, a living community under threat of closure or radical change. From this perspective the move away from 'home' and into the community at large can be feared as a kind of banishment into invisibility, Hansel and Gretel abandoned in the woods.

The confusion with names and places is reflected also in how we name the large institutions that are undergoing change or closure. They were built as hospitals and are still run on a medical model. The word 'hospital' is now no longer considered appropriate, and is often changed to 'unit'. 'Wards' have been renamed 'homes' or 'bungalows' to reflect changing attitudes to the client group and in some cases changes in actual lifestyle. The old identities and roles, however, run deep; I use the terms 'resident', 'home' and 'unit' in the text, except where the more old-fashioned terms 'patient', 'ward' and 'hospital' more truly reflect the roles, identities and dynamics of the situations described.

Life on the Margins

As a client group, people with learning disabilities find themselves on the margins of society by virtue of their difference. Even professionals have tended to focus on the fact of their learning disabilities at the expense of addressing the wider issues of emotional suffering within a holistic view of the person. Mainstream psychotherapists have historically considered this group of people incapable of making use of verbal psychotherapy. Valerie Sinason has made a major contribution to changing this perception both through her clinical work and her writing (1992). Psychotherapy for people with learning disabilities is now on the map.

By contrast, dramatherapy in the UK has its roots in work with this client group. Sue Jennings' (1978) pioneering work in 'remedial drama', for example, was influential in establishing dramatherapy as a recognised profession. However, as the profession has grown and developed there has been a shift in focus to a wide spectrum of client groups, such that dramatherapy for people with learning disabilities is now a relatively small specialism within the profession. Dramatherapy is an immensely flexible and creative method, and is used within the full spectrum of mental health, forensic, educational and training environments. The specialist use of dramatherapy for people with learning disabilities does not play a central role in the professional training courses in the UK and even runs the risk of being placed on the margins of clinical dramatherapy work.

When I began my own clinical work with this client group I learnt quickly that expectations based on other client groups I had worked with were not always appropriate in this new context. Through a process of trial and error, and through reflection on what was working and what was not, I gradually learnt some approaches to the clinical practice of dramatherapy with people with learning disabilities. My invaluable teachers in this process were the clients. The looks of incomprehension at some of my suggestions for working structures, and the moments of creative delight I witnessed when the work was accessible gave me the direct and honest feedback I needed to develop the work.

My hope in writing this book is that other dramatherapists working with or intending to work with this client group will find encouragement and food for thought from the working practices and processes I describe. The non-dramatherapist may gain an understanding of the kind of work that the dramatherapist might facilitate, and of the points of connection and difference with the non-clinical drama worker or drama teacher. Professionals from other disciplines may see the potential for creative co-working projects.

Drama and Theatre Concepts

Dramatherapy has its roots in the processes of drama and theatre. Of all the art forms this is perhaps the most inclusive, incorporating elements of music, movement, design, story and performance. The experience of theatre is one in which people come together in a social context to witness another reality, to participate in a different world that exists within a special defined space for a defined period of time. There is something other worldly and magical about this, suggesting that the theatre is essentially a place of escape and fantasy. At the same time theatre gives form to questions and issues that are of real concern in the real lives, whether private or collective, of the audience members.

It is worth considering some key concepts from the worlds of drama and theatre in the light of dramatherapeutic process in general and of people with learning disabilities in particular.

Drama The word has its roots in the Greek 'dran', meaning 'to do'. A therapy based in doing is a therapy of action, as distinct from talking. In everyday life we express ourselves through action. At times this action is devoted to work, at other times to leisure or play. Dramatherapy uses all kinds of actions and activities to facilitate therapeutic processes; the body and senses are engaged as well as the mind and verbal function. An action based therapy has the potential to be more holistic than a purely verbal therapy. This is of particular relevance to people with learning disabilities, whose verbal skills are often limited, and who tend to have fewer options for self-expression through action in everyday life.

Performance In the theatrical context a performance is a special shared theatrical moment involving both actors and audience. In everyday life there are many moments in a day when we experience ourselves as actors engaged in action in the presence of an observer or witness. Similarly there are many times when we are the audience to another or others in action. Even when we are alone, it can be argued that we are our own audience, a part of us witnessing ourselves as actors in action. Dramatherapy can help us to look at the way we experience ourselves in action, and to examine how we sense the world as audience views us. Life as performance is in this sense closely allied to identity and self-esteem. These are core issues for people with learning disabilities, who often expect to be passive and to be seen as passive. These essential features of drama and theatre can highlight and challenge these assumptions.

Role This dramatic concept is closely linked to character and identity. Through drama a participant or actor can experience a wider variety of roles than would be available to be played in real life, and indeed can move in and out of them with flexibility. The expansiveness and fluidity of this process is profoundly therapeutic. By temporarily adopting roles that are alien to our habitual life roles we can learn something transformative about the possibilities of change. What we consider to be permanent features of our identity may be nothing more than habitual patterns of posture, breathing, facial expression and thought patterns. Dramatherapy is helpful in encouraging people to expand their role repertoire, the range of roles available to us in life. People with learning disabilities, whose role repertoires tend to be limited, can discover other modes of expression and new possibilities in their own lives through playing with role in the context of dramatherapy.

Rehearsal Theatrical performances are prepared through rehearsal. The moment of performance in front of the audience is a moment of great excitement and great risk. We would be foolish to enter such a moment without appropriate preparation. Even in improvised pieces, where spontaneity and the unexpected are a valued part of the end experience, there is a period of training and preparation that enables the emergence of something fresh and spontaneous in performance. Actual performance projects constitute only a small part of the range of activities included within dramatherapy, but the philosophy of rehearsal is applicable in a broader context. Dramatherapy applies the principle of rehearsal and skilful preparation to everyday life. Performance anxiety is a normal life experience. People with learning disabilities benefit particularly from the element of familiarity in rehearsal that is implicit in the French word for rehearsal, *répétition*. The ritualised, repetitious aspects of dramatherapy, that have their roots in the notion of rehearsal, help to provide a feeling of safety and adequacy in a client group that suffers from profound feelings of inadequacy.

Story/Plot Within the dramatic improvisation or the theatrical performance occurs the creation of a different world, an imaginary world where anything could happen. We all carry with us our own histories or narratives, through which we identify ourselves. Dramatherapy allows the exploration not only of these narratives, but also of other, different ones. We can explore what was in terms of personal experience, what might have been, and what might never have been. Subjective experience can be given expression through mythological and metaphorical means. The range of expressive form within dramatherapy is vast. For people with learning disabilities, stories created within dramatherapy open up new and different worlds. At this level story work gives the opportunity to expand life experience. Beyond this is the further level of power. In life the person with learning disabilities often experiences their story as written by others. Within the dramatherapy session the client can be author and director rather than an extra in their own story.

Levels of Dramatherapy Process – The Tree

The range of clients with particular needs, problems and levels of ability included within the classification of learning disability is vast. Dramatherapy offers a variety of working methods that are applicable to a wide variety of clients within the full spectrum of learning disabilities. Some of these methods are applicable across the board, others are relevant only to those with some verbal ability, whose learning disabilities are relatively mild but who may be described as having 'challenging behaviours' or superimposed mental illness.

I have charted the various levels addressed by different dramatherapy processes through the image of the tree. As a symbol of holistic growth, creativity and the life–death cycle, the tree is a fitting image to portray the interconnectedness of the several types of dramatherapy process explored in this book.

I have divided the tree into four zones: roots, trunk, branches and leaves. Each of these has associations with certain characteristics and elements, which are addressed by particular kinds of dramatherapy process, and by particular working methodologies.

> **Roots** The foundation for all dramatherapy work relates to the elements of earth and water. Roots anchor a tree in the earth, are largely out of sight, but are indispensable for receiving nourishment and facilitating growth. In terms of therapeutic process, the dramatherapist works towards giving the client an experience of safety. The therapeutic environment is one where a client may learn to trust. This trust takes the form of a trust of the space, of the therapist, of the group in the case of group dramatherapy and of the self. If the therapy space feels insecure, or the presence of the therapist is unreliable, it is difficult for the client to take in the nourishment that is offered.

Clients experience grounding initially through the basic containment of the therapy space and the presence of the therapist. In terms of an intrapersonal process a variety of structures using movement, contact and an exploration of the senses helps to put the client in touch with his or her own body, and the body's relationship with the environment. For the profoundly and multiply disabled client this work may be the most relevant focus for the entire period of dramatherapy. Indeed the more sophisticated processes higher up the tree may be inaccessible to many such clients. Root level work

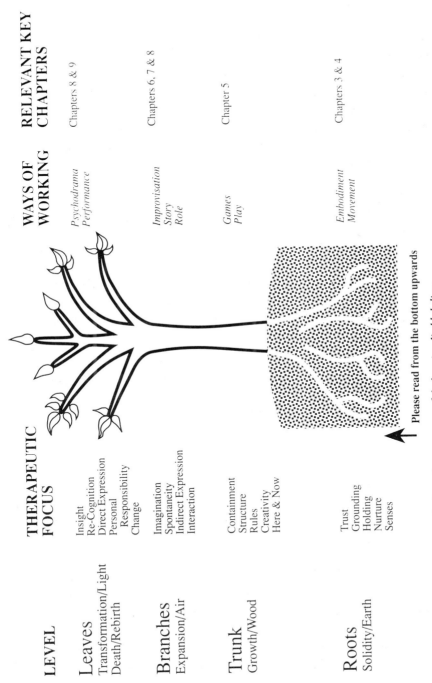

LEVEL	THERAPEUTIC FOCUS	WAYS OF WORKING	RELEVANT KEY CHAPTERS
Leaves Transformation/Light Death/Rebirth	Insight Re-Cognition Direct Expression Personal Responsibility Change	*Psychodrama* *Performance*	Chapters 8 & 9
Branches Expansion/Air	Imagination Spontaneity Indirect Expression Interaction	*Improvisation* *Story* *Role*	Chapters 6, 7 & 8
Trunk Growth/Wood	Containment Structure Rules Creativity Here & Now	*Games* *Play*	Chapter 5
Roots Solidity/Earth	Trust Grounding Holding Nurture Senses	*Embodiment* *Movement*	Chapters 3 & 4

Please read from the bottom upwards

Figure 1.1. The tree: orientation to the dramatherapy process of the learning disabled client.

can however effect profound change, often at an unconscious, subterranean level. A change in the degree to which a person can trust their own physicality, their own relationship to the immediate environment and to one or more significant others is a meaningful change.

Whilst for some clients the entire experience of dramatherapy will focus on embodiment and trust, for others the root level processes constitute an essential starting point for further work. Movement warm-ups and trust games can help to create a group space which is safe enough for a journey towards other, less concrete realities. Chapter 3 (on profound disability) and Chapter 4 (on movement work) refer predominantly to root level processes. This level of therapeutic process is also implicit as a starting point in the chapters on group dramatherapy (Chapter 7) individual dramatherapy (Chapter 6) and psychodrama (Chapter 9).

> **Trunk** The trunk of the tree is the part that emerges from the earth and provides the impetus for branching out and reaching upwards towards the light and the air. Its prime characteristics are growth and contained direction. Its form is apparently simple, but it contains the potential for the later complexity of the branches and leaves. It is a space of transition and transformation, the place between the hidden, sensory world of the roots and the full expressiveness of the upper part of the tree.

The trunk represents a vital zone of transition between the non-demanding dramatherapy processes of root level work and the highly complex possibilities of full dramatic exploration represented by the higher zones of the tree. The kind of processes that allow this transition are based in games and play. Working with games helps to develop simultaneously a recognition of form and an experience of freedom. When playing a game there are rules which should be observed, and which work as a container for spontaneous expression. Spontaneity without form may verge on chaos. Form without playfulness may be controlling and limiting. The combination of structure and fun that is implicit in playing games is a *sine qua non* for improvisational, story and performance based work. Trunk level work facilitates the mastery of a basic grammar or syntax out of which can grow a more creative use of the language of drama. Without an appreciation of boundaries, of turn-taking, give and take, and the spirit of playfulness there is little point in trying to tackle a free improvisation or a dramatic performance.

As with the root level work, there are some clients or groups for whom trunk level activities represent the extent of complexity appropriate for their therapeutic process. The level of imagination required is relatively low. The work takes place predominantly in the here and now (see Chapter 5 on games). Some clients will naturally expand the rules of the games into areas of make believe and role work. Others will be challenged and rewarded enough by the new shared language of the game, through which interaction with the group or therapist is facilitated.

> **Branches** At this point the form of the tree begins to express its complexity. As the roots spread themselves in the element of earth and physical solidity, so the branches expand through the element of air. This is the element of thought and expressiveness. There is an abundance of possibilities, of different routes or dramatic structures that can be travelled at this time.

Non-specialists attempting to 'do a bit of drama' without a full appreciation of the skills involved sometimes make the mistake of attempting to facilitate work at this level from the outset. It may be a long time before there is sufficient trust (anchorage in the roots) and sufficient discipline and spontaneity (mastery of the trunk) to support branch level work. For some clients or groups it may never be a relevant way of working. Its complexity and abstraction may be threatening or too demanding at a cognitive level.

This is the level of work in which there is an agreement to suspend disbelief, to inhabit a world of make-believe temporarily for part of the session. The make-believe world might be a well-known story, a story of the clients' own making, or a make-believe place in which the clients interact as themselves. The work usually involves taking on new characteristics and roles, or expressing new aspects of familiar roles. In this phase of work it is possible to inhabit a different world, and to express personal and interpersonal issues through the fiction or metaphor.

Processes at this level are explored in the chapters on group dramatherapy, individual dramatherapy and the use of fairy tales. In each of these modes questions arise as to the degree of conscious awareness clients bring to their therapy. Some issues may be addressed through the apparent disguise of the imaginary world that would be too threatening to look at directly. There may on occasion be an acknowledgement of the personal significance of an improvisational piece of work, but this is not always essential, possible or even desirable. An important part of the therapy at this level rests in the fact of creativity, which can be transformative in its own right. Whilst psychotherapy often focuses on problems or solutions to problems, the arts therapies, including dramatherapy, can focus on nurturing what is healthy and alive in the inner world of the person through creativity. Dysfunctional aspects of the person are sometimes more easily addressed within the context of an overall celebration of what is right in the client.

> **Leaves** At the far extremities of the tree the leaves represent the processes of transformation. Their medium is light, transformed into energy and growth. Their life cycle through the seasons epitomises the cycle of continuous change, of death and rebirth, that is integral to the larger life cycle of the tree as a whole.

In therapeutic terms the leaves are suggestive of processes that engage the light of conscious awareness, facilitating insight into self and others. This level of work presupposes some ability to take personal responsibility for change. A relatively high level of cognitive skills is necessary so that personal issues or patterns can be re-cognised, expressed and worked through. Dramatherapy structures that are suited to this sophisticated level of work include psychodrama and performance projects. In both of these, clients use expressive skills in a complex and sensitive way, taking responsibility for shifting between realities, and making connections between these different worlds. I refer to these methods in Chapter 9 (on psychodrama) and in Chapter 7 (on dramatherapy in groups). There are also moments of insight process within the individual dramatherapy work of Lucy (Chapter 6), and within the dramatherapy and fairy tales project (Chapter 8).

None of these levels is exclusive. The therapeutic process moves between the different zones and types of dramatherapy structure. It is useful for the dramatherapist to be able to articulate to herself or to colleagues the kind of therapy that a client is engaged in, and to notice when these levels change, or when there is a need for a change. It is not a sign of failure on the part of the client or the therapist to stay within one or two zones. Some clients will never have the cognitive or expressive abilities to benefit from branch or leaf level processes. Dramatherapy is flexible enough to work across the spectrum of clients with learning disabilities and it is the therapist's task to pitch the work at the appropriate level.

A Working Approach

Dramatherapy seems to be of value with this client group. Different clients my colleagues and I have worked with seem to have been supported by different aspects of dramatherapy process. As a dramatherapist I am often deeply moved by the creativity I witness in sessions, as well as by the content of what is expressed through one or other dramatherapy method. Sometimes I believe that I understand what is happening through the work. At other times I have a sense that what is happening is meaningful, without being able to define exactly what that meaning is.

I often experience doubt and uncertainty in this work. I used to feel rather ashamed of this, as though I should be more certain of the nature of each person's therapeutic journey through dramatherapy, and more certain of the precise nature of dramatherapy. My own attitude has changed. I am now more welcoming of doubt and uncertainty as friends or partners within the therapeutic process, that keep alive the need to question. I do search for meaning in the work, and I believe that the clients find meaning through the work. When I have an interpretation in mind, however, it is usually held quite loosely. I sense that too firm and exact an interpretation may be reductive and I could miss something living and complex in another person's experience as the price of my own comfort and certainty.

The dramatherapeutic journey happens on many levels. In this book I shine a light on some working methods, and some moments of group or individual process. The light is partial. Much of the journey still takes place in the dark, and with a sense of shared adventure.

CHAPTER 2

Preliminary Processes
From Referral to Goal-Setting

This chapter focuses on three processes which lay the foundation for a period of dramatherapy treatment: referral, assessment, contracting. Each of these help the dramatherapist and client in the setting of appropriate conditions and goals for dramatherapy.

Referrals

Whilst an informal, verbal or self-referral procedure has the advantage of enabling clients to take responsibility for their own choice of therapy, I prefer to back this up with a formal, written referral that involves other carers and professionals. This has a number of benefits.

(1) The referrer has the opportunity to share important information about the client: e.g. medical diagnoses and medication; physical abilities and disabilities and sensory problems; methods of communication; other therapies they are involved in, names of key workers, and the kind of social or family network of which they are part.

(2) The therapy is given a formal context and an official identity. This is particularly relevant in the light of dramatherapy being a relatively new profession – it may still be perceived as a leisure activity rather than a clinical intervention. The formality of the referral procedure encourages a more appropriate perception.

(3) The referrer is encouraged to consider the needs of the client, their own reasons for referring, and their expectations of the outcome of dramatherapy.

(4) The referrer is encouraged to support the therapy. Formal referral is the first step towards an agreement or contract for the therapy to take

place. The contract involves client, therapist and, usually, carer; at a very basic level the carer may need to be involved in helping the client get to the therapy sessions on a regular basis. It is also important for the carer to understand the possible reactions the client may have to the therapy, which can influence behaviour and mood in the home or work environment. The involvement in the therapy may go beyond this, in terms of the carer taking on the role of co-therapist or therapy assistant.

(5) Other people involved with the client are identified. It may be useful to liaise with other therapists, family members, carers or medical practitioners at some point during the course of dramatherapy.

What is on the referral form reflects attitudes of the referrer as well as providing information about the client. Reasons for referral may be specific e.g. 'to stop Claire screaming all day'; or generalised e.g. 'to help Charles develop relationships.' The way in which Claire's problem is perceived and described can give the dramatherapist some useful clues to the client's living environment. It is likely in this instance that Claire is a source of annoyance and distress to the staff and fellow residents of her home. The referrer, quite understandably, hopes for a behavioural change in Claire, or perhaps just some respite from being with her. The dramatherapist may wonder if Claire holds the identity of 'trying child', or 'the most difficult resident' in her home environment. The information on how the client is perceived by others indicates the kind of life roles she is likely to identify with. These roles are created and recreated reciprocally in a cyclical fashion. Claire perceives herself in a particular way and behaves accordingly. This behaviour leads to her being perceived by others in such a way that her self-perception is reinforced and the behaviour continues. An awareness of role helps the dramatherapist gain an appropriate perspective on the relationships as revealed through the referral form.

Assessment

Assessment has two main purposes. First, it provides an opportunity to begin to explore how the client presents, what her needs may be, and what therapeutic goals would be appropriate. Second, it aims to establish whether dramatherapy is an appropriate treatment for the client and whether client and therapist have the potential to work together. The referral itself constitutes the first phase of assessment of the client. It is usually indirect, coming from a third party and without necessarily involving face to face contact between therapist and client. This direct contact is the next phase: a preliminary meeting is arranged.

The preliminary meeting between therapist and client usually takes place on the client's territory, either the home or work environment. At an overt level this provides an opportunity for the therapist and client to introduce themselves to each other, and for the therapist to explain the reasons for the meeting. The meeting provides an opportunity for letting the client know that he or she is being offered the chance to take part in dramatherapy; to mention why they have been referred; to agree together how many times client and therapist will meet in order to decide whether to make a commitment; and to get to know each other a little.

At a more subtle level the meeting provides a wealth of information to the therapist, which forms part of the assessment for treatment.

Posture and body language

Habitual posture can be usefully looked at as a reflection of habitual identity, and habitual communication patterns. There are a number of considerations through which observations can be highlighted.

- **Posture** How open or closed is the posture? Is the client's energy dedicated to taking up as little space as possible, or is it expansive?

- **Dress** How does the client dress? Does she appear to take care of her appearance? Is she dressed in an age-appropriate manner, and is this a reflection of her tastes, or of the perception of her carers?

- **Eye contact** How extensive is eye contact? It may be avoided entirely, sought out eagerly, or fall somewhere between these extremes.

- **Mobility** How mobile is the client? Is she ambulant, how does she move around? Does she choose to be mobile or still during the meeting? How much control does she have over her movements?

- **Proximity** Does the client choose to be unusually close or unusually far from the therapist? If she is incapable of actively choosing her desired distance how does she respond to the proximity of the therapist? The client may reach out to grab and pull the visitor close. She may hit out, or shrink from proximity and contact.

- **Breathing** It is usually obvious if someone has breathing difficulties. We notice when someone wheezes or coughs. The dramatherapist needs to be aware also of the subtle breathing patterns of the clients, both at the first meeting and continually through the therapy. Is the breathing shallow or deep? Where does the client breathe from: throat, chest, belly? Is the breathing fast or slow, unobtrusive or laboured? Does the breathing communicate an emotional tone? Does it change noticeably according to different situations?

All observations about posture and body language at this stage must be seen in the context of this being a preliminary meeting. Although the client is on familiar territory she is probably meeting the therapist for the first time, and may be particularly anxious when confronted with an unfamiliar person. If her understanding is limited there may be all sorts of inexpressible fantasies about the therapist and the reasons for their meeting.

Communication methods

Some basic information about the client's ability to communicate may have been included at the time of referral, e.g. diagnoses of hearing impairment or autistic characteristics. Within the context of a one-to-one meeting with the therapist some preliminary first hand observations are appropriate, based on the following questions.

- Is the client verbal? Does she use single words, simple sentences, or complex sentences? Is she able to talk about herself and others ?

- Is the client vocal? She may not be able to speak but does she use vocalised sounds to communicate? What kind of voice tone is used?

- Does the client communicate by using methods of facial expression, and non-verbal communication, e.g. touch, pointing, gesture, either on their own or to enhance her verbal skills? Does the client use these methods to indicate an understanding of verbal communication?

- Does the client use/understand makaton sign language?

- Does the client avoid direct communication?

The sense of the relationship

Dramatherapy is essentially interactive, and it would be false to exclude the feeling responses of the therapist from the assessment, even at this preliminary meeting. The therapist has a number of roles on this occasion; visitor, professional, initiator, organiser, listener, observer of other, and observer of self.

The dramatherapist works at least partly in the realm of the subjective, and it is important that the therapist's own subjective responses be acknowledged from the outset in any therapeutic relationship. Throughout the preliminary meeting and after it the therapist asks herself, how does this interaction feel? What is my intuitive response to this other, and how do I experience them responding to me? Do I feel able to work with this person, and does the client seem able to work with me?

When a normally able person decides to go into therapy they may reasonably spend some time picking and choosing their therapist, on the basis of their reputation, their orientation, and above all on their sense of the therapist. In the case of someone with learning difficulties it may be very difficult to express a choice in this sense. Indeed, one of the common problems of people with learning disabilities is a lack of awareness of the possibility of making a choice, and then of expressing it. It is particularly important that the therapist encourage the client to voice a choice, if this is possible. If communication skills are inadequate the therapist can reflect on how workable the therapeutic relationship feels.

Moreno used the concept of *tele* to describe the interpersonal dynamic between people (Blatner 1988). Client and therapist alike have preferences for certain kinds of interactions and people. *Positive tele* describes the feeling of attraction and liking that may be experienced towards another or between two people. *Negative tele* describes a sense of repulsion or aversion towards another, or between people. *Neutral tele* refers to a more neutral chemistry in the interaction. In the context of the preliminary meeting between therapist and client, a mutually positive or neutral *tele* may indicate that there is a good starting point for a therapeutic collaboration. If the therapist experiences a profound aversion or negative *tele* towards the client she will need to consider carefully whether she can, or will, usefully work with the client. Similarly, if the therapist senses this kind of reaction from the client towards herself this needs to be acknowledged, and the same question asked. No hasty decision about the possibility of therapy needs to be made on the basis of one meeting. The important issue at this point is to bring the feeling quality of the relationship into the assessment picture, and to acknowledge that preferences exist for both parties.

Empathy has a role to play in the assessment meeting, as in all stages of dramatherapy process. The therapist may empathically 'tune in' to the feeling state of the client. This is an intuitive process, mediated by observations of posture, breathing, non-verbal communication, verbal communication and voice tone. The process mirrors that of the actor, who takes a script as starting point and feels his way into a character, attempting to find the appropriate physical and vocal style to embody the feelings, characteristics, and life of the role. In the case of the dramatherapist the starting point is the living physical presence of the person in interaction, and the therapist attempts to intuit the feelings experienced by the client.

The empathic connection is valuable in providing the therapist with a feeling sense of the client, a sense perhaps of sadness, anger, desperation or confusion. Assumptions must, however, be made with care. The therapist needs to question the origin of such feelings experienced during or after a session. Do they reflect the therapist's own conditioning or are they an authentic sense of the client's state? Such questioning is particularly important in the light of some clients' inability to correct verbally a false assumption made by the therapist.

The first few times I came across Paul, a non-ambulant, non-verbal man who seemed to scowl continually, and periodically made a deep growling sound, I sensed, or assumed, that he was angry, volatile and perhaps dangerous. I kept a careful distance from him. As I got to know him better I realised that the scowl was a permanent muscular characteristic, rather than an active change in facial expression signalling anger or dissatisfaction. I learnt to notice subtle expressions of his eyes that were a clearer indication of momentary mood changes and a method through which he could attempt to communicate directly. The growl seemed to be used to express interest, and as a statement of his presence, as much as to convey anger or fear, contrary to my initial impression.

So the empathic 'tuning in' to a client's feeling state needs to be accompanied by an open-minded attitude on the part of the therapist. Everyday social interaction depends on a complex web of signs and symbols, some of which the person with learning disabilities may not have learnt, or may not be physically capable of performing. It is only too easy to jump to wrong conclusions when interpreting what we see. We are used to creating meaning immediately and usually at an unconscious level. The therapist must learn to question some of these unconscious assumptions. If someone is physically incapable of smiling, does this mean they never experience happiness?

Studio based individual assessment

Following a preliminary meeting the client may be invited to come and explore the dramatherapy studio in a one to one context. This provides the client with an opportunity to familiarise herself with the space and the therapist. For the therapist one or two exploratory sessions in the fertile environment of the dramatherapy studio gives an opportunity to assess the client through action. The studio provides an environment in which the client is free to explore and express herself spontaneously, in relation both to the physical space and to the therapist.

The session is essentially client-centred and unstructured, except for the boundaries of time agreed in advance, and the boundaries of space provided by the studio. The space is prepared for the session so as to offer a variety of possibilities to the client. Pieces of equipment that may be of interest are set out in the space, or are left on view so as to be accessible if the client chooses to investigate them. Some parts of the room are left clear, so that there are spaces to move in or to retreat to. As a general principle the environment should give plenty of opportunity for choice, and the preparation of the space facilitates this.

(1) It is useful to create different different environments within the space as a whole. A soft area may be set up in a corner of the studio, using a combination of play shapes and gym mat. This space is suited to sitting or lying at ground level and offers possibilities for experiencing a sense of security, relaxation and enclosure. Elsewhere in the studio there may be bean bag chairs and more conventional chairs, one of which may be at a table. The varied use of coloured or dimmable lighting, as well as daylight, may enhance the mood of these different areas of the studio.

(2) The permanent decoration of the studio may provide unusual visual stimulus. There are two such areas in my studio, created as part of a client-centred community art project. At eye level in a large recessed alcove directly opposite the main entrance is a large tactile collage, depicting a night time scene, with fox, owl, spider, moths and tree against a moonlit starry sky. Above the central area of the studio is a recessed area of the ceiling, with small skylights and four walls. Here there is a bold daytime sky mural, depicting every kind of weather, depending on where the viewer is positioned. The whole is only visible if the viewer looks up. At a visual and symbolic level both dark and light, day and night are present in the space. This reflects the holistic principle that both positive and negative, conscious and unconscious material can be contained within the dramatherapy process.

(3) Musical instruments may be positioned around the space: some free standing ones such as drums and xylophone, some smaller ones, such as maracas or bells, perhaps on a table top, shelf, or inside a box. A tape recorder or hi-fi system may also be visible.

(4) Balls of a variety of textures, colours and sizes offer a multitude of possibilities for exploration and interaction. The largest foam variety, standing at about a metre high can be used as an aid to trust work, for leaning across, sitting on and being rocked. It can also provide an outlet for the expression of strong energy and feelings, by kicking or rolling it across the space. Smaller balls may be held, hidden, licked, rolled, kicked, bounced and used to engage in games with the therapist.

(5) Containers of different kinds provide an opportunity for the client to be curious. Baskets, boxes and bags, cupboards and trolleys may lead to the discovery of a collection of hats, masks, puppets, dolls, pieces of fabric, costume, pictures and small objects.

The possibilities for expressing choice in such an environment are virtually endless. It is a client-centred space and nothing is out of bounds. In home life, whether this be institutional or within the family, there is usually limited opportunity for the expression of spontaneity and curiosity. Other priorities, such as the domestic routine, staff duties, or the need for order take precedence.

The exploratory visit to the dramatherapy studio offers the client another kind of experience, one in which the process of discovery is the priority, and the role of the therapist is to support the client in this. How the client uses this time is an expression of his or her individuality and constitutes a core element in the assessment process, through which the therapist gauges what kind of issues may be relevant for the client to approach through therapy, and whether dramatherapy has something to offer them.

The therapist may consider several points during the exploratory sessions.

The client's relationship to the space is significant; preference for enclosed or open parts of the studio is individual. Sandy spent her session moving around the boundaries of the space, as close as possible to the walls, with an attraction for the most enclosed corner. She was so motivated to get to this corner that she climbed over a pile of bean bags to get there. She spent all her time on her feet, and was always on the move. Beside her need for walls and corners she was also keen to explore the three doors in and out of the space. Simon by contrast, found his way to the largest open space in the room and spent the session there, walking in a circle. He did not contact any other areas of the room, but did show interest in his own reflection, which he could see on a wall mounted mirror at a certain point in his repetitive cycle.

The degree of spontaneity and curiosity shown in the session varies across a wide spectrum. At one end of this spectrum is an entirely passive attitude.

Susie appeared to do nothing without a specific invitation/instruction, standing in the doorway or by a chair for extended periods of time until being 'told' to 'come in' or 'sit down'. At the other end of the continuum is the actively spontaneous and creative behaviour of Jo, who explored the whole space in a spirit of excitement and play, dressed up in a table cloth and witch's hat, discovered things from the back corner of a cupboard and actively drew the therapist into his world.

The specific objects or props which attract or repel a client can be noted. Therapeutic work can be developed through objects which interest a client, and changes in the variety of experiences or props used can indicate shifts or developments in the therapeutic process over time. The first time Harry visited the studio he sought out a doll at the bottom of an equipment trolley. This was quite a surprising choice for a middle aged man who presented as quite boisterous and confident. He sat alone holding the doll tenderly and murmuring to it. In subsequent sessions, in which he was part of a small group of three, he continued with this process. Initially he avoided any shared activities in the group. After some weeks one of the other men joined him as he held the doll, mirrored what he was doing with another doll, and they swapped dolls. In subsequent sessions Harry habitually began each session alone, holding the doll. This was his chosen warm-up to being in the group. When he felt ready he would put the doll away and join the group activity. I shall not attempt here to interpret his process with the doll. What is very clear, however, is that his relationship with the doll was meaningful for him from the outset. It facilitated his therapeutic process and was a significant part of his personal journey in therapy.

The balance between interest shown in the environment and interest shown in the therapist is also worth recording. It may feel less invasive to relate to objects than to a person. The therapist may be experienced as frightening. In the example of Sandy, above, she actively avoided proximity with the therapist, but always seemed to be acutely aware of my position. Other clients may need the therapist as audience or witness, to show something to, and for encouragement. Still others may direct most of their energy to the relationship with the therapist, through talking, physical contact, eye contact, games or even role play. The therapist may usefully note their own experience of the session, the tone or mood present between the client and therapist, and the kind of role or roles both parties played.

At this point the therapist may be in a position to create a preliminary role profile and assessment of needs of the client, from which some broad goals for therapy can be drawn up. A role profile is a way of describing in dramatherapeutic terms how the client presents, how he appears to view himself, and how he engages with his environment and the therapist.

A healthy and mature person has a wide role repertoire to draw from. Many of these roles provide satisfaction, fulfilling a variety of different needs for the individual and their social network. There may always be a proportion of roles which are dysfunctional or unsatisfactory, and it is part of an ongoing process of personal development to get to know these roles and to practice new ones. A narrow role repertoire indicates a lack of choice in life and a condition of being stuck; stuck with a particular range of feelings, stuck in certain familiar patterns of expression and behaviour, stuck in a particular self-image and stuck with the reflection of that self-image in others.

Role in this sense has little to do with 'playing' or 'play-acting', and more to do with a way of being in the world. It is at the heart of identity and self-expression. Moreno defines role as 'the functioning form the individual assumes in the specific moment he reacts to a specific situation in which other persons or objects are involved' (Fox 1987). It is the policy of many agencies working with people with learning disabilities to encourage a lifestyle where there is choice. Exploring and developing the role repertoire addresses this aim directly, and at a deep level, helping to equip the person with learning difficulties to make real choices in how she expresses herself in the world.

A sample role profile, made following a referral, meeting and two exploratory studio sessions.

Harry presents three striking roles:

- Harry as cheeky, flirtatious clown, keen to share a joke and to be liked. In this role he is quite adventurous, exploring the space, sharing his finds with the therapist, and initiating verbal/vocal interactions about what he has found.

- At the end of the session he presents a less playful, more demanding and controlling role, refusing to leave the studio unless arm in arm with the therapist. This role has elements of demanding child and masterful courtier.

- For a short period during the session, as mentioned above, he inhabits a more introspective, vulnerable role when he finds the doll. This role includes elements of nurturing parent and vulnerable baby.

On the basis of this role profile the therapist can consider how dramatherapy might serve Harry. It may be that he needs a space where he can express and integrate the vulnerable and nurturing role that he finds through the doll, a place where it is safe to let go of the clown mask for a while. It may also be relevant to explore his issues of control and of identity relating to age and sexuality. The therapy will not necessarily aim to tackle these issues head on. Dramatherapy process is seldom linear. It is, however, useful to bear in mind what his habitual roles are, and how Harry might develop more adequate ones. The role profile gives a framework through which the therapist can reflect on the meaning and process of the therapy. Imaginary roles played out in therapy can be seen in the light of these habitual life roles, highlighting the emergence of newness as well as the exploration of the habitual (Landy 1986).

Assessment Techniques

There follow three assessment techniques which can be used for more focused and investigative assessment of the individual, and some guidelines on group assessment.

Spectogram as assessment method

The spectogram or button sculpt (Jennings 1986) is a popular dramatherapy technique that can be used with adults or children. It provides a flexible and non-threatening form for the therapist to find out about the client, and for the client to reflect on their own world. It is essentially a projective method, through which the inner world of the client is projected onto external objects.

I have found it useful in the early stages of therapeutic work with a wide range of clients with learning difficulties. The form can be simplified or expanded according to the abilities of the client and the focus of the therapy. The way in which a client engages with the form helps the therapist assess the degree of abstraction the client can use, and gives some indication of their potential for reflection, insight and imagination.

A clear surface is required, either on the floor or on a table. The client is introduced to a box of small objects, collected by the therapist over time. My box includes marbles, shells, stones, beads, buttons and everyday objects of a similar size, such as a rubber, a small penknife, a small bell, miniature bottles of scent, screws and pieces of string. These objects should be of varying textures and colours, and appeal to as many senses as possible. I also include a couple of small toy animals, and a set of Guatemalan worry dolls. These are diminutive, thumb-nail size male and female dolls of which a dozen are kept in a small box. They are used traditionally to tell your worries to before going to sleep, so that you can rest peacefully, having let go of the troubles of the day. The Guatemalan people have an understanding of the significance of scale. However big your worries are, you can tell them one at a time to

towards, such as the desire to have friends, or to live more independently. Other changes can exist only at a fantasy level, such as the desire that someone dead were still alive. The expression of this desire through the spectogram can be seen as a statement of the strength of feeling around this relationship.

Step seven The client is invited to return the picture to the way it is in real life. The wished-for or magic change has been expressed and witnessed. It is now time to begin the de-roling process, by bringing the spectogram back to an expression of how things are in the client's life, and acknowledging the difference between wishes and reality. It may be appropriate at this point to talk about future goals for therapy.

Step eight The client is invited to put the objects back in their box, and to de-role them, so that they no longer represent the people in her life. A marble is a glass marble again and no longer her mother. Some people require longer than others to de-role the objects and distance themselves from the projected world. It is important to let the client make this transition at her own pace.

The method described here from step two onwards accesses the inner world of the client head on and explores it directly. This approach is fine for some clients who value the opportunity to talk about themselves, their history and their current life. Others may be more responsive to a more oblique approach, through which they ostensibly explore a fictional world, but one which nonetheless tends to express their concerns.

Variation of the method
Having explored the box of objects, the client is introduced to the idea that she and the therapist are going to make a story together, and show that story with the objects. Instead of choosing an object to represent herself, the client is asked to choose an object to represent the main character in the story. She may start with the idea of the character and find an object that suits it, or start with the object and then give the character a name. The therapist continues to elicit other characters in the same way, and to support the client in finding the spatial relationships between the characters. The setting of the story may emerge from the characters, or may be decided at the outset.

The role of the therapist is to facilitate the client in making the story, so that it is as far as possible a product of the client's imagination. This may involve asking a series of questions about what happens, and about what each character thinks, feels, wants and does. Therapist and client may share reflections about the characters and situations in the story as it unfolds. The therapist needs to be receptive to the story and sensitive to its subtext, the web of feelings and relationships the client expresses through it.

At the end of the story the client is encouraged to de-role the objects and put them away. Before this the therapist may invite her to find a title for the story. This helps to round off the process, and provides an opportunity for focusing on the essence of the story. A title also enables client and therapist to refer back to the story in the future. It symbolises an experience and language shared by them both.

Genogram as assessment method

This method is applicable only with clients capable of talking or signing. It is particularly useful for those who can read or write. Its value is in providing a pictorial representation of the client's perception of her place in the family. The genogram is essentially a family tree, and is drawn up by the therapist in response to the information about the family elicited from the client. Marriages, relationships and offspring are charted, using a square to represent male figures, and a circle for female ones (see Figure 2.1). I usually start with the client, and follow on with parents, siblings in order of age, grandparents, spouses etc. Deaths may be marked with a cross. The age, date and cause of death may also be noted. Separations and divorces may be marked with a single or double line respectively through the relationship line. The basic information can be supplemented by asking questions about those whom the client knows well, feels strongly about, likes or dislikes. The client may also be given the opportunity of choosing the colour for each person from a range of coloured felt pens. By considering the appropriate colour the client has the chance to express patterns, links between family members, and relationships where there are particularly strong feelings and attitudes. Conflictual feelings can be expressed with a zig-zag line, and particularly close relationships can be shown with a flowing line, or an extra thick line. Client and therapist can negotiate an appropriate code between them to highlight relevant aspects of the genogram.

The genogram can be useful in revealing factual information about the client's background and history. Its creation is a shared activity between therapist and client; there is an end product which is unique, and to which reference can be made in the future. Whilst some people are able to talk extensively about their extended family, and have a firm sense of their own place in it, others may have a more limited vision. I have observed that those with a strong sense of their place in the family tend to have a stronger sense of their own identity.

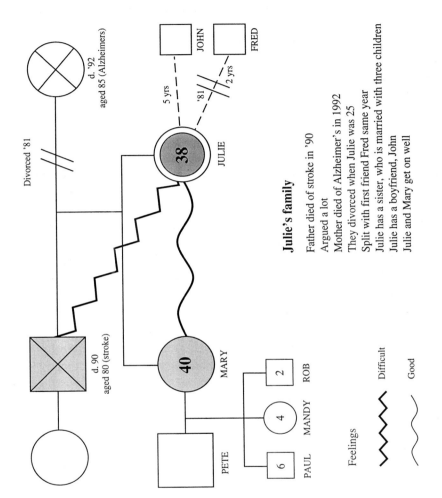

Julie's family

Father died of stroke in '90
Argued a lot
Mother died of Alzheimer's in 1992
They divorced when Julie was 25
Split with first friend Fred same year
Julie has a sister, who is married with three children
Julie has a boyfriend, John
Julie and Mary get on well

Figure 2.1

The genogram is not a specifically dramatherapeutic intervention, but as a shared creative activity in which client and therapist make something together it is very compatible with the spirit of dramatherapy. I first came across the use of the genogram in the context of group analytic psychotherapy. In this context it is used at interview to give the client the opportunity to talk about her family background, on the basis that familiar relationships tend to be repeated in the context of the group and through the process of transference. Patterns are replayed within the contained microcosm of the group, where there is the opportunity for confrontation, insight and change. Traditional psychotherapies tend to put considerable emphasis on the connection between the past and the present, and encourage the client to work towards coming to terms with past influences. The relevance of the technique to the dramatherapist working with people with learning disabilities is somewhat different. Whether the client lives within the family context, within a group home, or within an institutional setting, the opportunity to talk about personal origins and history can be valuable. Although subsequent therapy may address the issues indirectly through imaginative, creative and non-analytical processes, nonetheless the information shared through the genogram may help the therapist understand the client's therapeutic process. The work may reveal, for example, unresolved guilt, grief and confusion, which have a profound effect on the client's self-view. Later dramatherapy work may offer the chance to express and explore these feelings, at some dramatic distance, perhaps within the context of a story or improvisation.

Guided self-portrait as assessment

This method is suited to clients with some verbal facility and the ability to make a representational drawing. It is a table top activity, which provides an intermediary space between therapist and client that can help to alleviate the intensity of the assessment interview. The focus of the exercise is on self-image and image in the eyes of the other.

A selection of coloured felt pens and paper are laid on the table in preparation. As a first task the client is invited to draw a picture of himself, with an assurance that he does not have to be good at art.

The self-portrait reveals how the client sees himself. He is in a sense his own audience, and this is explored verbally using the drawing as a springboard. The client is invited to look at the picture and to offer some words to describe how the person in the picture appears. The client (if capable of writing) or the therapist makes a list of these words. In Vincent's case (Figure 2.2) he sees himself initially in terms of physical characteristics: as having

Figure 2.2. Self-portrait by a client

'ginger hair, blue eyes, very few teeth, a pointed nose', and then in terms of an overall impression as 'scary, in a rage, and weird'.

Since our self-image tends to be heavily influenced by how others have seen us in the past, Vincent is then asked to recollect how people have seen him historically. The words he gives are words he remembers hearing as a child: 'fat, spastic, look at him'.

A third viewpoint is elicited: how the client is seen by the people who know him now, especially the people he lives with or goes out with. This list is in Vincent's case a little more balanced than the childhood memories. He believes others would describe him as 'all right', 'a nice person', or 'a right sod'.

The fourth perspective is that of his family, who in Vincent's case see him as a bit of a Jekyll and Hyde, either 'nice' or 'a right sod'.

The assessment can develop further with the use of the spectogram, genogram, or conversation. The self portrait can be used again during or after a period of therapy as a way of noting any changes in self-perception.

Assessment for Group Dramatherapy

The composition of a dramatherapy group is important. With a compatible membership the group can become a real forum for creative work and personal change. With a slightly different mix of group members this chemistry may be absent and the group may never take off. There are no fixed rules to follow that will ensure a productive group chemistry. A group may be made up of people from the same home environment, or of people with apparently similar needs and issues. There is a place for single sex groups, as well as for mixed ones. It may be tempting to invite only verbal or non-verbal, ambulant or non-ambulant people into a particular group, on the basis that group members will be 'at a similar level' or have similar special needs. However, categorising clients according to these criteria is not necessarily relevant in the context of dramatherapy, and may limit the potential of the group. Some of the most productive dramatherapy groups in my experience have been made up of clients with a wide spectrum of need and ability in terms of mobility, verbal skills, and social skills. The very fact of difference can provide a relevant challenge to group members in overcoming their assumptions and prejudices about others and in finding ways to communicate together. After all, 'difference' is, paradoxically, something they have in common.

Particularly when setting up an open-ended or long term dramatherapy group it is useful to treat the first two or three meetings as group assessment sessions. Clients have the opportunity to vote with their feet, and withdraw from the group if they find that it is not what they want. The therapist can take the opportunity to consider the balance of participants and to make changes accordingly. There are usually some group members who are more dominant than others, and it would be undesirable to create a group where everyone felt equally visible and equally powerful even if this were possible. However, it may be that the particular behaviour or manner of one or more participants makes other, quieter group members too uncomfortable to use the group, and a different group might offer them a more favourable environment for finding their confidence.

Group assessment sessions are also useful for noting the level of social interaction within the group. A simple session structure, which offers a variety of experience, is set up; e.g. greeting song; greeting game; physical warm-up; parachute work; musical improvisation/circle dance; goodbye song.

After the session the therapeutic team reflects on:

- The level of contact between people during each phase of the session, in terms of eye-contact, physical contact, verbal communication. Expression of strong attraction or aversion between particular group members may be highlighted here.

- The level of cooperation between people. The parachute work reflects this directly as I have explored elsewhere (Chesner 1994a). If participants do not keep hold of the parachute it falls to the floor.

- The level of spontaneity. Appropriate spontaneity is evidenced where clients creatively add to, and go beyond, the structures suggested. Inappropriate spontaneity is shown where clients ignore the structures offered and follow their own impulses without consideration for the group.

- The kinds of activity that participants found easy or difficult, and enjoyed or disliked. Some group members may be particularly responsive to physical work, others to music or ball games.

The observations made at this point can be used to consider the compatibility of group members, and to inform the direction and goals of future work. Information noted at this stage becomes a useful reference point for noticing change. Since change tends to occur gradually it is useful to keep written records from the outset, both of individual and group activity.

Contracting

After assessment, the client and therapist decide whether or not to go ahead with a period of dramatherapy treatment. This should be a two-way negotiation, as far as is possible, although in reality some clients are more able to express their preferences and needs than others.

If the decision is to go ahead the therapist needs to consider the most appropriate form of therapy, one-to-one or group. One-to-one therapy is preferable where the client is too anxious to tolerate group work, or needs to focus on exploring their environment, or on building a relationship with one person. It may also offer a useful forum for in-depth, issue focused work, particularly where the material is inappropriate for sharing in a group, or there are time considerations that make a group approach inappropriate.

In other circumstances group dramatherapy can offer distinct advantages (Chesner 1994a). Instead of the client being dependant on one therapist/professional/expert/parent figure, the group itself acts as therapeutic agent. This empowers both the individual and group, and fosters self-esteem, which is usually a central goal of therapy with this client group. Too often adults with learning difficulties see themselves in a child role in relation to more capable and powerful parental figures. Carers may collude with this by being over-protective and encouraging behaviour based on the desire to please them as authority figures. The consequence of low self-esteem for the person with learning difficulties is that the peer group is also undervalued and viewed with disrespect. The people who could be a source of support and social enjoyment may instead be a reminder of inadequacy. If 'I' am a second class person, and 'you' are the same as 'I', then 'you' are a second class person too. Group therapy challenges this view of self and other.

The pace of this process is gradual, and this is reflected in the contract for group dramatherapy. Where possible I favour an open-ended contract, which allows for a group to complete its natural life-span. This may be up to two or more years. Shorter fixed-term contracts are used for groups with a specific goal, such as resettlement support groups, communication skills/makaton training groups, or for specific project work.

In the case of one-to-one dramatherapy I favour contracts for six to twelve sessions initially. This may be long enough to achieve defined goals, but would normally be an extended assessment period, prior to long-term therapy if appropriate. The pace of the process varies considerably according to the abilities of the client and the nature of the work. One-to-one sessions may also be used as preparation for small group work.

The contract for therapy is negotiated between therapist and client, and shared with the referrer, as are the broad goals of the treatment. Clients may be dependent on support from carers to get to therapy sessions, and to help them ground the therapeutic work in everyday life. A wholesome line of communication between therapist and carer or referrer can in some cases be a prerequisite for treatment. A three-way agreement or contracting process makes the expectation of team support explicit.

CHAPTER 3

Dramatherapy and Profound Learning Disability

The area of profound and multiple disabilities poses additional challenges to the dramatherapist. These clients have more limited ability to communicate with the dramatherapist and with their peers. Mobility is often severely challenged; there may be sensory impairment, perhaps affecting both sight and hearing; and there may be 'challenging behaviours', often of a repetitive and obsessional nature; and little or no apparent ability to communicate through speech or signing.

The idea of establishing a therapeutic relationship with such a client can at first be daunting. For the dramatherapist many of the activities and approaches learned in training are irrelevant when working with this level of disability. However, by taking a flexible approach and following some broad principles the dramatherapist can establish such a relationship and do valuable and satisfying work.

The first principle is patience. Change is possible; development is possible. It is likely to take a long time. Short term dramatherapy is unlikely to be of any value with these clients. Patience is needed to embark on a relationship and process that may need to last several years. Within any session patience is also necessary in terms of allowing the client time to respond. It is a truism that we live our lives at a fast pace. Working with a client with profound learning disabilities challenges our habitual rhythm, and the degree of stimulation that we have come to regard as normal. The pace of the process is slow and the therapist should not underestimate the difficulty he or she may experience in adjusting to this. It can be frustrating when our expectations as therapists are not met, or when nothing seems to be happening despite our efforts.

The second principle is trust. Client and therapist both need a degree of trust for the other. The client is likely to find this harder than the therapist, who may need to earn the client's trust gradually over time. In group or individual dramatherapy with more able clients trust-building can be seen as a first stage in the therapy, the foundation for further, more adventurous work. With more profoundly disabled clients the development of a relationship of trust may be more of a long-term goal. In terms of the spectrum of processes within dramatherapy as expressed by the metaphor of the tree (see Chapter 1), we are dealing here primarily at the level of the roots, grounding and anchoring the relationship in safety.

One crucial way in which the therapist can facilitate this is by being reliable in terms of adhering to a regular time for sessions. We talk colloquially and figuratively about 'being there' for someone we care about. In terms of the therapeutic relationship 'being there' reliably at a concrete level is paramount. A further way to develop trust is to be attentive. The challenge is to find appropriate and acceptable ways of giving attention to the client. The other principles of working with this client group relate to this task.

The third principle is space. The dramatherapist can use observation and empathy to give the client the spatial conditions he or she prefers. This may mean spending the first few sessions going for a walk in the open air, away from the intrusive presence of others. At the other extreme it may mean finding a nook in the dramatherapy studio that feels cosy and safe. Similarly there is an optimal degree of proximity with the therapist. The client may need to know that the therapist is close at hand, perhaps even touching; alternatively the need may be for the therapist to keep a distance, physical closeness being perceived as invasive and threatening. By respecting the client's preferences, the dramatherapist gives the tacit message 'I am listening to you, I won't force you into a situation you do not want'. Ultimately it may be possible for the client to expand willingly beyond their habitual preferences, but a relationship of trust must be established first.

The fourth principle is containment and safety to explore. This is the underlying principle of all dramatherapy work. Privacy and lack of intrusion in the studio help to create a safe environment in which the client's needs come first. Containment is also a function of structure. With clients with multiple and profound learning disabilities the structure of a session tends to be more flexible than with more able clients. When conducting group work at the more able end of the learning disabilities spectrum the dramatherapist may impose the time boundary quite rigidly as a matter of containment. With people with profound learning disabilities the length of a session may need to be more variable, according to the client's ability to cope from week to week.

Nonetheless it is important to establish boundaries for the sessions. Certain behaviours, for example, may be clearly forbidden within the session. It is up to the individual therapist to decide where the line is drawn between acceptable and unacceptable behaviour in the context of therapy. Personally I draw a line at being physically assaulted by a client, and I discourage overt masturbation within sessions. Other therapists might be able to tolerate these behaviours and accept them as legitimate forms of communication within the therapy.

The fifth principle is to work with the dynamic of doing and being. Although dramatherapy is an action based therapy it is not helpful to overwhelm clients with the need to keep active. There must be a balance of activity and just being, whether this is just being in relation to the therapy space or just being with the therapist. Stillness and silence are not 'time out' from the therapy. They can be at the heart of the therapeutic process, moments when there may be an important letting go, an experience of trust, or a meeting between therapist and client. The dramatherapist needs to be quietly alert to the quality of such moments where nothing seems to be happening. This is a question of balance and rhythm. Stillness without activity may be lethargy; activity without stillness may be obsessional or manic. In each case the imbalance is an avoidance of being fully alive in the moment. A moment of breakthrough for one client may take the form of engaging in an activity; for another it could be more significant that he stops and allows himself to come to a point of rest.

When working with the less expressive client it can sometimes be useful to work on the basis that the therapist may be the active, expressive one in the relationship, whilst the client may spend time in the role of audience. This is a predominantly passive role for the client, but nonetheless of value. The role of audience in the theatre can be a stimulating one. Similarly in the therapeutic situation the client's interest can be raised by the dramatherapist taking on the role of performer. The 'performance' may be something as simple as putting on a hat, pulling a face, singing a song, making a sound, a movement – some spontaneous expressive response to being together with the client. If the client engages with what is happening he or she may find a spontaneous way of joining in – laughing, reaching out to touch, vocalising, mimicking, or perhaps just looking and listening. Even turning away or pushing away can be a positive statement of preference, whereby the client can acknowledge 'I see what you are doing and I want nothing to do with it. No.' If the client is in the role of audience then he or she has the right to like or dislike the performance. Either response can be recognised and appreciated by the dramatherapist, and this may help to build up a sense of self, and self-esteem in the client.

The sixth principle is to work towards the development of a shared language. Even if a client is unable to talk and appears unable to understand spoken language, it is helpful for the dramatherapist to talk to them. It can feel odd and quite challenging to conduct a one-way conversation. However, I feel it is worthwhile to assume that the non-verbal client has some understanding of spoken language. There is occasional painful evidence for this. On one occasion a man who was considered to have no understanding overheard two care staff talking about the death of a relative of his, in front of him but not to him. Only when he became acutely distressed did they realise how much he was able to understand. Some months later the same man began to use some language actively within his dramatherapy session. His father had died many years previously. He spent the whole session crying and asking 'Where's daddy?' Not only did this man understand more than was assumed, he also had access to his own words when he was in touch with his pain and early loss. It may be that the traumatic loss of his parent was accompanied by a loss of his will to use words, and that as he felt safe enough to express the feelings of loss in therapy he was also able to find his words.

Another reason to talk to the non-verbal client is that there is more to spoken language than the literal meaning of the words. The sound of a voice speaking respectfully with the intention to communicate is in itself a communication and a validation. The underlying message, quite apart from the actual meaning of the words, is 'I recognise you as a person, and you are worthy of my attention in the same way as other, speaking people are.'

However, there is more to establishing a shared language than conducting a one-way verbal conversation. The onus is on the dramatherapist to observe and listen to the client. The starting point must be the client and the present moment. Anything can become the foundation for communication. My colleague Pat McCulloch was working on building a relationship with a client, Bob. He was considered too difficult to work with in a number of contexts, because of his inability to stay in one place, and his obsessive concern with sticks. He liked to hold a twig and twiddle it between his fingers. This was his main occupation and he seemed more interested in the twig than in the people around him. Pat built the foundation of a relationship with Bob by taking him out for a regular stroll in the grounds of the hospital where he lives. She made no demands on him, and allowed him to discover and explore as many twigs as they came across. After some sessions run on this basis she clipped a couple of pegs onto the twig he was holding, and for a few moments he explored the new situation. He carried on twiddling but with an air of surprise perhaps that someone was willing to engage with him on his terms and that something different was happening. From Pat's point of view she had introduced Bob to something new, and was no longer simply an accessory to his solipsistic world. Over the next few sessions he was able to work in the studio and continue to extend his awareness into new areas on the basis of a trusting relationship.

The seventh principle is timing. The way in which a shared language is created is unique to the individuals concerned. In this sense the dramatherapy session is truly a dramatic improvisation, based on a balance between respecting the *status quo* and daring to risk something new. Without taking a risk and challenging the habitual way of being, people tend to remain stuck in the same old ways. Conversely if the therapist makes continual demands of the client to take a risk, the client may simply retreat in fear. The essential skill as a dramatherapist or as a dramatic improviser is to sense the moment to try something new, and to invite/challenge the other (improviser or client) to join you.

The principle of timing also relates to the principle of space. The moment when a client does something new, is able to let go of some inhibition and open up to some level of spontaneity, may be a moment when there is no apparent demand being made by the therapist. In a small group it may be the moment when the therapist is giving attention to one group member that another is able to reach out spontaneously and play a new instrument, handle a new prop, or communicate in a new way. In one-to-one work it is often helpful to have moments where the dramatherapist gives attention only obliquely. Unrelenting direct attention can be experienced as invasive and inhibiting. Whether the client is an adult or a child it is useful to remember the relationship of a mother with her playing child. If she is not experienced as present the child may not feel safe enough to explore its world. If she is too present, too involved, she may take over and deny the child its own space and process.

These basic principles can give the dramatherapist a sense of direction in the work with this client group. Since changes tend to happen over longer periods of time it is advisable to keep notes of sessions, particularly when something new occurs, however small.

Some Ideas for Working Structures

Sessions are designed around the individual needs and abilities of each client. There follow some suggestions for activities, which the dramatherapist can try out and develop if the client is receptive.

Working with the sense of touch

Explore the sense of touch, initially with hand to hand contact. Hands can be held, stroked, squeezed or massaged. The client can be the recipient in this, or may be able to explore the feel of the therapist's hands. Hands can dance together, be friendly or shy. A hand to hand conversation might develop. Or it may be enough for hands just to 'meet' each other. At a level of hand to hand interaction the client can have an experience of equal relationship, or of being the one who initiates and is in control.

Dependent clients are often the passive recipients of touch, particularly in the context of bodily functions and physical care. In the therapy situation it is important to afford the client the same physical respect as to anyone else, and to avoid being invasive. The client may be used to an invasive and functional approach to his or her body, and may cope with this reality of life by withdrawing, becoming apparently less sensitive and having less sense of self. Such a withdrawal may be quite appropriate as a defence in the context of everyday reality. If I am not master of my body and of my own physical boundaries, then how do I know who I am, and how do I inhabit my world?

In the dramatherapy session, where we are not dealing with dressing, feeding, toileting and cleaning, we can establish a different set of norms in terms of touch, and consequently in terms of relationship and role. We can take time and care, because the role of the dramatherapist is to focus on the relationship rather than on practical physical tasks. At the simplest level the dramatherapist can offer a hand to be held, and wait for the client either to take up the invitation or to refuse. In this moment an important interaction is occurring, the subtext of which is: 'I recognise you and your right to make a choice. I am prepared to make contact with you, but I won't force you. You have some power here, which I respect.'

The therapeutic process is an invitation to be vulnerable, to be open to feelings and contact. The client needs to know that the human condition is a shared one and that the vulnerability is not all on the his or her side. We have more in common than not. The dramatherapist can confirm this by a reversal of the usual relationship regarding touch. If there is sufficient trust the therapist might invite the client to touch the therapist's face or hair. This can be helpful not only with blind and visually impaired clients, but also with those who can see. If the therapist can trust the client to be appropriate and sensitive in this situation the client's own confidence and self-esteem is nurtured. The world of difference gives way for a while to a world of commonality.

Physical touch activities can develop into games. Some familiar childhood hand games may emerge. Variations of these as well as new and unique games may also arise spontaneously in the session. These become part of a repertoire or shared language between therapist and client, that may be repeated often or from time to time in the course of the therapeutic relationship. At this point the process moves organically from root to trunk level activity (see Chapter 1).

A caveat: adults with learning disabilities are sexual beings. Parents, carers and therapists may be tempted to turn a blind eye to this fact. Society's myth of the learning disabled person as the perpetual child has been challenged during recent years, but is not yet dead. While verbal psychotherapies tend to avoid any physical touch, action based therapies such as dramatherapy can and do use touch legitimately and usefully within the therapy. When working through touch the dramatherapist needs to be especially sensitive to the issue of sexuality. There is a responsibility not to overexcite or mislead the client about the nature of the relationship, and to maintain respectful boundaries.

The sense of touch can be used extensively to explore objects as well as the body. The dramatherapist can invite the client to touch a variety of objects, and through these to experience a whole range of textures, temperatures, shapes, sizes, colours and touch related sounds. Each experience can be developed into a game or improvisation, so that the relationship is not only client-to-object but client and therapist with each other through the medium of the object.

Texture

sponge	glass bead necklace	paint brush
velvet	hand cream	clothes brush
fur	finger paints	grass
lycra	tissue paper	leaves
net		

Temperature

metal	wood	polystyrene packing material
glass	wool	hair drier

Shapes

ball	rope	buttons
box	playshapes	bubbles
drum	hats	

Size

furniture	model car	babushka-type dolls of decreasing size inside each other
car	different size boxes	Guatemalan worry dolls

Touch-related sound

electronic keyboard	bells	most things that can be held and dropped
drum	cassette player	hands
cymbal	paper	

The kind of exploration that these objects facilitate can at the simplest level be fun, and enrich the life experience of the client. The relationship that is built up gradually with the dramatherapist is one of growing familiarity and trust, mutual discovery and adventure. The key issues for this client group are generally trust, spontaneity, empowerment and self-esteem, each of which can be nurtured through this work.

Working with the sense of smell
Some touch-based exploration can be enhanced by the use of fragrances. Perfumed cream can be used when massaging hands or face. Diluted aromatherapy oils can be used in a similar way, especially floral and fruity fragrances such as lavender or neroli.

It is also possible to scent the air directly with these oils, either in a special dispenser, or by splashing a few drops on a radiator. The client may come to associate the studio with a pleasant smell even though there may be no direct communication or interaction in response to the smell.

The sense of smell can be introduced as a surprise element into other activities. In my box of miniature objects I include a collection of small perfume bottles, some empty and some full. The smell is 'discovered' when they are opened. Miniature bars of soap can be used in a similar way, the smell becoming evident as they are unwrapped; a moment of sensory revelation.

The smell of everyday natural items that we take for granted might be unfamiliar to the more dependant client living in an institutional setting. The scent (and sight) of a real orange, or a real banana, being peeled can be a feast for the senses, quite apart from the possible enjoyment of eating these fruits.

Working with the sense of hearing

Music can be played to soothe, stimulate and change the mood. There is a wide variety of arrhythmic, electronic and 'new age' music on the therapy market that is associated with relaxation. Some of this includes natural sounds, of the sea, rivers and bird song. Music such as this can provide a pleasant background to a session. I am wary of using music unthinkingly as hypnotic 'wallpaper', however. Some clients may prefer silence and might experience even gentle music as quite invasive or disturbing. The therapist needs to be sensitive to the client's response, and perhaps alternate the use of background music with periods of silence.

In the spirit of dramatherapy as a broadening experience I like to choose music that the more dependent client may not have access to elsewhere. When music is played in the home or ward the choice is usually that of the staff, and may be limited. I have gradually built up a collection of well known and unusual works, and within a dramatherapy session different clients have been responsive to a wide variety of music: classical, opera, minimalist, folk, and 'world' music from other cultures. A positive response from the client might be a quietening of disturbed behaviours, attentive listening, singing/vocalising and dancing/moving some part of the body in time with the music.

The client can also participate actively in making sounds or music. Most objects can give a sound if struck or dropped. A ball that bounces combines sound with movement when dropped. A large ball held between therapist and client can be tapped with the hands, as if drumming. A whole conversation might develop. Paper or polystyrene packing pieces can be scrunched with the hands, combining experiences of sound and texture.

Musical instruments can be explored within the dramatherapy session. This has connections with, but is distinct from, music therapy. In dramatherapy the music is not the primary medium for communication. The focus is on the relationship and on the process of exploration, which may at times be expressed musically, and at other times in a variety of other ways. One of the benefits of working with sound and music is that the client can be empowered to make a huge sound from quite a small physical gesture. An electronic keyboard for example responds to a light touch of a button or key.

Denis, a non-verbal blind man in a wheelchair, delighted in pushing over a cymbal on a stand, and hearing it crash to the floor. He was not habitually a noisy person, and was known as someone who preferred quiet places away from large groups and loud activity. His response to the sound of the cymbal falling to the floor, however, showed that his aversion was not to sound or noise itself, but to other people's noise, to noise that was out of his control. He was pleased to find a way of making his own din, and to have a place to do this without incurring the irritation of the people he lived with. He also began to move himself around the studio in his wheelchair during dramatherapy sessions. In other contexts he was not known to wheel himself in this way and so it was assumed that he could not. The ethos of empowerment within the dramatherapy session, and the safety he experienced in making his own noise seemed to have encouraged him to take a risk in terms of being responsible for his own movements.

The soundbeam uses the principle of minimal movement for maximum effect and can facilitate exciting work with clients with profound and multiple disabilities. Even those people who cannot or will not touch or hold a musical instrument or beater can create their own symphonies of sound by moving whatever part of the body they can (see Chapter 4 on movement).

Working with movement

Physically dependent clients tend to lose their full range of movements. The dramatherapist can help to motivate these clients to use movement creatively, to relate to their environment and to the therapist. The benefits can be physical, emotional and social.

If physical movement is limited the dramatherapist may introduce concrete devices to extend the impact of any movement. A coloured silk streamer held between client and therapist allows a small movement to be transmitted along the fabric and felt by the person at the other end; visually the movement of the fabric is pleasing, and the texture of the streamer adds another dimension of sensuality to the experience. A combination of several streamers of different colours heightens the experience. The streamer concretises the relationship, the moving line between therapist and client. The distance between the two (or more) people can be varied by pulling in some of the length of the streamer, or getting wrapped up and tangled in it. The movement of the streamer draws attention to different directions, above and below, side to side, round and round. The quality of the movement is airy and fluid.

Another device for extending movement and concretising the space between therapist and client is the use of large pieces of lycra fabric. This comes in a variety of strong colours, and is soft yet strong enough to be handled roughly. Its elasticity allows it to be pushed and pulled into bizarre, amusing and mysterious shapes. Therapist and client can play with ideas of hiding, covering, transforming and uncovering. A musical commentary can be created by combining such a movement improvisation with the use of the soundbeam. As one shape is created and held still the soundbeam can reflect this with a sustained sound that only changes when the people and the fabric move and the shape is changed. In this way the music can highlight the contrast between movement and stillness, and between one position and the next.

The dramatherapist's body in movement can also be used to inspire movement in the client, to extend and build on movements the client makes, or simply to arouse interest. Initially this process makes more use of the therapist's creativity and spontaneity than that of the client. The therapist takes the mood, a movement or a gesture of the client as a starting point for movement and keeps an openness to any response from the client. At some point the client may find a way of joining in, perhaps through touch, vocalising or movement. The aim is to find a way of being together that reflects the quality of the moment, that allows participation at whatever level is possible, that builds on the relationship between therapist and client, and that nurtures openness and spontaneity.

In all the above activities an important contributor to the therapeutic value is the location of the therapy space. There is sometimes pressure with the more dependent clients to treat them *en masse* in the home environment. It may indeed be true that a visit from a peripatetic dramatherapist can serve to stimulate and brighten up the home experience of a group of such clients. However, the importance for a client of going somewhere different, away from the locus of their habitual passive or disturbed roles, cannot be overemphasised. It is similarly beneficial to be given time as an individual, either in a small group or one-to-one. The underlying message is one of valuing, and of recognition. This is particularly important for clients whose dependency and poor communication skills mean that they are regarded as groups of patients in terms of their daily care.

CHAPTER 4

Movement and Dance
in Dramatherapy

Rationale for Movement Work

Dance and movement have an important place in working with people with learning disabilities for a number of reasons.

First, the method is essentially non-verbal. People with learning disabilities may experience themselves as most handicapped in the context of verbal communication. We live in a highly verbal culture, where written and spoken communication are used in sophisticated ways. Most people with moderate and severe learning disabilities are denied access to the freedoms and powers of the verbally sophisticated and literate. Verbal communication is essentially abstract and symbolic. Movement, by contrast, is sensual, physical and more immediate as an experience. In terms of the broad range of dramatherapy activity described in Chapter 1, most movement work belongs in the area symbolised by the roots, and deals with trust and grounding.

For those with limited or no speech, expressive movement work offers the opportunity for communication, 'conversation' and contact of another kind. Without the hurdle of purely verbal communication they may find a new spontaneity, validity and freedom. A client may come to experience physical communication as an area of ability and success rather than disability and failure. While verbal language is bound by rules of grammar and pronunciation, physical communication may operate through a simpler and more flexible set of rules. This allows greater possibilities of contact without judgement.

Movement and dance provide an opportunity for personal awareness. The physical sensation of the body as a whole and of the separate body parts in movement is a direct experience of the immediate world of the person. A sense of personal connectedness with the body is essential for identity and for being grounded in the here and now. Clients with multiple and profound disabilities need an opportunity to explore the limits and possibilities of their bodies. Habitual institutionalised life styles (which may exist 'in the community' as much as in a hospital setting) take their toll on the physical skills of residents. If a person never needs to reach up for anything because this task is always carried out by members of staff, the muscles for this movement become lazy, and eventually the movement is experienced as difficult, dangerous or impossible. The limitation is not only physical, but is a limitation in personal effectiveness, and in a sense reduces the personal world of the client. Physiotherapy plays an important role in keeping the body mobile from a clinical perspective. Expressive movement work within the context of dramatherapy helps clients find their own spontaneous motivation for a wide range of movements.

Movement is holistic. The breath, the circulation, the emotions and the quality of energy are affected by movement and dance. This gives movement work the possibility to effect change at many levels. It is often apparent that a part of the body that is damaged is hidden, disconnected from the whole, perhaps disowned by the client and denied the possibility of contact with others. It seems to symbolise the whole issue of damage, not only the aspects that are physical, but also the mental, physical and existential aspects. The attitude to the damage or the dysfunction may be both rejective and defensive. The body itself is enacting a drama in which one internalised role rejects, whilst another feels rejected, withdraws and at some level even dies. Shame and despair are part of this internal drama, and the outcome is lack of integration, unresolved conflict, unexpressed pain, denial. Movement has a real part to play in challenging and healing this pattern. The painful inner drama described here is not, however, the only experience. I have also worked with multiply disabled clients who are more at peace with their body and themselves, who can openly acknowledge a physical dysfunction whilst challenging its limits in terms of self-expression and independent living.

Movement as Warm-Up

Within the overall framework of a group dramatherapy session the warm-up has several functions. The group warms up to being a group, to being expressive, and to issues of interest or concern which may be developed after the warm-up.

Movement-based warm-ups are usually popular and may even be requested by the group if omitted from the session plan by the therapist. It is fun to move, and it is fun to move together. Alertness is increased, spontaneity may be developed, and useful skills learned through the physical warm-up.

There follow some sample structures for warm-up through dance, movement and physical awareness.

Self-massage

This activity brings a focus to the senses of touch and hearing, and gives participants a guided tour of the body.

The group stands in a circle and follows the suggestions both spoken and, more important, modelled by the therapist. Start with the hands and rub them together. Feel the heat that is generated and hear the sound created by the group.

Bring the hands up to the face and place them on the cheeks, eyes, forehead and chin.

Take the hands up to the head and let the fingers tap all over the skull with loose wrists, like rain falling.

Stroke the neck and throat with alternate hands.

With the right hand make a long sweeping stroke from the left side of the neck down the arm and through the upper side of the hand and fingers. Repeat this, then make the same journey from neck to hand, but squeezing instead of stroking. Repeat again, but from the underside of the arm.

Repeat this sequence using the left hand working down the right neck, shoulder and arm.

Slap the chest (above the breasts) with the flat of the hand, using alternate hands rhythmically. Using the analogy of Tarzan, vocalise at the same time with an open mouth.

Stroke with the flat of both hands in large circling movements over the ribs, stomach and abdomen.

Make fists and use the flat of the fist to pummel the hips and buttocks.

Lean forward from the waist and use the flat of the hands to slap the lower back and as far up the back as you can reach.

Straighten up and use the flat of both hands to make large circular strokes covering the right thigh both front and back, inner and outer, from the groin to the lower knee. Repeat on the left leg.

Lean further over and stroke the lower legs from knee to ankle using the same long circular movements.

If appropriate, come down to a sitting position, remove the shoes and stroke and squeeze each foot. This is not always feasible. It may be too time consuming to get all the shoes off and on again, especially if participants need help with this. There may also be resistance to removing the shoes. In these cases finish the massage with an energetic foot stamp, drawing attention to the sensation of the feet against the floor and the noise created by the group.

Variations:

- Many variations will arise spontaneously in relation to the physical limitations and differences of participants. The massage can be a useful diagnostic tool in revealing areas of greater or lesser mobility and confidence for individual clients. Compare the exercise over a period of time; improvements in these areas may be highlighted.

- A shorter, gentler version of the self-massage involves the image of the shower. Start by stretching up, turn on the imaginary taps, and let the hands representing the warm water wash down the whole body from head to toe.

Exercise sequence

Warm-up exercises can be considered in two broad categories: those that involve the whole body in movement, and those that work on isolated body parts.

Start with a group yawn and stretch. A common tendency is for movements to be small, lacking in confidence and energy so it may be helpful to provide imaginative incentives to extend the stretch and encourage commitment to the movement. When stretching upwards challenge the group to reach for the ceiling or for something hanging from it. It is important that the challenge applies to the therapist as well. Mean it! If the therapist models making an effort and working with energy, the approach is infectious. Similarly, when stretching sideways aim for the walls or the windows, and when stretching or bending downwards aim for the knees, feet or floor.

Stretching the lower body from a standing position poses some problems in terms of balance. If the whole group can hold hands or wrists in a circle this helps to give some stability whilst standing on one leg and stretching the other leg forwards and backwards. It may be helpful to vocalise whilst stretching as this encourages breathing and a release of tension.

Exercises involving different parts of the body can be undertaken in a spirit of investigation. What movements are possible with the arm, the wrist, the neck, leg, hips, back? There will be swinging movements, rotations, stretches, bends, kicking and punching movements. The spirit of investigation opens up the possibility of movement suggestions from participants. The discovery of a movement and the desire to share it becomes the incentive and the language to communicate in the group.

Movement poem

One at a time each person makes a movement of their choice and the group is encouraged to focus on that person, and to mirror or copy the movement. When everyone has attempted the movement the next person becomes leader and the focus is moved to them. When each person has contributed a movement see if the group can remember all the movements and repeat the entire sequence. Each movement has become part of a whole group creation, a poem.

Variations:

- The movement poem depends on the group's ability to focus on different group members and to copy the movements. There may be an initial resistance to focusing on anyone other than a staff member, a sad reflection of the status of peer group relationships. If so, the necessary skills can be built up gradually over several sessions, by working on the exercise each week. Familiarity builds confidence and a sense of satisfaction as the form is mastered. The exercise encourages a new level of relationship within the peer group as the role of 'leader' is passed around and shared.

- Enhance the poem with sound. Each movement is accompanied by a vocalised sound, or a sound made with the body. This may be extended into a word or phrase. The group learns the full sequence, a choral dance poem of its own creation. If the exercise is repeated over several sessions the poem may remain the same as a ritualised expression of group identity, or it may develop and change as the group process moves on.

Circle dance

Traditional and new circle dances from around the world have become popular in personal development circles over the last 25 years, sometimes referred to as 'Sacred Dance'. Moving as a group in a circle within a learnt sequence of steps evokes a sense of communal celebration at several levels. The shape of the circle allows each participant to see and connect with all the others in a concrete and grounding manner. The circle as a whole is greater than the sum of all its parts, so there is also a sense of participation in something greater. The rotation of the circle reflects the orbit of the earth and the planets. Day and night, the seasons, birth and death, natural cycles, the cosmos are implied and evoked by the dance.

As a warm-up for dramatherapy the circle dance is a celebration of the group. The mood may be centring, solemn, soothing, harmonious, energising or fun, depending on the music chosen and the sequence of movements. The circle dance provides opportunities for listening to music from around the world and from different ages. Every continent seems to offer music suitable for the circle dance.

In terms of application with this client group, it is a question of choosing a dance which offers an appropriate degree of difficulty, and making adaptations to incorporate the use of wheelchairs if appropriate. The group may learn the step sequence first and then add the music, or the dance may develop spontaneously in response to the music. At the simplest level a dance may consist of holding hands in a circle, rotating in either direction; moving in towards the centre of the circle, and out again. Some people with learning disabilities find it hard to conceptualise, and therefore hard to create a circle without assistance. A therapeutic team, interspersed around the group may be necessary with more dependant groups to facilitate the circle dance.

Variations:

- These are infinite, such as breaking into pairs for a phrase and then returning to the circle.

- Another possibility is to break the circle at one point and invite the person at one end to lead the group as a snake on a journey around the room, eventually closing up again as a circle. This provides another contained opportunity for different group members to adopt the role of the 'leader'.

- Slightly more complex, but also more contained, is the creation of an arch by two people, and the 'leader' takes the group through and round to recreate the circle.

Elastic dance

A circle of strong elastic – a good four inches wide – provides the framework for this warm-up. Make sure that the two ends are joined together firmly.

Participants hold on to the elastic rather than each other's hands. This creates a circle without the necessity of physical contact. Rhythmic music is played and the group improvises in response to this. The dance is less formal than the circle dances described above. As one person initiates a movement others may pick up the suggestion and copy it or respond with something new. The elastic maintains the connection between people, and exercises a pull as people move. The delight of this form is that group members make spontaneous suggestions to each other which are often picked up by the group as a whole without the use of words, or having to take on the role of 'leader'. The elastic provides an impetus to exploration and risk taking.

Some of the experiences prompted by the elastic: stretching it to the limit, making the circle as large as possible before the inevitable tug inwards; one person at a time rushing forward into and across the circle and back again; taking the elastic as high and as low as possible; taking the elastic up and over the head, so that the whole group is inside the elastic. This particular development allows the participants to let go with their hands, and to feel the support of the elastic across the back. Learning to lean against the elastic takes the dance firmly into the area of trust building and relaxation.

In both the elastic dance and the circle dances the circle can operate as a container and audience for one or two people at a time to 'perform' a solo or duet at the centre of the group. The group may clap or hoot in support of those in the centre. There is a ritual element in this which simultaneously supports group identity and individual expression.

Movement for Trust and Contact

The session warm-ups described above help to create confidence and trust. This goal may be the focus not only of the warm-up but also of the central core of a sequence of sessions. The work of Veronica Sherborne (1990) is well known in this field. The body in movement and relationship is at the heart of this work. The application of contact improvisation in special needs groups as developed by Claire Russ provides a complementary source in this area, as does the performance and improvisation work of Wolfgang Stange and the Amici Dance company.

Key concepts in this work are grounding, pushing, pulling, balancing, leaning and supporting. By working on these physical tasks participants are implicitly tackling the issues of relationship with self, other and environment.

Grounding

By grounding I refer both to the relationship of the individual through gravity with the earth/floor/ground, and to the inner experience of the earth element within the body. This means in particular the sense of the body's solidity, its spatial presence and weight. There follow some suggestions for facilitating this exploration.

A good place to start is at floor level. Lay a mat or rug on the floor and invite group members to lie down.

(1) **Sensing the body.** Draw attention to the sensation of the body resting on the floor. There are parts of the body which are in contact with the floor – the back of the head, the back, buttocks, backs of legs and feet. Feel for a

sense of letting go, of giving the weight to the floor, and feeling the support of the ground. Notice the breath coming into the body through the nose or mouth, and notice it leaving the body as you breathe out. Feel for a quality of letting go and relaxation, particularly on the out-breath.

(2) **Sensing through touch.** This is a variation of the above in partners. One partner lies while the other gently helps them to contact the sensation of the body through touch. First, the facilitating partner lays a hand on the belly of the partner and lets it rest there, rising and falling as the partner breathes. The touch operates as a magnet to the attention, helping to bring the focus to the breathing. Second, the facilitating partner moves down to the feet and holds them whilst the partner focuses on the feet. Third, the head is held, firmly and not very high, with just the hands between the floor and the skull. This gives the opportunity to let go of the neck muscles and to trust. The facilitating partner could be the therapist or preferably a client, who thus has the experience of being in a helping and trusted role.

(3) **Rag Doll.** This sequence explores relaxation, letting go and giving support in pairs. Partner 'A' lies on the floor, facing upwards, arms a little distance from the body, hands facing down, and attempts to let go of tension by imagining him- or herself as a floppy rag doll. Partner 'B' raises A's lower arm from underneath, just a few inches, so that the arm pivots at the elbow. B feels for the weight of A's arm and lets go of it; if the arm is relaxed it will drop easily to the floor or into B's other hand. If not, it remains held up, and B can encourage A to drop the arm gradually by taking the weight and lowering it gradually to the floor. The principle of giving and taking the weight can be extended to the whole arm, which B can shake rhythmically for A, encouraging the elbow to remain loose, and exploring the range of movement in the shoulder joint before lowering the arm to the floor. The weight of the leg may also be taken by holding the foot and ankle, lifting from the floor, and replacing gently, taking care not to drop it. The knee may also be raised, allowing the leg to bend and relax. B does this from the side, lifting A's knee a few inches from underneath using both hands, and encouraging A to transfer the weight of his or her leg to B, who then lowers it again to floor level. The point of these movements is not in the extent of the movement but in the quality of relaxation and trust that develops in both partners. Participants need close supervision from the therapeutic team during this process. It is important that B knows what is required, so the different parts of the sequence should be modelled first step by step, and verbal explanation used to augment what is shown. The implicit message is

that the dramatherapist views the clients as trustworthy and able to be a helpful resource to their peers.

(4) **Rolling.** Take it in turns to roll, in a lying position, from one side of the room to the other. This provides an excellent opportunity to feel the floor, and to move with a sense of letting go, building trust. The exercise can be extended to pair work: one partner rocking the other in a lying position and increasing the energy of the push until the lying partner rolls over. Where there is a good quality of relaxation and no medical contra-indications it may be possible to explore rolling over another person – an exercise involving a higher level of risk and trust.

(5) **Standing your ground.** It is easier to build trust in the earth and gravity from a lying down position, where a large body surface area is in direct contact with the floor. Standing, by contrast, involves only the smallest surface area, the soles of the feet, being in contact with the floor. Fear of falling influences the habitual movement and posture of most people. One way of working towards a sense of groundedness in a standing position involves pair work. Partner A stands, and is invited to feel the top of the head stretching upwards the full length of the spine, the feet 'planted' in the ground. Partner B facilitates this journey of awareness through touch; beginning at the top of the head, moving down the body through the shoulders, the length of the back, the legs and finally holding the feet on to the floor. It is no coincidence that the term 'standing your ground' refers to assertiveness and self-confidence in interaction. The physical act of standing with ease and confidence has a positive influence on sense of self and effectiveness of communication.

(6) **Further exploration.** From a stable standing position further exploration may involve stamping, jumping and running, each of which is dependent on a confident relationship with the ground.

Pushing
Pushing is an expression of will and strength. A common feature of many people with learning disabilities is an uncertain relationship with their own personal will and strength. A client may be afraid of his or her own power, which may be disguised and denied, only to emerge in uncontained and frightening ways. A vicious circle is set up which is disempowering and confusing.

Movement work in dramatherapy offers contained and safe structures to test out and play with the dynamic of pushing. What begins as an exploration at a physical level may enhance self-image and confidence and have a real-life impact in terms of communicating in everyday situations.

A relatively non-threatening approach to pushing is back to back. Pairs stand back to back and 'massage' each other's back with their own, by bending the knees and moving up and down and side to side. This involves a mutual level of pushing. If one pushes and the other does not the exercise does not work. When an appropriate degree of pressure is negotiated physically the experience is energising and fun.

A variation of the above involves sitting at floor level, in pairs back to back, with the hands on the floor, knees bent up towards the chest and feet firmly planted on the floor. At the word 'go' each has to try and push their partner with their own back, using the rest of the body for leverage. An appropriate level of mutuality allows each participant really to 'go for it' and to feel contained by the partner. The exercise can be set up in a competitive framework, with the entire group in a line down the centre of the room. The task is to push the partner as far as the wall they are facing. A variation of this includes the use of the voice and the words 'yes' and 'no'. All those facing one way are given the power word 'yes', and all those facing the other way are given the word 'no'. The word is used to add force to the physical pushing. A second round might involve using the contrasting word, and participants are invited to comment on which word worked best for them.

Pushing face to face is more threatening and needs careful structuring. An intermediate object can be placed between the pushers. A large and strong foam ball, such as might be used for lying on in trust work, can be used. Participants stand on opposite sides of the ball and push.

Face to face pushing with bodily contact needs to be tightly structured. Both partners stand with legs apart in a firm stance, place their hands on their partners' shoulders and push, trying to match and gradually increase the level of push. Through this exercise participants can learn trust in their own and their partner's strength, and can practise being in control of their own level of pushing to find an appropriate balance with their partner. Fear at a fantasy level of the client's own strength or that of other people is replaced by an honest and safe investigation of the reality. The exercise is often accompanied by laughter as participants challenge the fantasy. The habitual role, based on the message 'good girls/boys/patients aren't pushy' is challenged at a physical level. This may be the first step on the way to more generalised assertive behaviour.

Pulling

As with pushing the physical dynamic of pulling reflects a psychological dynamic, and involves the exercise of will. Whilst pushing is associated with creating boundaries and limits and holding our own space, pulling is associated with desire and a commitment to striving to get what we want or need.

Many people with learning disabilities learn to deny the extent of their desire and need. Acknowledging needy feelings puts us in a vulnerable position, open to disappointment and rejection so it may seem preferable not to want or not to care. Someone who habitually makes such a choice risks the generalised loss of spontaneity and energy. Even the physical activity of pulling may be difficult alongside the psychological dimension.

I have mentioned the use of elastic which may encourage pulling as part of a dance. A team game of tug of war using rope can also facilitate pulling. Team members may hold on either to the rope or the waist of the person in front.

The use of an object rather than direct physical contact may be less threatening for some clients, and a gentle exercise can be set up using a hula hoop. Each partner holds opposite sides of the hoop and the leader guides the follower on a tour of the room by pulling gently.

Pulling face to face in pairs can be addressed as a trust exercise rather than a competition. Partners stand facing each other, with legs apart and knees bent and flexible, whilst holding on firmly to their partner's wrists. The idea is for both people to pull equally, so that they stand their ground whilst being pulled. Before finding this point of balance it may be helpful for each to pull in turn whilst the partner remains passive. The dramatherapist or therapeutic team may need to support and encourage each pair separately.

Leaning, supporting, balancing

There follow a number of cooperative activities using the dynamics of leaning, supporting and balancing.

(1) **Cradling.** This exercise, developed by Veronica Sherborne (1990), involves one partner cradling another. The cradled one, 'A', sits on the floor, with legs curled up. Their partner, 'B', provides support with their own body, moulding it in such a way that A can rest within it as a cradle or comfortable armchair. B sits just behind A, on the floor, legs open and bent like the arms of the chair, whilst B's chest and belly represent the back of the chair, against which A leans. For A the exercise gives an experience of being held, with the opportunity to relax fully. B benefits from being trusted, responsible, holding

and caring. In terms of the physical position, the centre of gravity for both partners is in the lower belly, around which the body rests. Cradling allows both partners to centre themselves physically, to feel in balance and in harmony.

(2) **Sticking hands.** This is taken from the Tai Chi exercise. Partners stand opposite each other and explore letting the palm of one hand rest against the palm of the partner's hand so that each is mutually supportive. Try with both hands, and with the back of the hand instead of the palm. This is a preparation for the main exercise, warming the participants up to the idea of leaning and supporting. The actual sticking hands requires the use of diagonally opposite hands (i.e. both left or both right). Let the wrists balance against each other. Make a circle together with this connected hand, and let the point of connection shift subtly from one part of the wrist to another as the circle is drawn. Shoulders and elbows remain loose and flexible so that the movement is smooth and each person responds to the other so subtly that it is impossible to tell who is leading and who following. The image of a bird circling and soaring may be used to capture the lightness and grace of the movement.

(3) **Leaning back-to-back.** This is a variation of the back massage exercise described above. Partners stand back to back and feel for the warmth and sensation of the contact and a sense of resting against each other. The same exercise can be more restful done sitting on the floor, and it may be used as a winding down exercise after strenuous movement work. Those with good mobility can try extending the exercise. Starting from a back-to-back sitting position the knees are bent and feet placed as close to the body as possible. Arms are linked together and the pair comes up to a standing position by using a combination of leaning through the back and pushing through the feet.

(4) **Leaning back.** In this exercise one person stands and leans back to be supported by the hands of one or more group members. The idea is not to prove how far you can lean back, but to allow yourself to give your weight to those who are supporting you. For this reason it is helpful to place the supporting hands no more than a centimetre or two away. If the hands are further than this the leaner is likely to simply bend backwards at the waist, without giving the weight at all. The exercise has value for those in a supporting role as well. They have responsibility for 'being there' for the leaner in a concrete way, and being strong enough to ensure the leaner's safety.

(5) **Free flow leaning and support.** The concept of leaning and supporting can be developed imaginatively using all parts of the body. Partner 'A' places him- or herself in a stable position, perhaps on all fours, sitting, lying or standing. 'B' finds a position of in which he or she leans with any part of his or her body using A for support. The pair may try out a variety of positions in a spirit of investigation. The exercise can be developed into a group improvisation. A begins in a stable position, B uses A for support; 'C' joins the sculpt by leaning against A or B and so on until the whole group is involved in a spontaneous and mutually supportive sculpt.

(6) **Playing with balance.** In this exercise one partner provides physical support whilst the other explores positions that require balancing skills and risk-taking, such as standing on one leg, leaning, twisting, pivoting, whether from a standing position or closer to the floor. Unusual ideas can be performed or shown to the whole group.

(7) **Improvisation with contact.** The skills of leaning, supporting and balancing, once practised, can form the foundation of a free flowing improvisation. Pairs are invited to make a journey across the room using the floor and each other for support, incorporating any movements they like, being responsive to each other's suggestions and having moments of contact as often as they like. The whole group can improvise together coming into moments of contact and moving on in their own journey spontaneously.

'Soundbeam' and Movement

The musical background for dance and movement work is usually pre-recorded on CD or tape. The dramatherapist and clients may choose a piece of music to fit the mood as closely as possible. The music then influences the kind of movement and dance that follows. Live musicians, where available, can respond to the spontaneous subtleties expressed through movement almost instantaneously. This will inevitably be according to their interpretation of what is happening. There is the potential for a satisfying creative interplay between musicians and dancers. It is unlikely, however, that many agencies would be able to fund such a facility on a long-term basis.

Soundbeam (See Useful Addresses) is a recently developed electronic system which enables an individual or group to create complex and varied music through movement. The system involves the transmission of ultrasonic beams, which constitute an invisible keyboard. The length of the beam is adjustable and the intervals between the notes of the invisible keyboard can be selected by the therapist according to the degree of mobility of the client or group, and the kind of scale or mode that is to be explored. As someone moves into or through the beam the information is fed into a keyboard and there is an instant musical response. As the person leaves the beam the music stops, and as they move up and down it they can 'compose' their own piece of music.

The system can be used by people with profound and multiple disabilities. Clients who may not be able to actually hold a beater or touch an instrument to create music in a more traditional way can create music by moving perhaps the head, one hand or foot in the beam. The smallest movement can be rewarded by an immediate musical response. The experience is one of power and effectiveness. The moment of realisation that 'I am making/stopping/shaping this sound' can be a profound and joyful experience, and provides a creative incentive for the client to explore his or her movement potential.

Jack presented as a depressed and unmotivated man in a wheelchair. His habitual posture was slumped with his head forward. He had good use of one hand, and was capable of moving his wheelchair himself with that hand. He tended not to. He had very limited active verbal skills but understood quite well. I introduced him to the soundbeam as part of an ongoing process of dramatherapy, and it effected some significant changes. First, he found himself in a position where he was still and slumped, and there was a long sustained single note. I was standing outside the beam and said, 'If you want the music to change, Jack, try moving your head.' After some moments he moved his head slightly, and there was an immediate shift of musical note. He moved his head again, and laughed as he realised that he was creating the music. The exploration developed over several sessions. He began to wheel himself in and out and along the beam, sometimes for as long as fifteen minutes without losing interest. My role as therapist was to witness, encourage, and make adjustments to the mode or programme of the soundbeam and the keyboard. We could also dance together in the beam, and developed a game with the long band of elastic (see above). Jack would hold one end, I would hold the other and pull, enabling Jack to freewheel to the accompaniment of the music.

Soundbeam in group work

Soundbeam creates the possibility of dancing or moving to create music in a group. Individual group members can take it in turns to perform a solo, exploring different movements and patterns of movement and creating an entirely individual musical accompaniment at the same time. Pair work brings in the element of interaction. Partners can move in relation to each other using contact, mirroring, or the use of an intermediary device. Whole group dance improvisation can be developed using a simple structure of free movement through the space and moments of holding a position like a statue. Musically this creates a fluid commentary as people move, contrasting moments of sustained chords during the still phases of the dance. Participants are encouraged both to watch each other and to listen to the music.

The soundbeam can be used to support dramatic improvisation and role play. One of our more memorable experiments was 'A journey into outer space'. The soundbeam and keyboard were programmed in advance with evocative echoing bells and flute. The improvisation began outside of the beam with the creation of a space ship. We mimed dressing in space suits, helmets and space boots, fastened our seat belts, held hands and counted down to ignition and lift off. We arrived at the moon and took it in turns in pairs to leave the space ship, and explore the surface of the moon in an atmosphere without gravity. This was an exercise in slow motion modelled at first by the therapeutic team. The music began on 'climbing down' from the space ship and helped to create an other worldly atmosphere. At one point, one of the participants found a baby (a doll) floating in outer space, rescued it and brought it back to the ship. Another found an interesting moon rock to bring back. As the last pair returned to the ship the music stopped and we began our return trip to earth. On arriving back we de-roled by removing our imaginary spacesuits, helmets and boots. As with real journeys the improvisation left the participants with strong impressions to share and reflect on.

Personal Dance Expression in Dramatherapy

The creation of a personal dance may be used to express the feelings of the moment in a direct and physical way. I have used this method mostly in one-to-one dramatherapy (see Chapter 6), but it can be adapted to use in a group context.

The principle behind the method is that many clients with learning disabilities have difficulties expressing their feelings in words. At one level they may find it hard to access the feelings, and at another level there may be problems of vocabulary and speech. The posture and movement of the body may provide a more accessible vocabulary for communicating at this level.

There is no need to provide music for this dance. The dance can be developed in stages, starting simply in the here and now with 'the way things are'. The client begins simply, perhaps with a deliberate movement, perhaps a habitual or unconscious one. The dramatherapist receives the movement, accepts it and repeats it with the client. An organic rhythm is developed through repetition and the movement may be extended or exaggerated. The momentum may lead spontaneously into another movement, or the therapist may invite the client to add the next movement of the dance. The process may be facilitated by offering a verbal commentary of the feelings whilst performing the movements with the client. As the feeling and movement is validated and held by the therapist, further movements and developments may begin to flow. The process gives form to feelings which the client experiences as formless and potentially overwhelming. The ideas come from the client, who should have the experience of being heard and understood through the dance without judgement.

In individual dramatherapy the personal dance can be used at the beginning of the session as a method of arriving, checking in and re-connecting with the therapist. In group dramatherapy a shorter version of the method can be used as a warm-up; each person is invited to show with a movement how he or she feels or what kind of week it has been. Later on in the development phase of the session the personal dance can be used as a central piece of work. This is particularly relevant if one group member is emotionally warmed-up to an issue and needs the opportunity for exploration and expression of feelings.

Whenever one person is the focus of group dramatherapy it is important that they have the permission and backing of the group as a whole to take centre stage. At best the issue of the individual touches others in the group as a group concern. If this is the case the individual works on behalf of the group, and is more likely to have the full attention of other group members. The issue of focusing on the individual within the group context requires sensitivity when working with any client group. In the case of people with learning disabilities the dramatherapist needs to take special care to maintain group interest and concentration. This can be done by directing the commentary to the dance out to the group as a whole and by inviting the group to let the individual client know if they have experienced similar feelings. There may even be moments when the whole group can join in the personal dance of one individual, provided that the client or therapist directs the other group members to be true to the subjective feelings being explored.

CHAPTER 5

Games in Dramatherapy

Games have a special place in the work with this client group. A game provides a framework, a form for social interaction. There are rules to be mastered, and a discipline to be followed. The game represents a shared language for the players. In terms of the broad range of dramatherapy structures that can be used with this client group, games correspond to the trunk of the tree: there is a certain degree of sophistication, beyond the sensuality of root level processes, which is a prerequisite for the complex dramatic activities of the branch and leaf level work. Games provide a focus for concentration, and reward the players with a shared experience of fun, spontaneity and challenge. Particular games may have an added educative or training function, working on verbal communication, imagination or touch.

Simplicity in a game is important if it is to be mastered. It is rewarding to manage to play a game in an acceptable way; we become part of a group of players, with a sense of belonging. In addition, once the rules of the game have been mastered, we can explore variations, and contribute spontaneously to the interaction taking place through the game. The game as shared language develops over time within a group, until the variations become new rules, and new variations develop.

The dramatherapist will soon realise if a game is too complicated: it will fail to engage the players. It is advisable to simplify a game to the most basic level, and build up complexity in response to the needs of the players. There follow some examples of tried and trusted games that have worked with a wide variety of people with learning disabilities engaged in group dramatherapy.

Pass the Ball

A game for cooperation, and peer group cohesion. A good starter game, requiring concentration and awareness of the group.

Preparation. Set up a circle, initially sitting. The therapist encourages the group members to look at who is present. It can be helpful where people are distracted to start by holding hands, concretising the connection between people in the group. In particular ask group members to notice whose hand they are holding on each side.

How to Play. Introduce a ball into the group and explain the idea of the game, which is to pass the ball to the next person in the circle. Support the verbal explanation with physical gesture, pointing the direction in which the ball is to be passed. A large foam ball has the benefit of being soft and warm to the touch, not too bouncy and easy to hold. It may be helpful to comment on the progress of the ball round the circle: 'Andy is passing it to Mary, who's passing it to...'. The combination of physical action and verbal commentary supports concentration and validates each person's contribution to the game.

Variations

- Try sending the ball round the other way.
- Change direction half way round.
- Anyone can change the direction at any time, either by calling out 'change', or just doing it.
- Change the speed, by challenging the group, 'Let's see how fast we can do it.'
- Introduce a second ball when the first ball is half way around the circle.
- Try it with one ball going one way and one another.
- Introduce a number of objects of different sizes and textures to be passed around the circle. This involves adapting the manner of receiving, holding and passing, and dealing with change.
- Challenge the group to see how many different objects can be passed around in both directions. Fun when two objects come to one group member from different sides at the same time!
- Try the basic game in the context of a larger standing group.

Ball 'Hello'

Preparation. A greeting game for the start of a session. Play it in a seated circle. It can even be played before everyone has arrived, with latecomers joining in as they arrive.

How to play. Say 'hello' to someone in the group by looking at them, calling their name and then throwing the ball. Each person chooses who they throw the ball to. This may be the same person each time, or different people in the group. The pathway of the ball makes a web of connection between the group members, and a record of who throws to whom over a period of time can be revealing of developing group dynamics.

Variations. Many of these arise of their own accord as participants gain in confidence and spontaneity.

- Look at one person, but call and throw to someone else, who may not be expecting it.
- Throw the ball very high, very hard or with a bounce.
- Stand, turn round and throw the ball to a named person over your head.
- Find other unusual ways of throwing the ball.
- Play the game with eye contact only, in silence.
- As well as (or instead of) saying the person's name say something else about them, e.g. what they are wearing today.

Changing Places
This game is an exercise in observation, spatial and group awareness.

(1) Names

Preparation. Form a standing circle. Hold hands briefly to concretise the shape of the circle, and ask participants to hold their place, and to notice where other group members are standing. Each person could call out their own name, or make a gesture to indicate their presence. Get a gong or similar hand-held percussion instrument. Invite each person to strike it in turn.

How to play. Explain the rules. The dramatherapist or leader of the game will call out two names of group members. 'If you hear your name look for the other person, make eye contact and when you hear the gong strike, change places across the circle.' The sequence may need to be modelled by helpers or experienced players. Some participants may need to be talked through the process step by step, and other group members may help them find the right place.

Variations

- As you pass the other person find a way of greeting them.

(2) Characteristics and clothes

This game arose in response to noticing how unobservant group members were in relation to themselves and others. There may be a combination of factors influencing this, e.g. institutional life, an emotional defence to personal shame, developmental problems etc. There is therapeutic value in encouraging clients to look, at themselves and at each other, within the safe framework of a game. Self-acceptance presupposes self-awareness.

Preparation. Form a circle, either sitting or standing. Encourage group members to look at each other in turn, noticing what each person is wearing and characteristics such as hairstyle.

How to play. Explain and model the rules. The therapist asks a question, e.g. 'Who is wearing a watch?' Allow a moment for the group to establish who is wearing a watch, then ask 'Everyone who is wearing a watch, change places.' Sometimes this will involve two participants, at other times several, and ultimately, perhaps, the whole group.

Variations

- Group members choose the characteristic, and take on the role of conductor of the game.
- Try speeding up the process if the group masters the basic rules. Challenge the group to identify who is involved as quickly as possible and to change places as quickly as possible, perhaps in response to the striking of the gong.

Statues

This game encourages listening, movement, balance, stillness and motor control.

Preparation. Ideally you would have a live musician. My colleague Pat McCulloch plays the accordion, which has the advantage of allowing her to move around and play at the same time. Otherwise, a music system with a remote control allows everyone to participate.

How to play. Introduce the basic concept. When the music plays, move, dance freely. When it stops, freeze or make a statue. It may help to call out 'statues' as soon as the music stops, and it certainly helps to model the game continually by playing along with the group. The non-verbal cues then support the verbal ones, and there is a sense of satisfaction all round when the entire group manages to stop at the same moment.

Variations

- Whilst the music is playing encourage pairing or interaction in the dancing, by modelling this and developing ideas that come spontaneously from the group.
- The game can be made competitive by calling out the last person to stop each time until the most proficient person is left.

In the Hoop

This game has elements of musical chairs, but is cooperative rather than competitive. Participants practise listening skills, coordination, observation, and negotiation of physical proximity. Concepts of 'starting and stopping', 'inside and outside' form the foundation of the rules.

Preparation. Hula hoops are laid out around the floor, one per person. A musician or music system are needed.

How to play. The rules are explained. When the music plays, move around the room; when it stops find a hoop and get inside it. After each round one hoop is removed so that some players need to share. Eventually there is only one hoop and everyone needs to get one foot or wheelchair part inside it. At this point everyone is a winner!

Throwing the Voice

This game and the following one were developed in the context of a shared dramatherapy and speech therapy intensive week. The aim of this week was to develop communication skills, particularly makaton and speech. This game was devised to help those participants who had some speech but who lacked the confidence to use sufficient volume. It could equally well be used to help someone who speaks too loudly to reduce their volume.

The basis of the game is that voice work is best approached through body and breath work. In acting training this is the premise for much vocal training.

Preparation. A large ball, perhaps an inflatable one, is used. The larger the ball, the more the whole body is used to throw it.

How to play. A circle is created. Group members are invited to throw the ball to someone, whilst calling their name. The size of the circle is increased and the therapist models throwing the ball a further distance, while throwing the voice with it, loudly so that it reaches the other side of the circle. Individuals may be asked to repeat an attempt, with every improvement acknowledged. The size of the circle may be changed, with the smallest circle used to practice whispering or quiet speech.

Variations

- Make the ball invisible. Mime throwing it, and make appropriate changes to vocal volume.

- Use a large heavy ball, such as a four foot diameter foam 'playshape' ball. (These are expensive to buy, but double up as invaluable supports for trust work.) It takes considerable effort to roll such a ball, and the physical push can help with pushing the voice out. The exercise promotes confidence and the fun of risk-taking.

'Calling' Footsteps

This is another, more competitive game involving throwing the voice. It draws on the familiar grandmother's footsteps, but the focus is not on creeping up silently, but on making yourself heard, and taking the initiative in communication.

Preparation. A group warm-up helps to liberate the voice and generate confidence. 'Group shout' involves the group forming a circle, and shouting 'hello' as loudly as possible, perhaps loudly enough to be heard at the end of the street. For the game itself a clear, long space is required. A starting line could be useful. The game requires more than one staff member.

How to play. Initially the therapist stands at one end of the room, facing a wall. The participants line up at the other end of the room. They are invited to call 'hello' so that the therapist can hear them at her end of the room. When the therapist hears someone calling she turns round, names the person she heard first and invites them to take one or more steps forward. A helper in the role of guardian of the rules may be needed to ensure that only the invited person moves, or that only the prescribed number of steps are taken. When the therapist turns her back again there is a new opportunity to call, and so the game continues until someone manages to get to the other end of the room, and touch the therapist on the shoulder. The helper may encourage and prompt those who need it, and model the game by participating.

Variations

- Therapist calls out 'ready' to indicate that it is time to call out.

- Whoever gets to the therapist first takes on their role for the next round of the game.

- Instead of calling 'hello' participants call the name of the person at the end, or any other word or phrase agreed upon by the group.

Hide the Ball

This game has elements of role play, and as such explores the interface between the here and now centred trunk processes and the more imaginary branch level work. It could be called Sherlock Holmes and Dr Watson. The game requires observation, the ability to keep a secret, and the negotiation of physical boundaries.

Preparation. A small ball or bean bag is required. The group sits in a circle. The ball is passed around the circle so that each person has the chance to look at it and handle it.

How to play. One person volunteers to be Sherlock Holmes. If a deer-stalker is to hand, they may like to wear it. Accompanied by a member of the therapeutic team in the role of Dr Watson this person leaves the room until called back into the group. Meanwhile one person in the group volunteers to hide the ball on their person, by tucking it into a sock, cuff or pocket, or placing it somewhere on their chair or wheelchair. The group calls out 'ready' and Sherlock Holmes and Dr Watson knock on the door. On the reply 'come in' they enter, and have to try to find the ball. This is an opportunity to look carefully at each person in the group, and to follow up hunches by questioning, pointing and touching as appropriate. The group may give clues if necessary. In practice this game reveals who can and who cannot keep a secret. It may be more fun for some people to show Sherlock Homes immediately who has the ball and where it is. The enjoyment in this case is in knowing and sharing the answer rather than in watching Sherlock Holmes look for clues. It is interesting to consider the opportunities for 'secrets' in an institutional setting.

Variations

- Revealing the ball as the detectives enter is clearly one variation, although not one I would have thought of myself.

- Hide the ball anywhere in the room and encourage the group to use verbal feedback such as 'warmer/colder' or 'yes/no' to guide the detectives.

Guess the Picture

This is a communication game involving observation, listening, and a broad range of communication skills, both verbal and mimetic. It is a challenging game, and meeting the challenge builds confidence.

Preparation. Select several pictures of varying themes (about six). A collection of photographs from magazines, mounted on card, is a useful aid to discussion and improvisation work.

How to play. Pass the pictures around one by one and ask each person to tell the group what they see. This can be done verbally, through makaton, mime or pointing. It may be necessary to elicit information by asking questions initially, such as 'show me where the house is in this picture' or 'how many men are there in the picture?' One person takes all the pictures, and selects one to describe. The pictures are then laid out on a table where all can see them, and the group is asked to identify the picture that has been described.

Variations

- The describer selects one person from the group to be the guesser. That person then becomes the describer for the next round of the game.

- Follow up with a discussion, role play or improvisation based on the themes of the pictures.

- Invite the describer to recreate the scene from the picture using the group and props from the studio.

Fairground Games

This activity is a combination of games, which can be played individually for their own sake, and can form the basis for an improvisation based on the idea of a fairground. Games form a useful stepping stone towards imaginative improvisation. The concept of an imaginary place, such as a fairground, may be difficult to grasp in some groups. The games can be played in the here and now initially, and then transferred quite easily into the 'as if' world of the fairground. This constitutes a movement from trunk to branch level work.

(1) Ball in the box

This game involves turn-taking and coordination of hand and eye.

Preparation. Place an empty box on the floor. Collect together a large number of balls.

How to play. Take turns to throw a ball towards the box, and applaud or acknowledge each successful throw. It may be appropriate to allow participants to stand at different distances from the box, as physical limitations make this game more challenging for some than for others. A 'fielder' may be needed if the number of balls is limited.

(2) Quoit on the stick

This game also involves aiming.

Preparation. Some rubber quoits are needed. Set up a stick in a box, or a mop in a bucket, or one of the therapeutic team can use their extended arm.

How to play. Each person takes it in turn to try to throw the quoit on to the stick. Allow plenty of opportunity to practise. If the therapist's arm is being used instead of a stick the game involves two-way cooperation. Other members of the group have the opportunity to watch as each person has their turn. As audience they may cheer, encourage each other and applaud as appropriate.

(3) In the stocks

Aiming skills are required in this game. The reward is the sight of the therapist wet and bedraggled.

Preparation. A bucket of water with a sponge, or a water pistol are required. 'Stocks' can be built out of playshapes, tables, or whatever is to hand. They should be positioned so that only the head is visible.

How to play. Each person in turn shoots the water pistol, or throws the sponge. Delightful.

Variations

*   Other group members may volunteer for the dubious privilege of being in the stocks. It is not advisable to push anyone into this role, as it could be experienced as humiliating. The main source of humour as in all 'lord of misrule' activities is the licence to debunk those in authority.

(4) Coconut Shy

This is another game involving hand–eye coordination, and a legitimate forum for destructive impulses, contained within the boundaries of the game.

Preparation. Toy spring-loaded guns with ping-pong balls are ideal, but small balls for throwing serve the same purpose. Set up a table with a triangle of polystyrene cups balanced on it.

How to play. The players take it in turns to take three shots at the cups from an appropriate distance. This distance might vary according to physical abilities. The mountain is reconstructed for each player.

Variations

*   *Leaning Tower of Pisa* Build a tower out of playshape cubes, preferably involving the group members cooperatively in this task. It could be several feet high. Individuals may either take it in turns to aim some larger balls at it from an appropriate distance, or the group as a whole may bombard it from all angles in a celebratory explosion of destructive energy. Bombs away!

(5) Fairground Scene

The four games above can be placed within the context of a fairground, created with the help of music and a couple of simple activities.

Maypole dance:
Using a set of streamers on sticks one person stands in the middle holding the ends of the streamers, while each group member holds the other end. The group winds around the central figure and back again to the accompaniment of waltz, polka or fairground music. If one member of the group is tall enough to function as a maypole use a large round parachute instead. The maypole stands in the middle and group members hold the edge of the parachute, winding in each direction and letting the canopy billow.

Carousel:
Play some rhythmic, cheerful music, and create a circle dance. Include moments of pairing up and turning with a partner, and encourage the dancers to change partners.

Board Games

The rules of most board games are considerably more complex than the games described above. This does not rule them out from use with this client group, as long as the therapist is flexible in how they are used.

I discovered *Cluedo* in the context of a small group of three men with severely challenging behaviours whom I saw on a weekly basis together with a male nurse from their home/ward. One of the men was autistic, very obsessive and spoke only very quietly and after considerable encouragement. Another had a hearing problem and a history of violence, but had a good vocabulary and comprehension. The third was very uncontained, loud, boisterous, spontaneous and egocentric. They all seemed to value coming to dramatherapy. It must have been a relief to be in a small group rather than a locked ward together with other men with similar problems. The dynamics of the group, however, were such that the first, quieter man would become isolated, whilst the other two engaged in loud chatter, spontaneous play and ultimately play fighting. This was not unhealthy. The group was providing a forum for letting off steam. There seemed to be a boisterous male camaraderie and friendship in the relationship between these two, but they had problems with boundaries and tended to get out of control.

We decided to work directly on the issue of boundaries and rules. Each session centred around a table, and we developed activities that involved listening and turn-taking. One of these was a version of the picture game described above, with the added ingredient of a tape recorder. We recorded the game and then played it back in the group, which encouraged some useful reflection on the interaction within the group, as well as on individual communication style. The microphone itself had the function of a 'talking stick', and facilitated turn-taking and listening.

A further table top game involved listening to a tape of everyday sounds, and matching them with pictures. Each player has a card with a number of pictures on, and some counters. The first player to place a counter on each picture is the winner, and the game can also be played non-competitively, as emerged in this group. The players helped each other to complete the game and the satisfaction of completing the task was shared.

On the basis of this success we attempted *Cluedo*, which became a popular activity in this group, requested on a regular basis. It was played non-competitively, as the conventional game requires complex memory and deductive skills that were beyond the ability of the group in question. Nonetheless the board game provided a physical focus for communication and turn-taking in the context of a shared imaginary world. Dice, cards and small props were useful concrete elements to handle. The different characters were renamed after known characters in the hospital community (e.g. the hospital chaplain, who was a significant figure for them), and in this sense the game was given an individual identity by the group.

It would have been interesting to explore extending the imaginary world of the board game into short moments of role play, contained by the overall structure of the game. The challenge for this group would be in facilitating work with a high degree of spontaneity and possibilities for creative expression balanced by clearly understood boundaries and structures for containment.

One-to-One Games

One-to-one work with clients with profound and multiple disabilities can include the simplest games. These often arise spontaneously in the interaction between therapist and client, in the development of a shared language (see Chapter 3 on profound disability).

Facial mirroring, eye contact games such as peep-bo or hide and seek, hand games and vocal games can be developed. These games depend only on the presence of two people in relation to each other. Further opportunities arise if objects and props are used, such as give and take, a gentle tug of war, hiding and finding, building and destroying. The key to developing these games appropriately is in the relationship between client and therapist. It is particularly important for the therapist to empathise with the client, to be patient and to attune to the rhythm and pace appropriate to the client.

CHAPTER 6

One-to-One Dramatherapy
A Journey With Lucy

Lucy was referred to me for individual dramatherapy following her participation in a short term music therapy group with colleagues. In that context she had seemed withdrawn and disturbed, and unable to use the group experience to work through her problems. Her contribution musically had been a regular and repetitive drum beat on a particular tambour, and she had been unwilling to explore other instruments. In her home environment – she lived with a dozen other women in a residential house within an ageing hospital unit – she was also seen as restless, anxious, unhappy and lacking in confidence.

When I first met Lucy I visited her in her home environment and we sat in the garden away from the other residents. She was a woman in her mid-forties, slight and mousy looking. She was able to walk, but in a shuffling way. Her posture was withdrawn, arms held closely to her sides, and head looking downwards. She had a bad tremor that was most obvious in her head, which was held low and to one side, and this affected her speech. I had difficulty understanding her, and had to ask her to repeat herself a lot. She was able to appreciate my difficulty in understanding her and was motivated to communicate. We talked about therapy, and I was struck by her ability to recognise her own need and her own unhappiness. She talked about a colleague in a work placement with whom she had some problems. It was clear that she welcomed the chance to be in a one-to-one situation with someone, and that she had some insight into herself. I felt that she might be able to use individual therapy to share and work through some of her troubles, and we agreed to try out a couple of sessions together.

The process extended into longer-term individual therapy. Our shared journey was both emotionally painful and creatively rich. There follows an account of the first year of this journey, with some reflections on technique and therapeutic process.

A Brief Background

Lucy was adopted as a baby shortly after her adoptive parents had lost a child. They did not know that she had disabilities at the time of adoption, and she grew up as an only child, unaware of her adoptive status. She learned to walk when she was four, with much help from her parents, and also received speech therapy. They wanted her to be as normal as possible, and provided her with a very sheltered home environment. There was little open recognition of her difference or problems.

She was admitted from there into the hospital for people with learning disabilities. Her parents could no longer cope with her at home due to their failing health. She was in her mid-twenties. A few years later, her mother died, and ten years later her father died. She was 'protected' from both these events, only hearing about them some weeks after each death. The regular family visits were taken on by an aunt and uncle whose trips to the hospital followed a similar format to those of her parents – a picnic of predictable favourite foods in the grounds of the hospital. Whereas her father had visited weekly, they came about once a month.

There are certain features of this background that are quite characteristic of the client group. The shift from protective home life to large institution is a major one and often traumatic. It often takes place as the client reaches puberty or adulthood when the protected child role within the family system is challenged by the uncomfortable realities of sexual development; or, as happened in Lucy's case, when the parents are too old to continue supporting the adult child. In either case the change in circumstance is often perceived by the client as a punishment for being 'bad'. Feelings of guilt and anger are fed by this perception and interpretation of events, often despite explanations of the move being 'for your own good'.

Death of the parents is a profoundly disturbing experience for most people, even after leaving home and creating their own life. For a person with learning disabilities brought up to remain dependent on a protective family well into adulthood, death of the family constitutes an even greater loss. For an only child such as Lucy brought up without a network of friends outside the family, the loss of the parents is of enormous significance. By 'protecting' her from the reality of their death she was denied the opportunity to attend the funerals and to come to terms with her pain and loss.

Loss and bereavement often emerge at the heart of the therapeutic process when working with this client group. The loss of the chance to lead a 'normal' life, the loss of freedom to fulfil dreams, and the loss of loved ones through changes in residential situation or through death – these are painful realities that are difficult to face and difficult to work through.

Establishing a Shared Language

The first five weeks

During the first few weeks of therapy my task was to find out how Lucy and I might best communicate with each other. For me it is one of the joys of dramatherapy that any number of forms may be used in the creation of a shared language. Lucy had no previous experience of dramatherapy, so it was up to us together to define and refine what dramatherapy would be for us in the context of her sessions.

During these early sessions I introduced her to a number of possibilities for personal expression, and she used these to introduce me to her inner world and her concerns. In a sense, we were casting a broad net together, made up of themes, and forms for exploring these themes. As the work developed, certain themes and certain forms emerged as most useful.

In the absence of a dramatherapy studio on site the sessions were conducted in a music therapy room. This meant that I did not have access to my usual range of props and creative stimuli. The room was smaller than my usual workspace, and more sparse. It was an empty space with a variety of larger instruments, and a cupboard full of smaller ones, a few chairs, a small table and a desk. I made only one addition to the space, which was a set of coloured pens and a small drawing pad, which I put on the small table.

Session One

For Lucy the room was also the space where she had experienced her music therapy group. In the first session I invited her to show me around the space and she chose to show me how to play the tambour. This was the instrument she had played in her music therapy group and she was clearly still in touch with that experience as something positive. She said that it was strange being in that room with me. I asked her if she knew where the music therapists were, and she said, 'On holiday'. Despite having worked towards an ending of the group Lucy had not dealt with it. Our presence in the room revealed her fantasy version of the ending. It is not uncommon for absences and endings to be seen in terms of holidays as a way of avoiding the reality of the loss and the feelings of being left. I talked to her about my music therapy colleagues, and let her know that they had spoken of her to me, that they were still around but that the group had finished.

In addition to playing a musical instrument we also worked with drawing, dance, mime and talking in our first session. She noticed the pens and paper, sat down and drew me a picture of the house she used to live in, and of her parents and her (Figure 6.1). I noticed how she positioned her parents together, with herself standing somewhat apart. The dynamic of a threesome, with its potential for jealousy, rivalry and Oedipal issues was to figure extensively in her therapy as it developed. For the moment she described the picture as 'a happy day' and told me that her parents were now in heaven. I asked her if she could draw heaven and she said that she could not, as she had not been there. She was bringing her background and the death of her parents into the therapy from the outset. There was a sense of 'paradise lost' and a recognition of something unknown/unknowable about the nature of death.

Figure 6.1 Lucy and her parents

She drew a second picture (Figure 6.2), a happy memory of herself paddling at the seaside with her parents looking on. She smiled at the picture and the memory, and I invited her to move into our first piece of role play. This was a simple piece of mime work, in which she joined me in miming paddling in the sea, scooping water with our hands and splashing our faces. This lasted only a minute or two, but it was enough to establish her openness to working dramatically, and her ability to use her imagination to create a new reality. In establishing the method it was important for me to model the mime initially, as an invitation to her to join me. It was safer to be 'actors' together at this stage, than for me to ask her to act alone with me as therapist/audience looking on. It was important to establish the possibility of shared play initially as a foundation for dramatic work. At later stages in the process either of us might be actor, audience or director.

Figure 6.2 A happy memory: paddling at the seaside — symbolically we were also 'getting our feet wet' in terms of engaging in dramatic representation

We sat down again, and she talked about how the visits of her aunt and uncle were not the same as seeing her parents. (Perhaps she was also telling me that working with me was not the same as her earlier relationship with the music therapists.) I asked her if she missed her parents and she replied, 'Yes, terribly'. I asked if she could imagine being happy again. She was thoughtful and eventually answered, 'I would like to be.'

In our initial meeting Lucy had told me that she enjoyed dancing, so I suggested we dance together. I was keen to find out whether she could open up in movement terms, and I modelled a variety of movements, without music, which she was able to mirror accurately, and enjoyed doing so. At the end of the session I asked her what she had enjoyed most, and it was the drumming and dancing. I asked her how she wanted to finish, and she chose to beat the tambour, whilst I moved to her rhythm. The tambour, a symbol of her earlier therapeutic experience had been used as a containing ritual at the beginning and end of the session.

Session Two

In this session we began to develop the movement work. After warming up by moving around the room, touching and naming the objects there, I asked Lucy if she wanted to draw. She said no, and chose to dance instead. This time the movements were her own and I mirrored them. The dance that emerged consisted of three movements, the first of which was a reaching upwards with each hand: we decided to name this a 'happy movement'. The second movement was her habitual, unconscious head lowering, which I exaggerated and incorporated as a movement into the dance. We decided that this was a 'sad movement'. The third movement consisted of small stamping steps, which we decided were 'angry movements'. I was trying to develop the idea of communicating feeling through movement, and I wanted to give her permission to bring any of these feelings into the therapy. It was a method that we developed more spontaneously the following week.

We reached a sticking point in this session, where Lucy could only say 'no' and 'I don't know' to anything I suggested. She was giving me a taste of a very bleak, and despairing experience of herself, one of disability. It was a mode that we returned to periodically during the course of her therapy, and which she needed me to experience with her.

There was nothing she could do, no way of being active, and no way of expressing. After making several unsuccessful suggestions, I asked her if I could tell her a story, and she was at last able to say yes. The structure allowed her to be in a receptive and relatively passive role. I made up the beginning of a story as an intuitive response to my experience of her. It was a way of letting her know I had seen her, and an invitation to her to embark on a creative and therapeutic journey.

ANNA: Once upon a time there was a beautiful princess. She had long blonde hair and was very lovely. She lived in a large palace. She would walk through the rooms of the palace, and look admiringly at her reflection in the mirrors on the walls. What was her name?

LUCY: Nilag.

ANNA: You would think that she would be happy in that lovely palace, but no, she was sad. She would wander in the gardens of the palace, and sit by the fountains listening to the water. One day she was sitting looking at her reflection in the water and she watched as a tear fell into the pool. She asked herself why she felt so sad, but she did not know.

One day she heard a strange voice, and it was a wise old frog, who told her, 'Princess, you are sad because you are lonely.' Do you think the frog was right?

Figure 6.3 The Princess Nilag/Maglab

.he frog told the princess that she must leave her lovely palace, and go on a long journey, and that she must find a friend. The princess Nilag didn't even know what a friend was, but she decided she would go.

Lucy ...d managed to make a contribution to the story in terms of the princess' rather strange name, and had been given the chance to influence the direction of the story. She drew a picture (Figure 6.3) of the princess' face, half hidden and with an ambivalent expression. We left the story at this point, and I had no idea if we would return to it, or whether it had any real relevance for her. In fact it was left fallow for a month, and I thought it had been forgotten. When Lucy brought it back into the therapy it became the central form for her dramatherapeutic journey. In its original form the story was my creation, and her contribution was simply the name of the princess and a drawing of her face. Gradually she made it her own creation and my role was more to facilitate her in telling the story, and exploring the themes and relationships within it.

The two trial sessions were over, and we agreed to continue on a regular open-ended basis after a one week break.

Session Three

Breaks in therapy, even those that are planned for, and that happen so early on, are often disturbing, particularly where the client has issues of loss, death or abandonment. After only two sessions Lucy and I had established a meaningful relationship; and the break of a week between the second and third sessions may have been a contributory factor to Lucy's condition when she arrived for the third session. She was very agitated, and full to overflowing with worries. On entering the room she went and stood in the corner, shaking and talking rather incoherently in an anxious voice.

I had difficulty hearing the content of what she was saying, although the emotional tone was clearly enough one of distress and anxiety. I gradually made out that she was worried about the hospital, and about why she was there, and why her parents had left her. She wanted to go 'home'.

I encouraged her to come away from the corner, and to move around the space as a way of arriving in the room and grounding herself. She took the tambour and began to play it as she walked around the room. She was saying 'no' quietly and repetitively as she played. I asked her to say it louder, and she said 'No, I'm all right.' I decided to try and explore this internalised message of denial.

ANNA: If your mother was here what would you say?

LUCY: I'm all right.

ANNA: And if your father was here?

LUCY: I'm all right.

ANNA: Perhaps you wouldn't want to worry them.

LUCY: Yes.

ANNA: So what do you do with your worries?

LUCY: I don't know.

ANNA: Shall we make a dance to explore this? What part of your body knows about worrying?

Lucy lifted her right hand up and forward toward me. Standing opposite her I mirrored this movement until our hands met. She repeated the movement with her other hand, and I mirrored likewise.

ANNA: So your hands know about worry.

We held the worry in our hands, cupped in front of us.

ANNA: What other part of your body knows about worry?

LUCY: It's gone.

ANNA: Where to?

LUCY: I don't know.

She touched her head, and I mirrored this movement. As in the previous session when I had incorporated her unconscious head movement into the dance I considered her unconscious touching of her head to be part of the dance, and I included it both in my mirroring and the commentary that I was making.

ANNA: So I put the worries in my head. They feel so heavy there.

I let my head swing down, which was Lucy's characteristic movement, and this time she readily mirrored my movement.

ANNA: They feel so heavy there.

I exaggerated the head nod, letting the whole of my upper body swing down with the weight of worries in the head, and she mirrored this and echoed my words.

Lucy yawned and this too was incorporated both into the dance and the commentary.

ANNA: It's so tiring carrying all these worries around.

LUCY: Yes, so tiring.

My aim was to facilitate Lucy in finding a form for the feelings that were overwhelming her when she arrived in the session. I took my lead from her and we created a language together. One of the possibilities of a formalised language such as a dance is that it can be repeated and modified. I suggested we repeat the dance and the commentary together, and in so doing the feelings were given containment and space. They were something expressible, that could be known and shared.

The second time through she felt enough in control to be able to explore a little further. She showed me how her whole body felt an overwhelming sadness; and began to talk about her feelings of not being like other people. Her parents seemed to have denied that she was different, and she could not understand why she was in a hospital as she shared their denial. I felt that this denial had been intended to protect her from pain, but that she was in touch with the pain anyway, along with confusion as to her condition. I decided to challenge her. I asked her if she was like me and she said that she was. I questioned her about ways in which we were not the same – I drive a car, earn money, live alone etc. She acknowledged the differences between us, her need for help in some parts of her life, and her lack of independence. She seemed quite relieved to have this reality in the open and it put her in touch with her anger.

She said 'My memory is going over the hills and far away' and when I asked her what she remembered she drew a house, similar to the one in the first picture, and coloured it in angrily, blotting out the doors and windows. She was continuing to say 'yes' and 'no' a lot, and claimed that she could not say anything else. I asked her about her anger, and suggested she could be angry with me. She said 'No, I'm angry with myself' and as we talked about her feeling of inner conflict she added 'I've got to face it you know.'

There is a characteristic contrast here between the language used by a client when feeling stuck and inadequate, and the richer, clearer vocabulary which can be accessed at moments of breaking through.

Session Four

In this session Lucy worked mostly through drawing. She drew a sequence of three pictures (Figure 6.4a, 6.4b, 6.4c). The first represented her family home in the past; the second her current home in the unit; and the third was a potential future home. It was striking that she obliterated the windows angrily in her current home as she coloured it in. The potential future home looked remarkably like her original home. Although she was able to name a

Figure 6.4 (a) Lucy's family house of origin

Figure 6.4 (b) Her current home in hospital

Figure 6.4 (c) A possible future home in the community

couple of real acquaintances with whom she might live if she moved into the community, my sense was that the idea of a future home was rooted in the fantasy of a return to the past.

At this time there were no overt plans for Lucy to move from her home within the hospital unit. Nonetheless, the relationship between her past, her present circumstances and her potential future was clearly of some concern to her. The current culture of moving people from institutional settings into the community creates fantasies for those who remain within the institution. They can feel left behind and this may trigger memories of the earlier 'abandonment'. The community is often 'sold' to clients as 'a better place' and there is a collective excitement about moving into the community, often shared by staff and residents. The community comes to represent a brighter future and the way forward. For many clients the fantasy image of this brighter place can only be based on past memories of living in their families of origin.

There is perhaps another significance to the series of drawings of homes. They can be seen as images of containment, and as representative of herself. Perhaps this sequence of houses was a symbolic representation of Lucy's preparation to branch out into the imaginary world of the story. In this sense they represent metaphorically the trunk stage of her therapeutic process.

Session Five

Although we had explored some mime and dance in previous sessions, this was the first time we entered an improvised role play. Lucy remembered the story of the princess, but not in the way I told it. I asked her to tell me the story so far, and as she did so she made it her own. Instead of the princess dropping a tear in the fountain it was a needle from her embroidery.

We enacted hunting for the needle in the pond (both of us in the role of the princess) by miming removing our shoes, and feeling for it in the water with our feet. I checked if we had found it and she chose the moment when we did. We lifted it out of the water and embarked on our journey to find a friend, armed with the needle and the tambour. I took on the role of narrator of the story, and asked questions to elicit as much of the content as possible from Lucy. She took me into an imaginary wood, and was able to make this into a strongly shared reality. We got down to floor level to drink from a stream, ate berries from trees and bushes as we continued our journey, and lay under a tree to sleep at night. As the princess she was frightened, being all alone in the woods at night. I asked her for the solution to this problem, and she suggested that she would call the frog. I took on the role of the frog, reassured her and suggested she beat her drum when frightened.

Dawn came and we carried on our journey. We were approaching the end of the session and I suggested that we could see in the distance the place where the princess must go. She could see it too, and named it as a castle.

We left the role play and sat down together. I suggested she make a drawing of the story so far. In so doing we could create some distance between ourselves and the enactment. We could discuss what happened in the story and in that sense de-role from the roles of princess and frog, and establish ourselves as Lucy and Anna back in the room and reflecting on the story. She made a drawing of the princess and the frog arriving at the castle with her tambour and needle. The drawing was pink, and the castle seemed inviting, full of windows and a large door. This door was also a door into the world of Lucy's dramatherapeutic journey. We had gathered shared experience and expressive skills enough to embark on this journey. We had found a common language. The journey could begin.

Working through the Metaphor

Once we had established some ways of working together sessions began to fall into a regular pattern or structure.

- Physical warm-up, arriving in the room or straight into

- verbal feedback about the week, or current concerns and a discussion of options for working methods and a choice made by Lucy
- enactment of the story using dramatic role play, movement and music making
- pictorial representation of key moments and reflections on the story
- closing ritual of Lucy's choice based on music or movement.

This was a form we arrived at together over the weeks. It remained flexible and open to change from week to week in response to Lucy's changing concerns. I saw my role as both facilitative and directive; facilitative in giving Lucy as much choice and responsibility as she could accept, directive in providing ways in which we might explore the dynamics and feelings of the imaginary material she presented.

Session Six – the people in the emptiness

Lucy kept her coat on all session. She requested to go on with the story, and took me to the castle that we had seen in the distance in the previous session. If we had been working in the dramatherapy studio she would have been able to build a concrete representation of the castle. Without any props we walked along an imaginary path until she decided we had reached the castle gate. We opened it in mime and called out 'hello'. I did not know if her castle would be peopled; as a product of her inner world Lucy would have to decide who, if anyone, was there. We continued to call 'hello', then waited, listening for an answer. None came. We mimed opening the door into room after room. Each time we called, listened, and Lucy said 'It's empty.'

Eventually I asked whether anyone lived there and she said 'Yes, a witch.' I gave her the choice of being the witch or casting me in that role. She decided I would be the witch and that she would continue as the princess. She told me in role that she was cold, and as the witch I suggested she light a fire, which she mimed. The encounter was a brief one and the relationship between princess and witch was developed more in the following session.

I checked with her whether she needed me to continue being the witch and with her permission moved out of that role. She continued to look for other people in the castle and found a young man. I asked her to take on the role of this man, and she sat in a chair whilst I interviewed her in role.

ANNA: What's your name?

LUCY: Robert.

ANNA: Tell me about yourself. What do you look like?

LUCY: I'm ugly.

ANNA: In what way?

LUCY: I've got big feet.

ANNA: Big feet?

LUCY: Yes, and very long legs, and a big nose, a big mouth.

ANNA: Anything else?

LUCY: Ugly.

I was using the interview in role technique to find out about this character. Having found out about him I asked Lucy to choose whether to stay in that role, or to return to the role of the princess, trusting that she knew where she needed to be. She chose the role of the princess, and I was to be Robert. Once I had taken on the role, she, as princess turned her back and walked away. I asked if she wanted to say anything and she said 'No'.

From the role of Robert I felt she had expressed herself to me quite clearly through her physical gesture. I was, I felt, holding the role of a strange and monstrous aspect of herself; perhaps her learning disabilities and difference from other people. Her gesture was rejective. She walked away and I was left to experience being weird, monstrous, alone, abandoned and ignored.

The picture Lucy drew to illustrate this session (Figure 6.5) shows the relationships slightly differently. For the first time in all the buildings she had drawn characters were placed inside the castle and visible. While the princess had walked away from Robert in our enacted encounter, in the drawing these two figures are shown facing each other within the container of the castle. It is the witch rather than the princess who seems rejected or rejecting. She is placed on the outside of the castle and faces away from the figures within. In describing the picture Lucy said that Robert was angry with the princess and that Nilag was angry with the witch.

There are many possible interpretations that could be made in relation to the session, the development of the story, and the pictorial representation of it. The characters within the story can be seen as 'inner objects', aspects of Lucy in relation to each other. In this sense the princess, witch, and ugly man are inner roles. These roles may be based on a known repertoire of fairy stories together with an internalisation of her experiences of herself and others in her past and present life. It was not entirely clear which aspect was angry with which, given the contradictions between the enactment and the picture. What is evident however is that we were beginning to deal with relationships that contained anger and conflict.

Figure 6.5. The Castle

It must be taken into account that the story arises in the context of therapy. It is a means of communication with me, her therapist. As such it offers her the opportunity to show me how it feels to be her. In this session we shared an experience of aloneness and emptiness when we first arrived at the castle. In a sense Lucy was taking me on a journey into her emptiness and coldness. In the encounter with Robert it was from the role of the princess that she turned her back on him. Perhaps this was an expression of her desire to turn away from the painful reality of her disabilities. My sense was that it was more than this. It was important for her that I should be in the role of the one who is rejected. In this way she could show me how it feels for her when I turn my back on her metaphorically at the end of a session, and in showing me how that feels I may represent the many other perceived sources of rejection in her life. The elements of dependency, closeness and authority invite the process of transference to take place, whereby the client's perception of the therapist is heavily influenced by earlier, often parental figures.

We were again in a dynamic of three. As in the very first picture she had drawn there were two female figures and a man – the family configuration she had grown up with. This time however there was the beginning of conflict between the characters, and the situations we explored were uncomfortable. Perhaps the picture shows a wished-for Oedipal situation in which bad mother/witch is pushed out, allowing daughter/princess to be together with the male figure/father. The story as fiction offers an apparent disguise and distance from reality. Paradoxically, this often facilitates the exploration of real life conflicts within dramatherapy. It would be a mistake, however, to be reductive or too precise in interpreting the story and the session. We may have been exploring Lucy's relationship with herself, her relationship in her family of origin, and her relationship with me, all at the same time and behind the veil of a fantasy world. As a dramatherapist I try to be aware of the many possibilities of meaning at the end of a session, while maintaining a position of openness.

Session Seven – in the dungeon

Lucy arrived wearing unusually strong colours: a black sweatshirt and red skirt. The design on the front of the sweatshirt was a black, empty heart, delineated by brightly coloured flowers.

We began the session by Lucy telling me that her 'people' had not come. She had waited for them all Sunday. She had been confused and angry, but had not checked with a member of staff if they were due to come. In the context of the hospital culture, having 'people', usually family, who visit is a major source of comfort, identity and even value. I was struck by the possibility that Lucy had isolated herself with her hopeful fantasy that there would be a visit rather than subject the fantasy to reality testing, and face the disappointment that it might be another week or two before they would come. She had suffered, but characteristically kept her suffering to herself.

She chose to continue with the story, and we reminded ourselves of the events of the previous week by looking at the picture. She remembered the castle, the princess and the witch; but she renamed the male figure as Peter, pronounced Pater. As such he may have contained elements of father (Latin *pater*) and her uncle.

I asked some questions to help us get back into the story.

ANNA: Where are we?

LUCY: In the castle.

ANNA: Whereabouts?

LUCY: In the dungeon.

ANNA: What's it like?

LUCY: It's dark and eerie.

We made eerie sounds together, by tapping on some wooden temple blocks with our fingers. This was the first time she had played anything other than the tambour in our sessions. It sounded uncannily like dripping water.

ANNA: Who is in here?

LUCY: A monster.

We negotiated who should play the monster and Lucy decided that she would be the monster. She stayed in this role for the whole enactment. It was agreed that I would take any other roles.

First, I was put in role as the witch, and the monster said I had to be put into an oven. I suggested she use the piano as the oven. She mimed turning it on, then stuffed me as the witch into the space between the piano stool and the piano. I was instructed to 'rise', and so I began curled up at floor level, and gradually rose up to standing position, howling with pain all the time. The monster was delighted, and when the witch was cooked to a state of charred blackness, she opened the oven door, instructed me to come out, and proceeded to push me out of the castle, and banish me into the woods.

I was now asked to take on the role of the princess, and the monster pushed her out, too. I asked questions from the role to find out why the princess was to be banished to the woods. The monster said she was bad, and could not remain in the castle. She had to go.

My third role was as Peter, and Lucy's spontaneous reaction to my entering this role was one of fear. The monster seemed to lose its power. She hid behind the piano. I tried to find out why I was so frightening by asking some questions. She replied that I did not play and that I chastised the monster. I felt that these wrongdoings were rather mild compared to her reaction, but she was not willing to say more. I asked her what I was to do, and she told me to sit down, before she would come out from behind the piano. With some encouragement she decided that I was to be caged. She put me in a chair by the wall and mimed locking the cage door. She then returned to behind the piano, peeked over the top and watched me with some pleasure moaning and groaning about being in the dark, locked up and all alone in the dungeon. I asked if I was supposed to get hungry, starve, die. She replied, 'No, just to be alone.' We stayed in this position for some minutes, until we decided to leave the story at that point.

We de-roled and Lucy made a series of drawings (Figures 6.6 to 6.9). These were quite primitive compared to her previous drawings, and she used dark

Figure 6.6 The monster in the dungeon

Figure 6.7 The witch, cooked and banished in the woods

Figure 6.8 The monster merged with the Princess

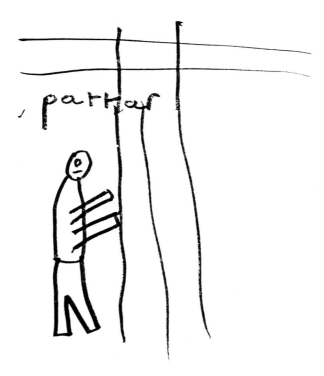

Figure 6.9 Peter/Pater behind bars in the dungeon

brown and black colours. The dungeon and the events we had enacted seemed to arise from an unconscious, dark and regressed part of her inner world. The interaction with the witch had seemed the least ambiguous. The witch was to be punished, transformed (cooked) and banished. The picture of her afterwards, alone and black in the woods was clear. It was noticeable that the drawing of the monster pushing out the princess was less clear. It showed these two characters as merged. My sense was that the monster represented a monstrous aspect of the little girl/princess that was split off but part of the same character. The picture of Peter showed him behind bars, as we had left him at the end of the enactment. I wondered about why the character of Peter was so frightening. Was this to do with her father's death being the final abandonment? Or her uncle not visiting? Was the cage an image of her own subsequent sense of imprisonment in an institutional life? As in the previous session I was left at the end in the role of the abandoned and alone one. She was showing me what it was like to be in that position. There was also the possibility that a male figure had been physically or sexually abusive to Lucy, that someone was so frightening and uncontained that they needed to be made safe by being locked up.

I had to bear all these possibilities in mind, but chose not to ask any direct questions at this point that would ask for meaning outside of the metaphor of the story. We finished with a dance, first, a dance of Nilag, which consisted of a restrained stamping movement, and then a de-roling dance to let go of the various characters in the story.

Session Eight — murder and abandonment

I was put in role as the princess, so that Lucy could take the role of Peter in the cage. I was to rescue him and the two of us were to go to the woods to kill the monster who was in the woods. I asked her which role she needed to be in, and she chose to be the monster again. It was only from within this role that she could contact her murderous feelings. The monster wanted to kill Peter and the princess.

I took on the role of Peter, and Lucy as the monster mimed killing me with a sword. She was energised and enjoyed watching me fall to the ground and die. As the dead Peter I asked what the monster wanted to say to me.

LUCY as monster: You're dead.

ANNA as dead Peter: What did I do?

LUCY: You were cruel, you left me. You are dead now.

We left Peter on the ground in the woods. She did not want to bury him, and still in role as the monster decided not to kill the princess, but to go to the castle where the two of them would live together. I took on the role of the princess and we returned to the castle and played a bongo duet together, before leaving the story. Lucy drew the monster killing Peter (Figure 6.10), and the monster and princess leaving the corpse lying dead on the ground.

Figure 6.10 The monster killing Peter

The different characters within the story lacked definition, and their characteristics changed to some extent from week to week. When I asked questions to clarify my understanding, the answers were often contradictory and increased my sense of uncertainty and confusion. There was a lack of consistency and clarity of thought in this sense, and perhaps a deliberate attempt on Lucy's part to disguise the personal meaning of her enactments, but certain dynamics and themes were repeating themselves. The energy of particular moments of enactment pointed to the key issues and themes. Lucy was expressing murderous and vengeful feelings. There was also a desire to destroy the triadic relationship and be in a dyad. This may have related to the Oedipal theme mentioned above. In terms of her relationship with me she was both killing me as Peter, and having me to herself in the final scene.

Session Nine – loneliness and rage

The session began with a spontaneous musical duet on chime bars and temple block. We were playing together, as we had been at the end of the previous week's enactment. Lucy said that she was happy, that her people had been and brought her sweets. She was very much in touch with the story and wanted to go back to the dungeon in the castle.

She was alone in the dungeon in the role of the princess. I questioned her and she replied that it was dark. She was standing, and mimed warming her hands at a fire. She said that she felt happy, but was standing alone in the dark in a dungeon with nothing but a fire. I asked her where the others were, and she said that she had sent them to the woods so that she could be alone. This could be understood as a reversal of her family situation, in which she was the one who was 'sent away'; or as a wished-for situation in her current life, where she was having to share a home with twelve people not of her choice.

We stayed for several minutes in this solitary scene, with me as audience or witness to the aloneness of the princess. Since there were no other people in the scene I asked her if this was a fire that could talk. She said that it was, and that I could take on the role. I crouched down in the place where she was miming warming her hands, and she remained standing slightly bent with arms outstretched towards me. She was reluctant to move the scene on, apart from fetching some more fuel for the fire. I commented on it feeling cosy. She agreed, saying that she felt warmer, but that she would keep her coat on. I suggested she might sit comfortably by the fire, but she refused. The feeling was a strange combination of intimacy and discomfort, as she maintained her stooping position for several minutes.

She drew a picture of the princess at the fire, using cold blue and grey colours. The fire seemed to be a multi-layered symbol: of warmth, comfort and life on the one hand, but also of cold, anger and destruction on the other. I asked her about the image of Nilag, and she said again that she was happy. I said that she certainly did not look happy to me, and I asked her where the other characters were while she was at the fire. She said that they were in the woods, and that Nilag was there too, looking for the monster to kill. I invited Lucy to return to the story to enact this scene, and she accepted.

I was to be the monster and stand in the exact place in the room where I had been as the fire. She came up to me and made stabbing movements, as I fell to the ground, dead. She continued to stand over me, and I watched her shadow out of the corner of my eye as she carried on stabbing at the air in a regular rhythm that reminded me of the way she had habitually played the tambour in her music therapy sessions. She was in control of herself in so far as she never actually touched me, and was able to observe the formalities of working with mime. At another level she was taken over by her 'act hunger' to stab me/the monster/whoever we represented for her. Eventually I turned my head to ask her how long she was going to carry on killing me, and her response was to laugh and say 'Forever.' I carried on asking some questions about which roles we were both in, but her responses were as contradictory and confused as her act hunger was clear. The story was emerging as a creative pretext for moments of symbolic enactment rather than a coherent linear process.

Session Ten – Misery

This was a difficult session, blocked at a level of creativity. We were unable to work with the story. Lucy was again entrenched in a position of disability, saying 'I can't' and 'no' a lot. I asked her about the story and she said 'Everyone is dead.'

Figure 6.11 Lucy feeling bleak

I said that she seemed miserable, and asked if she knew why. She said 'No, I can't say why.' I made some suggestions as to why she might feel miserable: because her parents were dead and no longer with her; because she only saw me once a week and would like to see me more often; because she had to live in a hospital and could not be independent; and because her people only visit once a month.

She agreed with each of these, and drew a picture of herself feeling bleak (Figure 6.11).

We had established a way of working in the previous weeks, and a rich metaphorical language. It was important for me not to be attached to that way of working, but to be able to respond to Lucy in whatever way was possible. Although she found it hard to name and express her unhappiness I felt it would be useful to let her know that difficult feelings can be named in the therapeutic situation. What is unmentionable in the everyday context is not taboo in therapy.

Making Changes

I looked back over the roles Lucy played in the first ten sessions. Within the story she was often murderous, vengeful, spiteful and monstrous. In terms of her real-life roles spoken about at the start of the session she presented as passive, child-like and lacking in confidence. In relation to me she was sometimes open and creative, and at other times stuck and despairing.

She often wore her coat throughout the session, and I felt that this related to the theme of emotional coldness, and also to the issue of exposure within the therapeutic process. I wondered if it might be useful to explore this, so I arrived at the next session with four large pieces of brightly coloured cloth.

Session Eleven – confronting the witch

I began the session by asking Lucy about her week, and she replied 'Nothing special whatsoever.' She responded to other questions by saying 'I don't know' and 'I don't know anything.'

She wanted to return to the story, and put herself in role as the princess sitting by the fire. Her name had changed from Nilag to Maglab. I offered her a piece of fabric to drape about her as the princess' dress. She chose the yellow one immediately, but was uncomfortable about my draping it over her coat. She said 'The princess wears nothing.' and wanted me in role as the princess.

We created a fire by draping yellow and red fabric over a xylophone, and I sat by it, complaining about being naked and cold. She took on the role of Peter, who on this occasion was the princess' father. As the princess I asked for help, and Lucy as the father said that she could not help. He himself was warm and had a coat but I would be better off alone and cold. I continued to complain and demand quite forcefully that he should help me. The response was Lucy's characteristic 'I don't know'. I continued expressing my need for something to wear and she eventually mimed giving the princess a yellow dress. I said that it was better than nothing, but that it would not keep me as warm as a coat.

The role Lucy played in this scene was punitive and withholding, qualities that were developed in the next scene. I asked if anyone else was in the scene and she pointed to the corner of the room, saying that the witch and monster were there. I asked if they should come over and share our fire. She said 'no' in a way that showed pleasure in her having something that they did not. I followed this mood, by calling across the room 'You can stay over there. It's our fire and you can't share it'. She joined in the shouting, rather quietly, but with definite enjoyment.

In the next scene Lucy chose to be the monster whom I approached from the role of Maglab.

ANNA *as Maglab:* What are you wearing?

LUCY *as Monster:* A yellow coat (*the same colour as the princess' dress*).

ANNA *as Maglab:* Are you warm enough?

LUCY *as Monster:* Yes I'm fine.

ANNA *as Maglab:* I'm cold, I've just got this little dress. Can you help?

LUCY *as Monster:* No.

ANNA *as Maglab:* But I'm cold.

LUCY *as Monster:* I don't know. I can't.

ANNA *as Maglab:* Oh, I'm sure you can.

LUCY *as Monster (walks over to the fire, removes the yellow and red cloths and brings them back):* Here you are.

ANNA *as Maglab:* You didn't think you could, but you did help me.

Within the make-believe of the story I had challenged Lucy to move beyond her position of 'I can't' into a more competent and active role, a helper. Having established an alliance between the monster and the princess I asked her as monster what he thought of the witch, who was still in the corner and who had been ignored in the story for several weeks.

LUCY *as Monster:* I don't like her.

ANNA *as Maglab:* Why not?

LUCY *as Monster:* She works me too hard.

ANNA *as Maglab:* How?

LUCY *as Monster:* She makes me carry wood for the fire.

ANNA *as Maglab:* Do you want to tell her how you feel?

LUCY *as Monster:* I'm afraid. But I want an argument.

ANNA *as Maglab:* Shall we go together?

LUCY *as Monster:* Yes.

We went over to the corner, created the witch out of a piece of black cloth draped over a chair and I took on the role of double for the monster. I modelled confronting the witch, calling her cruel and wicked, and Lucy as monster joined in. She was enjoying it, but was characteristically restrained. I began to exaggerate the feelings, and kicked the chair/witch. I encouraged her to do the same. She looked unsure, then reached forward laughing and shook the chair with her hand. We carried on throwing insults at her, and then I asked what we should do with her, chase her away, kill her? Her choice as in previous sessions was that we should turn our backs and walk away. We did this, and ended up playing a duet together on the xylophone, during which she repeatedly said 'yes'.

At the time when we were confronting the witch I felt that this character represented the cruelty of the therapeutic process. As Lucy's therapist I also made her work, carrying fuel for her emotional fire. It was hard work for her, but she did make a significant shift during the session from a position of saying no, to one of saying yes. The emergence of a competent role, one that could actively solve a given problem, that is, the princess' coldness, was an important step. I also felt it was healthy that she took the risk of facing the witch. The change in energy during this session was reflected in the colours Lucy chose for her pictures. We had moved into a pink phase.

Session Twelve – to the tower

Lucy arrived with news of having seen her people at the weekend. She was positive, described their picnic in detail and talked of her feelings as 'happy and cheerful' even when they left. When I questioned her further she mentioned some 'sadness' too, but she seemed reluctant to include any difficult feelings in what had been a predominantly pleasant experience. Although she had been able to express very negative feelings within the drama, in 'real life' she had a tendency to be either unrealistically positive or stuck in overwhelming negative feelings that were inexpressible. In

Kleinian terms she was in the less mature paranoid schizoid position, as opposed to the more reality-based depressive position in which both good and bad can co-exist.

She remembered the previous session in terms of the dynamics rather than the specific characters. I asked her if she remembered what we had done to the witch. She lowered her head, laughed and said 'no.' I challenged this as she was clearly enjoying remembering something. She said 'We put her on the fire.' In terms of our angry attack on the witch this was an accurate symbolic version of the story.

I asked Lucy how she wanted to work today, and she chose another drama with Maglab. The change of name had continued, and may have indicated a shift within the character. Certainly the ensuing drama was very different. The setting was still the castle, but we had moved out of the dungeon and were now high up at the top of the tower. We walked several times around the room, as if ascending a spiral staircase to get to the top of the tower, and I asked her which role she was in. She was Maglab and she was alone. She carried on alone up the spiral until she arrived at the top and I encouraged her to look out of an imaginary window.

ANNA: What do you see?

LUCY *as Maglab:* Mountains, woods, fields, hills.

ANNA: Are there any animals, birds or people down there.

MAGLAB: Yes, a big red bird, an eagle.

ANNA: Does he come to the tower?

MAGLAB: No, he's ill, he's very ill.

ANNA: Well perhaps he can come anyway.

> *I took on the role of the eagle, flew to a window in the tower, and perched there (on the piano stool) looking into the room.*

ANNA *as Bird:* Am I a special bird? What makes me special?

LUCY *as Maglab:* That you can fly.

ANNA *as Bird:* Would you like to be able to fly?

LUCY *as Maglab:* No. You are ill.

ANNA *as Bird:* (extending a wing) Can you make me better?

LUCY *as Maglab:* I don't know.

ANNA *as Bird:* Can you try?

LUCY *as Maglab:* Yes I can try *(miming bandaging the wing).*

ANN *as Bird:* Thank you. Can I still fly with this bandage on?

LUCY *as Maglab:* Yes.

ANNA *as Bird:* Can you say anything to help me?

LUCY *as Maglab:* Yes. Be better.

> *I flew off, and returned some moments later. I asked if I was better and she said that I was, and took off the bandage, in mime.*

ANNA *as Bird:* Thank you for helping me. Can I do anything for you in return? Carry a message, or use my claws or beak in some way?

LUCY *as Maglab:* No. Nothing.

ANNA *as Bird:* What do you do in this tower all alone?

Figure 6.12 The Princess healing the wounded eagle's wing

LUCY *as Maglab:* Nothing

ANNA *as Bird:* Do you make music?

LUCY *as Maglab:* Yes, plenty of music.

ANNA *as Bird:* May I hear some?

LUCY *as Maglab:* Yes.

> *She played the xylophone, a quiet tune of three notes and we vocalised together as she played.*

Lucy had introduced several new elements into the story: the tower, the eagle, and the themes of illness and healing. The theme of illness was of real concern to her, and she insisted on bringing it into the story, despite the fact that I had initially misunderstood the word 'ill' as 'real'. The role of the bird allowed Lucy to bring her own condition into the therapy, whether her learning disabilities or her sense of spiritual and emotional damage. It was positive that she entered the role of healer or helper in the story in an active way. In terms of her learning disabilities, however, the reality is that some 'illness' is permanent. The struggle to come to terms with this was an inevitable part of her therapeutic journey to become more whole and more integrated. As Lucy began to draw a bright picture of the princess bandaging the bird (Figure 6.12) she pressed so hard that the tip broke off the felt pen. I felt this was an unconscious reminder that some damage cannot be undone.

Session Thirteen – healing the tree

The central concern of illness and healing continued within the context of the story, but with different characters. From the tower Lucy as Maglab looked through a window, and found a deer from the woods. As the deer, I came up to the tower, and invited her to come to the woods.

We explored the woods together until she found a tree that was 'cold', 'ill' and 'keeps falling over'. She chose a wooden desk in the corner of the room to represent this tree. She felt it, and said 'It has trouble with its roots.' I asked if we could help it, and she replied 'No. Only the witch can help.' I asked if we should go and find the witch; 'Yes.'

Lucy chose to be the witch and cast me in role as Maglab. I found her, took her over to the tree and asked her if she could help.

LUCY *as Witch:* I can't. I've lost my magic.

ANNA *as Maglab:* But it is cold and ill.

LUCY *as Witch:* Yes.

ANNA *as Maglab:* Will it live?

LUCY *as Witch:* Yes.

ANNA *as Maglab:* Maybe it will just have to accept being ill.

LUCY *as Witch:* No, I need to go and find my spells.

She took me over to the other side of the room, and chose a cymbal on a stand to represent her lost spells. I carried it for her over to the tree and she took charge of a magic ritual, directing me to help as necessary. We each had a beater, and she beat on the cymbal in front of the tree. She told me that I was to beat on the leg of the desk. We made a solemn duet in this way. I asked if she had any magic words to say. She said 'This is so that it will grow again. And it will.' From my role as the princess I thanked her for helping the tree, and for teaching me some magic.

We left the enactment, and as she drew a picture of the scene (Figure 6.13). I reflected that the princess was getting on better with the witch than she had previously. The witch had changed from persecutor to helper, a transformation that occurs in many traditional fairy stories. In Hansel and Gretel, for example, the time spent with the witch in the woods is a time of transformation and growing independence for the two children. Their stay with her helps them separate from their parents and from each other (Opie 1974). In the story of Vasilisa and the witch Baba Yaga, the latter is similarly a device for the young girl's initiation into intuitive wisdom and her own power (Estés 1992).

Dealing with Current Life Events

We had reached a point in Lucy's therapeutic journey where certain role changes were apparent within the context of the story. She was more active in directing the story, and she was taking on more positive roles. We maintained an apparent distance and separation between the make-believe world of her story and the reality of her life within the hospital. In the next session we began to work directly with 'real life'.

Session Fourteen – the screaming bomb

Lucy arrived talking about her people not having been. She was disappointed again, and I asked her why she did not find out exactly when they were coming. She replied 'I don't know.' I asked her if she ever told them how she felt when they did not come. She answered 'no, it's a secret.'

I suggested it did not need to be a secret, and that she might talk to them about her feelings. With Lucy's permission I set out two empty chairs to represent her people. I was going to sit in one of them and she was to practice

Figure 6.13 The witch instructs the Princess in healing the tree

letting them know how she felt. I sat in the chair indicated to represent her cousin's wife, and waited for her to say something about our visits.

Her response was unexpected. She certainly began to talk about her feelings, but the focus was not the visits of her people. As the door into her feelings opened she became intensely agitated about a 'girl' in her home, a 'patient' who was noisy. Lucy launched into a long and articulate tirade about this woman who had been screaming all day. 'It goes right through you. It's like lightening. She goes on and on... I wish she was dead.' I asked Lucy what she would like to say to this woman. 'Shut up, stop this performance. I can't drink my tea in peace. You're like a screaming bomb. I wish you were dead.'

I moved out of the chair representing her relative, and into my own. I encouraged Lucy to consider what she could actually do about the situation, who she might actually talk to in her home. She practised telling the nurse that she wished to have her tea in her own room 'away from that screaming girl.'

I felt that Lucy's strong reaction to the woman had something to do with the contrast between them, and the fact that she keeps her own feelings secret. She made a striking drawing of the two of them (Figure 6.14), which I used as a basis for some questions.

ANNA: How do you think she must feel?

LUCY: Unhappy, distressed.

ANNA: I guess you know what it feels like to be unhappy and distressed. Do you?

LUCY: *(laughs)*

ANNA: You don't scream though, do you?

LUCY: No, I'm quiet and don't scream.

ANNA: Not even if you wanted to. Are there things inside you that make you want to scream?

LUCY: Yes.

ANNA: If you screamed, who would it be at?

LUCY: Me, mostly.

ANNA: And perhaps sometimes at me? At the patients in your home? At your people? Perhaps your parents?

She agreed with each of these suggestions, but it was significant that her first line of attack was habitually herself.

Figure 6.14 The screaming bomb. Lucy, on the right, looks out in horror

I pointed out to Lucy that the two characters in the drawing were opposites, the one who screams and the one who keeps her feelings secret. I suggested she might learn something from the other character. At least that one lets people know how she feels. Lucy was amused at this idea, and we returned to the initial role training exercise in which she was invited to let her people know how she felt when she was expecting them and they did not come.

Before leaving she asked for us to play the temple blocks together. As we played she talked about not wanting to go back to her 'ward'. She said she wanted to go back home again, to where she had lived as a child. In her mind's eye this house still existed, despite the fact that her parents were dead and it was no longer their home.

Session Fifteen – the meeting

That morning Lucy had attended a meeting about the possibility of her being resettled into the community. Her people had attended, and had expressed a preference for her remaining at the hospital. She had expressed the same preference.

The experience had made her disoriented, and she did not arrive for her session with me until ten minutes before the end, clutching a handful of chocolate wrappers. We talked a little, and she mentioned that her people had been, but denied that there had been a meeting. Something was deeply disturbing to her, but she was as yet unable to look at it. This difficulty coincided with the approach to the Christmas break, the first major break in her dramatherapy sessions.

Session Sixteen – the Princess dies

Lucy was still reluctant to talk about the meeting and the issues around it. She said that she wanted to work with the story, saying 'I love the story'.

She cast me as Maglab, and created the situation of Maglab leaving the castle and going into town. The theme of leaving home and approaching the community could apparently only be broached through the medium of the drama. Lucy was in role as director of the story. As Maglab I came down from the tower, left the castle grounds and began to walk towards town. Just before reaching the town I had to pass through the woods, which she described as 'eerie and frightening'. In terms of the room they were located behind the piano, an area that had been associated with fear in previous sessions. I asked her what to do in these eerie woods, and she said, 'Go back'. I returned to the castle.

The journey into town was perceived as dangerous, and by returning to the castle Maglab was able to avoid the danger, but was also stuck in the castle. From the role I asked whether I should try again, and Lucy directed me to do so. This time I got to the town, and went shopping in a few shops, Lucy playing a series of shopkeepers. After a while it was time to return to the castle, and Lucy directed me to return through the woods. The story took a spontaneous turn at this point. I was passing behind the piano, when Lucy approached, saying that the woods were full of owls. She took on the role of one of these owls, and made appropriate hooting noises, that were indeed quite eerie. I tried to talk to her from the role of Maglab.

LUCY *as Owl:* I have killed Maglab.

ANNA: Why?

OWL: I just wanted to.

ANNA: What did she do?

OWL: Nothing.

ANNA: Well how did you do it? With your claws, your beak?

OWL: With my beak.

I was no longer in role as Maglab, but was there more as facilitator of the story. I suggested that if Maglab was dead the owl might bury her. We mimed burying her, but she refused making any ceremony over the body. We were to just leave her.

We left the enactment and Lucy made some drawings of the scene (Figures 6.15 and 6.16). I asked her how she felt about the death of the princess, and she replied 'Happy, I've got my happiness back.' I checked with her whether the death of the princess meant the end of the story, and she said that it did not, but that there was a change.

What was this change about? There were a number of possible ways to understand the events of the story, and they may all contain an element of truth to a greater or lesser extent.

(1) The community is a dangerous place. It is safer to stay put.

(2) The community may be a dangerous place, but there are times when it is right to face the fear, and risk letting something die.

(3) The owl as death swoops unexpectedly and takes people away suddenly and without apparent reason, as it had with Lucy's parents In Shakespeare's poem *The Phoenix and the Turtle*, reference is made to the screech owl as the foreteller of death:

> 'But thou shrieking harbinger,
> Foul precursor of the fiend,
> Augur of the fever's end
> To this troop come thou not near'.

(4) The owl as the wisdom of the unconscious has killed off the little princess, a regressed little girl part of Lucy that is not in touch with the real world, and that she has outgrown.

(5) As Lucy drew the owl she said it was called Robin. Indeed it looks more like a robin than an owl. As a composite of two birds it may be a multiple symbol. The owl has associations of the night time and of wisdom. The robin is cheery and courageous. Through its association with Christmas it contains promise of birth or rebirth.

(6) Lucy's idea of moving into a home in the community had been an unrealistic one, a fantasy of moving in with her people or moving back to the family home. The resettlement meeting had revealed

Figures 6.15 An owl called Robin

Figure 6.16 Killing the Princess

these fantasies as unrealistic. Her people did not want her to live with them. An infantile hope had died.

(7) The approach of Christmas and the break in therapy is death-like. Killing Anna in role as Maglab is an expression of anger at the arbitrariness of the break.

Session Seventeen — the grave

In this last session before the Christmas break several themes were drawn together. Although we had enacted many killings and deaths over the preceding weeks Lucy had consistently turned her back on the dead. There was always a sense of unfinished business, of a difficulty in really facing the reality of death and endings. This pattern was reflected in the shared musical improvisations that took place either within the story or at the end of a session as a parting ritual. In these Lucy would characteristically stop playing very suddenly. I would be left hanging, having to come to terms myself with the abruptness of the ending.

It is fitting that the last session before our break, an ending in its own right, provided the forum for Lucy to look at death and loss. She arrived looking different, wearing a purple dress and a light jacket instead of her usual brown coat. She remembered the story and the fact that Maglab was dead. I suggested we might visit Maglab's grave, and she agreed.

I created a grave out of a folded blanket and a brown chiffon scarf that were in the room, and checked with Lucy if anything else should be there. She said that there should be an oak tree by the grave. I asked her to choose an instrument to represent the tree, and she placed a large xylophone at the head of the grave. The scene was set and we stood and looked at the grave. I asked her how she felt looking at the grave, and Lucy said that she did not know. I suggested we could spend a moment remembering the princess, so we sat on the floor by the grave, and looked at some of the pictures that Lucy had drawn of the princess. This enabled us to recap on the work she had done during this first 'term' of therapy. We placed the picture of the princess' face on the grave and reflected on her life. Lucy's contribution was to talk of how lonely the princess had been.

I said that we needed to say goodbye to the princess. Lucy's reaction to this suggestion was to laugh.

ANNA: Did you never say goodbye to your parents when they died?

LUCY: No.

ANNA: Did you not go to their funerals?

LUCY: No.

ANNA: Did you ever visit their graves?

LUCY: No, never.

ANNA: Have you ever said goodbye to the part of yourself that you were as a child, when you lived with them? Before you were an adult?

LUCY: No.

I talked of how people sometimes put flowers on a grave to pay respects and say goodbye to people who had died. I suggested we might do that within the drama, and she agreed to this. I took responsibility for structuring this ritual, whilst giving her choice as to the details. I asked her first of all to pick flowers for the princess. She moved to the side of the room and we mimed picking flowers. I asked her what colour they were; they were 'green', the colour of unripeness, and of growing. At her direction we placed them in mime at the foot of the grave at either side. I asked her to gather some flowers for her parents, and this time she chose blue ones, which we placed a little higher up at the side of the grave. Finally I asked her to pick flowers for the part of herself that was a little girl. She chose yellow daffodils (a colour that she had associated with the princess in the story) and we placed them at her request on top of the grave.

I suggested we stand by the oak tree at the head of the grave, and look at the grave with all its flowers from the tree's point of view. I felt it was important to include this symbol of growth and vitality that Lucy had contributed to the setting. I asked her if she could show in a movement how the tree felt as it looked at the grave. She stood with one arm pointing downwards to the ground, and the other reaching up towards the sky. We talked about this gesture, about death being part of growing.

I asked if we might play some music by the grave. Lucy chose to play the oak tree/xylophone, and I checked with her whether I should play with her. She directed me to take another, smaller xylophone and to set it at the foot of the grave. We played, and the music was quite different than on previous occasions. Lucy's playing was stronger and she was using more of the notes on her instrument. The improvisation was evocative, longer than usual, and significantly we found a natural and mutual moment to end the piece.

Lucy's drawing of the enactment (Figure 6.17) began with the tree, which she saw as having strong roots (unlike the sick tree of some weeks before), enormous and blowing in a strong wind. She added the grave, in pink; and then the flowers, which are tall and bright. The feeling of the picture is vital.

Figure 6.17 The Princess' grave, with trees and flowers

By facing and acknowledging death and loss she was more in touch with life and her own energy.

Working Through

We had arrived at a turning point. The image of Maglab's grave was a marker for us both, signifying the several deaths and losses that Lucy would need to come to terms with in order to mature and move on in her life.

Lucy's dramatherapy during the following six months addressed this need gradually; sometimes obliquely through the story and metaphor, at other times more directly through discussion. At the end of these six months there was another turning point. The organic pace and natural rhythm of Lucy's therapy was emerging. Although the issues of death and loss were highlighted as significant within the first six months, it was closer to a year before I felt Lucy was integrating the work.

This second period of six months can be looked at as one process, with a strong sense of continuity between sessions. Some sessions stood out as holding particularly meaningful moments for Lucy. There were four main threads to the work, and the focus could change within any one session or from week to week to one of these threads.

(1) The grave as location for the action.

(2) The tree as a symbol of life/death, growth and transformation.

(3) The relationship with Anna as therapist.

(4) The relationship with real-life relationships outside the therapy situation.

The grave had initially been set up by myself in the middle of the room. As Lucy brought her own inner world to the staging of the story she found a more accurate place for it. This was at the back of the room, between the back of the piano and a storage cupboard, and next to a wooden desk. There were already associations to these places. Lucy had hidden behind the piano when she first confronted Peter in the dungeon. This was also the locus of Maglab's death in the dark forest. The desk was the same one that had represented the tree that needed healing, and that the witch had indeed healed with Maglab's help. The area as a whole was rich in associations of fear, darkness, death and healing.

The general pattern of sessions was that Lucy and I would talk for a while, and then she would ask to go to the story. Asked where the story would be set she usually replied 'Maglab's grave' whilst looking at the relevant area of the room. She chose who would be in the scene and decided who would

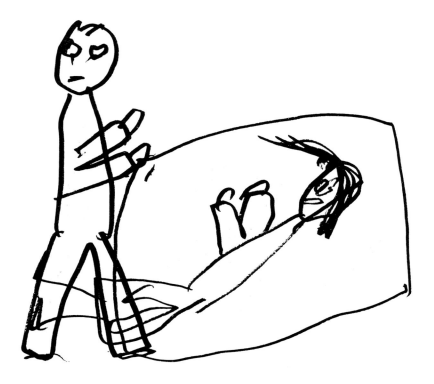

Figure 6.18 Peter visits the grave

play which role. She never played the dead Maglab herself. Sometimes I was put in this role, at other times I accompanied her as facilitator and the part of the dead princess was imagined. She visited the grave several times from each of the roles that had appeared in the story, and each of these appeared to allow her to access a different perspective or different feelings. She went as Peter, the witch, the monster, and also eventually as herself.

Burning

Two of the earlier visits to the graveside from the role of Peter involved setting fire to the grave (Figure 6.18 and 6.19). I held the role of the dead Maglab, lying on the blanket behind the piano. Lucy as Peter stood at the foot of this 'grave', just looking. Although I was playing the role of a dead person I allowed myself a voice, to ask questions and to facilitate the story. The direction this took was that Lucy as Peter would collect firewood from

Figure 6.19 Peter burning the Princess' grave

Figure 6.20 Peter chopping down a giant tree

the forest, pile it on the grave and set fire to it. As the grave burned she would hold out her hands to warm them on the flames, and described her feelings as 'glad' and 'happy'.

My own feelings from the role of someone who was not only dead and buried but also being burnt was that Lucy was expressing her vengeful and angry reactions. She recollected arguments she had had with her father when young. Another aspect to the image of burning, which became increasingly apparent, was that it is a means of transforming energy, of incorporating the old and dead into the new and living. This level of meaning was given clear expression in one session when Lucy as Peter took an apparent diversion from her trip to the grave.

On this occasion Peter used a massive axe to chop down a large tree in the forest (Figure 6.20). It fell to the ground, and he proceeded to set light to it. It burnt for a long time. I asked Lucy if it had finished burning; she said 'no.' She stood warming her hands on this fire for several minutes. Eventually she said it had finished burning. I questioned her.

ANNA: What happens next, now it's finished burning?

Figure 6.21 New life growing from the ashes of the old

LUCY: A new tree grows in the ashes.

ANNA: Show me.

(Lucy 'grows' as a tree, starting low and reaching up).

ANNA: How big are you?

LUCY: Quite small.

ANNA: Do you have anything in your branches, little tree?

LUCY: Yes, leaves, and fruit and nests.

Out of the ashes of the large old tree had grown something small, and new, and fruitful. I was reminded of the phoenix that rises from the ashes (Figure 6.21).

The fire of anger

It was difficult for Lucy to acknowledge her feelings of anger. Within the story they found expression through images of murder and destruction, but whenever I suggested one of the characters might feel angry this was vociferously denied. When Lucy finally allowed her anger to be visible in a session it was in the context of her relationship with me two weeks after the session described above, and after a break of one week.

When Lucy came through the door she was already talking energetically about a trip to a show that everyone from her home was going to except herself. It was unclear from what she was saying whether she was staying behind so that she could wait for her people to visit, or whether she had been asked to volunteer due to a shortage of tickets. As I questioned her gently to try and make sense of this she protested furiously that it was all her choice. She was literally shaking with rage and when I reflected back that she seemed angry, she shouted 'I'm HAPPY, I'm HAPPY.'

Twice during this conversation she demanded quite desperately to 'get on with the story' or to 'go to Maglab'. The story offered itself as a refuge from her painfully rageful feelings. I felt it was important not to use the story as an escape, an avoidance of the drama of what was happening in the here and now. Before going into the make-believe world of Maglab I made sure that she knew that I was not running away from her anger. I told her that I knew she did not like feeling painful feelings such as anger and sadness. I added that if I were in her shoes I would feel upset and angry if my people did not come, if there was a break in my therapy, and if everyone else was going on an outing except me. Even if she could not admit to her anger I needed her to know that I could see her pain and anger. She accepted this and we moved into the story.

She returned to the small tree that had grown from the ashes of the older one and she put me in role as this small tree. She addressed me from the role of Peter.

LUCY as Peter: It's okay to be you. You're okay just the way you are.

ANNA *as small tree:* You mean it's okay to be small and new and vulnerable, and to have angry or painful feelings.

LUCY: Yes, absolutely.

I saw this message as affirming and positive, so I asked Lucy to role reverse with me. In this way she could hear Peter/me giving this supportive message. Once Lucy had given herself permission to be herself in this way she began to access other feelings in the story, as the focus returned to the grave.

Sadness and longing

It was in the session following her angry outburst, and from the role of the witch, that Lucy first began to acknowledge the feelings of sadness that were present at the grave. She stood at the foot of the grave for some time. She had asked me to be with her rather than taking on the role of Maglab. I tried to double for her, speaking the thoughts I sensed might be there in the silence as she looked at the grave.

ANNA: It's quiet without you.

LUCY *as Witch:* Yes, deadly quiet... I'm sorry you're dead. I wish to
  heaven you weren't.

The following dialogue was spoken entirely by Lucy, as if she were both asking questions and then speaking the answers she heard to them. My part was simply to encourage her to continue asking the questions and to listen for the answers.

WITCH: Are you still happy, Maglab?

MAGLAB: No, I'm unhappy.

WITCH: Are you miserable?

MAGLAB: Yes.

WITCH: Why?

MAGLAB: Because I'm dead.

She stood in a solemn and dejected way, in silence as if she were taking in what she had heard. I asked her if we could explore her feelings as the witch at the graveside. She showed me in movement terms at first, her head and body drooping further and further down towards the ground. Between us we found some words: loss, sadness, despair, miserable and weighed down.

LUCY: There's a difference between the happy me and the sad me. I
  prefer to be happy, mostly. But this is a time for sadness. I'm
  really sad.

After a pause I asked her if she was ready to move on, and she was able to say no, to take her time and be with her sadness until she was ready. She was again giving herself permission. I brought a xylophone over and she played her feelings of sadness.

I asked her what other feelings were important to express as the witch at the grave. She mentioned anger, using the line 'No, no, it's not fair' and helplessness or resignation, using the line 'I can't – I have no magic to change death.' As the witch she gathered some flowers and laid them on Maglab's grave. The gesture was a familiar one, but it felt more meaningful in the context of the range of feelings that we had recognised in this session.

As we approached the time to leave the enactment I asked Lucy what else she needed to do.

LUCY: I can't say.

ANNA: Then show me.

LUCY: I can't.

ANNA: Just do it.

Lucy picked up (in mime) the flowers she had laid on Maglab's grave and placed them on my chair. She was making a connection between the drama of the story and the drama of her relationship with me. She had given herself permission to express her feelings. Some belonged in the alternative reality of her story, others belonged to the here and now relationship with her therapist.

Entering the grave

After several sessions of gazing at the grave from the edge Lucy eventually felt the need to get into it herself. She entered the room at the start of the session repeating under her breath 'Gone away and never coming back.' I suggested that was the case with her parents, and she agreed that her relatives were no real substitute for her real parents. Another week had passed without a visit. Her expectation was still that visits should happen on a weekly basis, as her father had managed. It felt like 'ages' since she had had a visit. The weekly disappointment that she created by maintaining an expectation of a weekly visit kept her sense of loss alive.

Before we embarked on the story Lucy wanted to make herself comfortable. It was a warm day, and she took off her cardigan and her tights, which she gave me to keep for the session. I thought of the imaginary flowers she had given me the previous session; of how she had even kept her coat on for many weeks earlier in her therapy; and of how accepting her clothes put me in a maternal role.

She put me in role as Maglab in the grave and came and sat next to me as the witch. Since we were clearly in the grave I repositioned the blanket so that it was draped between the piano and the cupboard. This created a kind of roof or top to the grave above us. It felt quite cosy, like a den.

ANNA *as Maglab:* Are you dead too?

LUCY *as Witch:* No, I'm alive. You are dead.

(Lucy sits looking in the other direction, out of the grave, in silence for several minutes.)

ANNA *as Maglab:* What are you looking at, witch?

LUCY *as Witch:* Nothing, myself.

ANNA *as Maglab:* How do you see yourself?

LUCY *as Witch:* I'm boring. Peter keeps leaving me. The monster is no company.

ANNA *as Maglab:* How do you feel?

LUCY *as Witch:* Numb.

ANNA *as Maglab:* What do you need to do?

LUCY *as Witch:* Nothing, just be here.

ANNA *as Maglab:* Why did you come?

LUCY *as Witch:* I was so lonely.

(after a long, sleepy silence)

ANNA *as Maglab:* How long do you intend to stay in this grave with me?

LUCY *as Witch:* I want to stay a whole week.

ANNA *as Maglab:* How will you live?

LUCY *as Witch:* Peter will bring one meal.

ANNA *as Maglab:* What's it like in this grave?

LUCY *as Witch:* The soil is rich. There's going to be a storm, with thunder and lightening but it will be warm and dry here (Figure 6.22).

The feeling of mother and child had stayed with me during the enactment. I wondered if Lucy wanted to curl up and lay her head in my lap, but said nothing. The idea of staying buried in the grave for a whole week seemed to me to be a statement of her attachment to me and to what I represented, the inner child, the dead parents as well as her therapist. She did not want to leave me, or me to leave her. She wanted to be with me, but also for me to know that the space between the sessions is for her a kind of death; a lonely space relieved perhaps once by a visit from her relatives. The strength of her feelings must be understood partly in the light of her transference. She was working through the issues of loss and separation from both her parents. The story provided one transitional arena for this; her relationship with me another.

Figure 6.22 The witch shelters for a week in Maglab's grave

Passing through

The following session started with the witch and Maglab still in the grave.

> ANNA *as Maglab:* How do I experience it here in my grave? What do you think it's like being dead?

> LUCY *as Witch:* It's peaceful and cosy, but I don't want to stay here forever. I can see a path with flowers on it, leading away from here towards my house.

Lucy chose her own moment to leave the grave. When she did so she said 'Goodbye' simply and clearly to Maglab and moved up the path alone.

I wondered if Lucy would need to spend more time inside the grave. In the next session it was evident that something had shifted in Lucy's relationship with the grave. The enactment started with Lucy as the witch walking through the woods, into the grave and straight out of it again, without any interaction with Maglab. She paced in a circular journey through the woods and the grave five times during the session, as if practising the process of passing through, letting go and moving on. It was a spontaneous dance or ritual, as she lowered her head to go beneath the roof of the grave and raised herself upright as she came out the other side. Each time she passed through the tunnel of the grave I was reminded of the birth process.

As she walked through the woods she showed me a tree, represented by a cymbal on a stand. This was her favourite tree, that she described as having golden leaves, that fall to the ground, and that comes back to life each year. As the witch she waited with it for a whole year while it went through its cycle. She then passed on, through the grave and returned. This second time the witch stayed 'seventeen days', watched the leaves fall, and then the whole tree was to fall to the ground. She lowered the cymbal silently to the ground, and this was where it was left at the end of the session.

The metaphors of the tree and the grave were coming together in this session. Both were part of Lucy's concern with life and death. By passing through the grave and into the woods she was perhaps affirming her own ability to move on in her life, having spent time working on her issues of loss and bereavement. The natural world itself seemed to be in a continual process of living, dying and being reborn. The leaves on the tree were transient, but also precious, golden. The final image of the fallen tree that would not rise again was perhaps a statement of the paradox of death. It is seen both as part of a cycle that repeats and as something permanent and irrevocable.

Hope of transformation

The next session began where the last one finished. I was put in role as the fallen tree, and lay on the floor twisted and groaning, waiting for directions from Lucy. She put herself in role as Peter, and instructed me with some authority to stand up. I said that I could not get up without help. She reached out her hands to pull me up, but did not pull. I told her she would need to pull harder than that. Without hesitation she did, and the tree was reinstated in a standing position. She gathered golden leaves from its branches, took them home and burnt them, warming her hands on the fire in the now familiar fashion.

The scene changed. Lucy stood as Peter looking at the grave. I asked if he would be going through.

LUCY *as Peter:* No, I'm not going through. I don't need to go in there. I will wait. One day Maglab's chair will be gone from in there, and on that day a great big lorry of a tree will grow through and up and out of the grave.

ANNA: When will that be?

LUCY *as Peter:* Not for a while yet, but it will happen. I'll wait. It will be a tree with cockle shells, nutmeg and silver bells. A place where I can go.

ANNA: Can you see anything happening yet?

LUCY *as Peter:* No.

ANNA: Can you hear anything?

LUCY *as Peter:* Yes, underground there is a 'biffing' sound, a low slow
  sound of things happening.

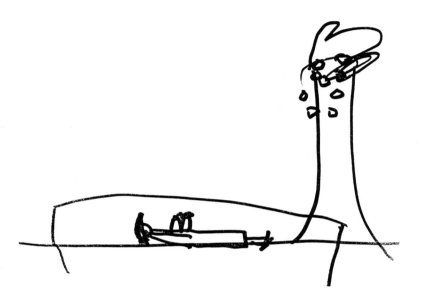

Figure 6.23 The promise of transformation

Lucy drew Maglab in the grave, and then the 'great big lorry of a tree' that
would eventually grow out of it (Figure 6.23). This is a tree with fruit. As
she drew Maglab Lucy said 'Maglab is dead.' It was as if she were realising
the meaning of this in a new way. My own sense was that she was becoming
aware of her own maturation. The 'little princess' was preparing to be
superseded by a more up-to-date, upstanding and fruitful identity.

We played music together as we usually did to close the session. As usual she
finished abruptly and I was left to adjust very suddenly. I mentioned this to
her and asked her if she liked me to be left playing. She replied 'No, I want
you to stop.' I told her she would need to tell me to stop so that I could be
ready at the end of the piece when she was. We played again and this time
she instructed me clearly to stop when she wanted to. This was a new and
assertive role in action.

Lucy would normally have left at this point, but she went back over to the picture and sat down.

ANNA: Is there more?

LUCY: Yes.

ANNA: Let me have a look at that picture again. Tell me about it.

LUCY: Maglab is lying down and feels miserable and lonely.

ANNA: How will the tree feel when it grows into place?

LUCY: Lonely, but not quite as miserable.

This may also be a realistic prognosis for Lucy. The loneliness may continue, but as she matures and becomes more familiar with her feelings her relationship with it and with herself may become less miserable.

We had reached another marker in Lucy's therapy, and I decided to give her some feedback and encouragement. I had the impression that different levels of her therapeutic process were coming together. Some deep processes of change were continuing at an underground, invisible, root level. At the same time there were clear signs that Lucy was beginning to apply new roles to her way of communicating with me. If the developing relationship with me could give her confidence to be more assertive and more honest about her feelings and needs with other people in her current world, this would constitute significant change in her life. There was a feeling of optimism as I addressed her.

ANNA: I'm thinking about the start of the session and how you got me
        to stand up as the tree. I'm looking at this picture of Maglab
        lying in the grave and waiting for the tree to grow and stand
        up tall. And I'm thinking that you just stood up to me your-
        self in the music and told me what you wanted. There has
        been a lot of standing up for yourself in this session. It's a
        good thing to learn to do. Well done.

CHAPTER 7

Group Dramatherapy

A Conceptual Framework

Most dramatherapy interventions take place as group therapy. It is worth considering why.

There are therapeutic as well as economic advantages to group dramatherapy. At the heart of these lies a paradox: the dramatherapy group is a place that is both the same as and different from other experience. It can be seen on the one hand as a microcosm of the larger social group. It raises the same challenges and frustrations as are experienced by the clients elsewhere in terms of their relationship with others. On the other hand it has the advantages of being a special culture, a place where different rules apply and a different experience may be possible. This combination of characteristics enables participants to engage in a process whereby habitual identities and issues are brought to the group; the impact and contribution of these can be seen and explored within contained conditions; and new life roles can be encouraged and practised within the context of a defined group membership and a creative group culture.

As I have explored elsewhere (Chesner 1994a), group dramatherapy has the ability to address the core issues of low self-esteem and low regard for the peer group which characterise this client group. Being part of a small and creative group culture, where each person's contribution is valued as part of the whole, has an impact on identity and self-perception. At best this is carried through into other areas of life. The extent to which change is integrated into the wider context beyond the special culture of the therapy group varies. There is perhaps always a leap to be made to integrate change made in the therapy context into the wider social reality. One advantage of group dramatherapy is that the distance of this leap may be smaller when the starting point is a group rather than the dyad of one-to-one therapy.

Dramatherapy as an action method reduces the distance even further. We live and express ourselves in action, and as social beings. Group dramatherapy has the advantage of using both these realities as the starting point of the therapy process.

Recent ideas in the field of clinical psychology for people with learning disabilities highlight the limitations of relying solely on IQ tests, behaviourism, normalisation and cognitive therapies, and point towards a more inclusive, social constructionist approach (Clegg 1993). Such an approach is philosophically much closer to the practice of dramatherapy, than the earlier approaches to clinical psychology with this client group. The interchange between the individual and the social environment is an important focus: '... abilities and processes, formerly located in individuals, are now seen as products of human community' (Shotter and Gergen quoted in Clegg 1993). Leont'ev even suggests that shared activity should be 'the essential unit of analysis' (quoted in Clegg 1993). Dramatherapy has always focused on shared activity as both an expression of habitual roles and the locus for change.

Five levels of relationship between individuals and society are suggested by Doise (quoted in Clegg 1993), who is interested in the links between the levels. These levels and the relationship between them can also shed light on the issues and processes dealt with in group dramatherapy.

The intrapersonal level

One intrapersonal level is the biological one. Many clients live with biological factors such as Down's syndrome. Personal history can also be looked at as an intrapersonal factor, a part of the client's inner world. Clients may bring their history of social disadvantage, abuse or poor bonding with an early attachment figure with them into therapy. These historical factors affect the clients' perception of self, other and the world, and so inform their experience of the group. Heard writes of the phenomenon of 'continuing unassuaged need' as a common characteristic of this client group at the intrapersonal level, one that is often dismissed as 'attention seeking behaviour' (quoted in Clegg 1993). This phenomenon is usually revealed within the dramatherapy group as a continuous *Leitmotiv* in the work. The therapeutic arena of the group in action brings out the intrapersonal world, expressed directly as it informs interaction in the group and also metaphorically in the drama.

The interpersonal and situational level

All interactions experienced by people with learning disabilities must be seen in the light of their context. Common problems have a tendency to arise in certain contexts, reflecting a pattern in society. It would be wrong, for example, to attribute the narrow social network and the experience of isolation often experienced by adults with learning disabilities solely to intrapersonal problems. There are clearly family and societal factors involved, to do with our collective attitude to difference and disability.

Dramatherapy recognises context as a relevant factor in understanding problems and facilitating change. The dramatherapy group itself creates a new context for interpersonal contact. Unfamiliar and imaginative structures invite something fresh to happen in the group. At the same time clients bring with them identities, expectations and patterns based on other experiences in the contexts of family, residential setting, workplace and wider community. The group explores and plays creatively with this material through games, improvisation and role play. Protected by the specific context of the therapy group and the idea of make-believe, the group can enact habitual or new responses to any number of situations recreated in the group.

The positional level

'By the positional level, Doise means the influence of relative position or power between people on their actions and thoughts' (Clegg 1993 p.397). People with learning disabilities are currently politically and socially disadvantaged. Some professionals suggest the appropriate way to tackle this inequality should be through political rather than therapeutic action (Fine and Asch quoted in Clegg 1993). While the political approach may well have value, the contribution of dramatherapy is within the area of therapy, but with an awareness of the broadly political perspective.

The positional perspective is central to a theatrical or dramatic view of interaction. In preparing a scene for performance actors and director analyse the power dynamic, present in any interaction. This is a core process of rehearsal, without which they cannot do justice to the theatre piece. All interaction, on or off the stage, can be similarly analysed from the positional perspective.

Dramatherapy offers many opportunities to explore status and power within the group. The clients' view of self and peer group tends to perpetuate the habitual positional level, but can be challenged by the experience of dramatherapy. Within the culture of the dramatherapy group choices affecting the whole group can be made even by clients who are non-verbal. The working ethos of the dramatherapy group is one which values the creative contribution and ability of each person, rather than focusing exclusively on what is dysfunctional or disabled.

The usual staff–client relationship is more flexible than in other therapeutic forms. As a dramatherapist I often play lower status roles within games, improvisations and enacted stories. A reversal of the usual positional dynamic brings the issue of power into the group arena for acknowledgement and exploration, and the implicit message is that power dynamics are open to change. Games and improvisations permit a playful or oblique look at the issues of power within the group, and in the wider context as brought into the group through memory and imagination. Role play may help clients prepare for application of a new role in the wider setting. In this sense the dramatherapy group can be a rehearsal for political change in a wider context.

The ideological level

'At this level Doise is describing the influence of belief systems' (Clegg 1993 p.398). There are societal belief systems implicit in the way we treat those with learning disabilities, and subgroups within this broader category. As a society our expectations of what is acceptable for people with learning disabilities are lower than for many other groups. The underlying message must be heard, or unconsciously imbibed by clients, as 'You are less important, less valuable than others. You are not a top priority'.

Therapy needs to tackle the effects of these belief systems, and to nurture self-esteem based on a different ideology. This is not to deny the need for changes in attitude and ideology at a societal level. The dramatherapy group as special culture can create some distance from counter-therapeutic aspects of the institutional or broader cultural ideology. Within this special place a different perspective can develop and be internalised by the clients.

The boundaries of the therapy group are all the more important the more difference there is between the culture of the dramatherapy group and that of the wider community. Even with the observation of clear boundaries it may be impossible to avoid ideological clashes. The same action can be perceived very differently within the dramatherapy context on the one hand and the nursing environment on the other. Mary, a non-verbal blind woman slipped off her shoes within her small group dramatherapy session. This was understood within the dramatherapy context to be a legitimate expression of choice, perhaps a sign that she felt at home enough to make herself comfortable, and was open to exploring her world at a sensory level. After the session she was escorted back to her ward, still barefoot. Here she was met with an immediate reprimand for having removed her shoes and a description of herself as a 'naughty girl'. The client was caught between two ideologies, two contrasting sets of expectations.

Group Dramatherapy in Practice

Group composition

I have found a composition of up to eight clients and two or three members of a therapeutic team to be a productive number for group dramatherapy with this client group. Such a group is small enough to allow each person to be seen, and to contribute in a meaningful way to the activities of the whole. Smaller groups of three or four clients are preferable with the more profoundly disabled clients, who require more individual assistance to make the dramatherapy work accessible. These smaller groups lack the richness of ideas and interchange available to the larger group, but can still provide a meaningful group experience for participants. The ratio of staff members to clients depends on the degree of autonomy, dependence and self-motivation of the clients. The therapeutic team should be large enough to facilitate effectively; not so large as to take over and dominate the work.

Clients are usually members of other groups in other contexts. Members of a small group home, who already have the fact of living together in common might form a ready-made dramatherapy group with the focus of working on their relationships. In other circumstances the dramatherapist has more control over group membership and has to make more conscious decisions as to the mix of people in the group. In principle I favour the inclusion of a spectrum of different abilities and personality types within a group, but within a broad band of compatibility. One or two members without active verbal skills can feel at home in a group with talking members if they have sufficient verbal understanding and a willingness to express themselves in other ways. Clients with physical limitations can similarly find their place in the mixed ability group (see Chapter 2).

Particular challenging behaviours can be more difficult for a mixed group to incorporate and contain. In one new group the two female members felt uncomfortable in the face of two rather overpowering men, and withdrew from the group sessions before the issue could be tackled. There is a case for creating a group specifically for people with similar communication patterns and similar problems in groups. The work process can focus specifically on addressing these issues. I have worked with one such group through a performance project, as described below.

Session structure in group dramatherapy

Individual sessions observe a regular structure for containment and guidance of the process. The classic three-part pattern of warm-up, development and closure as described by Jennings (1986) is of value with this client group. The step by step structuring of the session provides a framework that encourages group cohesion and a gradual deepening of personal and inter-personal exploration. The three-part structure can even be expanded into a five-part model when considering the needs of this client group. The processes of arrival and departure on the boundary of the group can be given form and containment as part of the regular group process. On this basis the five stages of the session are:

- arrival
- warm-up
- development
- closure
- departure.

Following the ritual–risk paradigm of Jennings (1987) the movement is one which starts from safety, structure and the here and now during stages one and two. The underlying movement is towards spontaneity, imagination and risk at the heart of the session in stage three, and back out towards the here and now, with structured and ritualised activity in stages four and five.

Arrivals and departures

It is worth considering these processes to be distinct phases within each session and to pay attention to what happens. As boundary moments they may need specific structuring so that group members know what is expected and where the boundaries actually are. The way each client approaches arrival and departure can be diagnostic, revealing both ongoing patterns and changes over time.

Dan, a man with a diagnosis of autism, had a general tendency to stand inappropriately close to people, to grin and bombard them with a series of predictable ritualised questions, apparently with the intention of seeing people get confused and irritated. This outcome excited him, made him laugh and spurred him on to continue in this cycle. He was very responsive to group dramatherapy, particularly welcoming the highly structured working sugges-tions, within which he was able to challenge himself, and displayed a vivid imagination. At the end of the sessions, however he would linger in the doorway after other group members had left, approach a member of the therapeutic team and start the ritualised winding-up process. At first I felt frustrated and irritated that he seemed to want to finish the sessions on such a note. Then I reflected on his positive response to most of the working suggestions within the actual sessions and wondered whether the process of departure was simply too unstructured for him. The following session I asked him if I could make an agreement with him, a kind of bet or game, the essence of which was that he would not be the last person to leave. The suggestion worked. If he was in danger of falling into his old pattern I could remind him playfully of the agreement, sometimes simply with a look, and he would get on with the process of leaving, and enjoy doing so.

Arrivals can be just as difficult for some clients. Times of transition can feel risky. Clients may arrive with anxiety, excitement or confusion as they leave one environment and settle into another. The phenomenon of 'continuing unassuaged need' often reveals itself at this time. There is the opportunity to express anxieties and concerns, tell the therapist any news, and most importantly to be seen and recognised. The way in which this happens can be chaotic and hungry, generating more anxiety as other group members arrive and the group assembles.

Some of this excitement is probably inevitable and even desirable as preparation for the group activities. I have found it valuable to prepare the studio space before anyone arrives. Clients can predict that there will be a clear circle of the right number of chairs or bean bags waiting to be filled as they arrive. This simple preparation sets the scene dramatically and symbolically for the therapy group, and grounds the process of arrival. Each person's place is there, contained by the circle and contributing to the circle as container of the group. If possible the therapist or therapeutic team are already sitting in the circle when clients arrive, so that the expectation of coming into the circle to start with is very clear. The whole group is implicit even as the first person arrives. Seeing the empty chairs in the circle helps to focus the early arrivals on who the other group members are.

As people arrive there is opportunity for informal sharing and re-connecting. In early stages of ongoing group process much of this is focused on the therapeutic team. It is a sign of maturation within the group when the focus of informal contact shifts spontaneously to the peer group.

Arrival and departure rituals

Greetings and sharing of news can be ritualised at the start of a session, and goodbyes can be contained within a ritualised structure at the end. There follow some ideas for simple rituals, that ground the group in the here and now and encourage trust. They fall into the category of root level work.

(1) **Circle link**. Everyone in the circle holds hands, concretising the connection between group members. The group is encouraged to look around the circle and see who is there.

(2) **Hello song**. There are different versions of greetings songs. They may focus on each person in turn, and often use a combination of action and words. The level of complexity needs to be appropriate to the group. A simple, well-known tune with few words repeated several times can be more easily mastered than a new tune with more sophisticated lyrics.

One old favourite involves a handshake being passed around the circle. The names change as the handshake moves on:

> 'Ted is shaking hands with Max,
> Ted is shaking hands with Max,
> Ted is shaking hands with Max,
> It's nice to see you here.
> Max is shaking hands with...'

At the end of the circuit everyone holds hands together and sings:

> 'Everyone's shaking hands with everyone...'

Most clients will delight in the individual recognition a hello song gives them. The predictability of the structure helps to build participants' confidence. Even non-verbal clients sing along in their own way.

(3) **Ball greeting**. A ball is thrown or passed between group members after their attention has been attracted through eye contact or calling out a name. This structure is extremely simple. The connection between group members is expressed through the medium of the ball. Choices are made moment to moment about whom to greet next. As group members become more confident, imaginative and playful variations of the ritual emerge through which group members can express and develop their relationships.

(4) **Talking stick**. The talking stick is a device through which each person can check in to the group by sharing some news, a word or even a gesture. The 'stick' can be a ball, a maraca, paperweight or any object that is easy to handle. The person who holds the 'stick' has the whole group's attention as they share what they wish to share. They then choose someone else to pass the 'stick' and the focus on to. The value lies in encouraging appropriate listening within the group and ritualising the change of focus. Group members have control over

how long they hold the group focus for. The way the group approaches this activity gives the therapist information as to the needs of the group on this occasion, and ideas of what may or may not be possible.

(5) **Goodbye song**. This follows a similar principle to the hello song. As well as naming each person in the group, the song can include an action such as waving, bowing or shaking hands, and a reminder of the time of the next session. It can help to close a session as well as placing it in the context of a continuous process. The ritualised nature of the song, repeated on a weekly basis, enables group members to initiate it themselves and to feel that they have some control over the closure.

(6) **Goodbye shout**. If the energy in the group is low at the end of a session, as sometimes happens after a predominantly verbal closure activity, the goodbye shout can be useful. The group connect in a circle, preferably standing and holding hands. They shout 'Goodbye' as loudly as possible and in unison, whilst raising the arms in the air. The activity creates a positive sense of the group and leaves people in a position to get on with the process of departure.

Warm-up, development and closure

The content and structures chosen for the central focus of a session is dependent on the dramatherapeutic level at which the group operates. The same dramatherapy structure may be used as a warm-up in one group, and as the development in another, according to the level of dramatherapy experience and general ability in the group. Closure activities are designed to create distance from the central development and prepare for the processes of departure and transition to another situation. The specific ways closure is structured depends heavily on the main content of the session.

In terms of the tree metaphor (see Chapter 1) an entire session or sequence of sessions may operate at ground or root level. In the early days of a group, activities emphasising embodiment, physical awareness and trust are the most useful for establishing a stable foundation for future work. Some of these activities are described in the chapter on movement.

These movement and contact structures can either be explored and developed in their own right or used as a warm-up for activities higher up the tree and perhaps involving greater sophistication. At the level of the tree trunk most groups are capable of engaging in games of varying complexity, and these can be used as the central development of a session.

Imaginative enactment, whether based on story, improvisation or role play makes different and more complex demands on participants. At the level of the branches of the dramatherapy tree this work belongs clearly in the development part of a session. Participants need to be grounded within the session through the warm-up before embarking on enactment. They also need to be capable of working with the imagination, able to play with the notion of 'as if' and to make a flight of fancy.

Not everyone is able to make this leap. Those whose perceptions remain concrete and firmly based in the here and now can be confused by full blown imaginary work. They might still be able to find their place within a group enactment by relating at a sensory rather than narrative level to the activity. Where the majority of the group seems incapable of the imaginary leap it is more appropriate to pitch the session at a level lower down the tree and in the here and now experience of the group. This is particularly the case where cognitive limitations are the inhibiting factor.

With some clients it is not so much cognitive limitations as a lack of spontaneity and playfulness that blocks participation in a make-believe world. As I have described elsewhere (Chesner 1994a) there are ways of learning to use the imagination step by step.

A number of devices can be used in this process. A parachute, for example, can be used as a root level structure. As each group member holds on to the edge of a round parachute the connection between people and the fact of the group as a whole is made concrete and visible. As group members raise and lower their arms the parachute rises and falls in a way that is interesting or pleasurable at a sensual level. The colours and movement are visually interesting, and there are the added factors of the sound and the breeze created by the parachute as it moves through the air which is felt on the face and neck of participants. The experience begins to change level, to move towards one of creative imagination when the group creates the 'as if' of a storm by accelerating and intensifying the movements of the parachute. The here and now of the studio begins to shift by common consent, to include elements of the sea and the skies. The drama of the weather is projected into the group space, and is created by group members without them needing to hold any imaginary roles themselves.

The various stages of imaginary engagement can be seen by looking at the use of one of the dramatherapist's most accessible props, the ball.

(1) At the most basic, root level, the ball is a source of sensory stimulation. The client does not use it in the ways we habitually associate with balls. It

is simply touched, its texture explored, it is allowed to rest in the lap, put to the mouth, perhaps pushed away.

(2) At the level of the trunk there are an infinite number of games that can be played. The ball is passed or thrown in a way that conforms to simple rules of the game. When the rules are mastered the activity is fairly predictable and safe.

(3) The same basic rules of the game are followed, but are developed or re-interpreted in a way that is playful and spontaneous. The ball is perhaps thrown, but the force behind the throw is disguised, or the thrower looks in one direction and throws unexpectedly in another. There is briefly an element of pretence or make-believe, but within the containment of a game. In terms of the tree this is the exciting point, full of potential, where the trunk begins to transform into branches. The ball is still used as a ball, i.e. for throwing, passing or rolling, but is at the same time a device to express spontaneity.

(4) The ball is passed around the circle not as itself, but in role as 'hot potato', 'sticky bun' 'egg'. The dramatherapist chooses initially what role to put the ball in, and models handling it 'as if' it were hot, sticky or delicate. The group learns what is expected and so can participate within a defined moment in a shared imaginary world. The expressive skills to maintain this imaginary world are modelled by the therapist and practised for a short moment in the spotlight by each group member.

(5) Spontaneity, playfulness and expressive skills come together fully at branch level when the ball is passed around the circle and each participant puts it in role in an original way that is a personal contribution. It could be a baby, a banana, a bar of soap. The possibilities are literally endless. It is an exciting moment when a group realises that anything is possible within the world of the imagination. This is the foundation for story making and improvisation.

(6) At a level of the leaves, the ball can be used consciously as a symbol. This is a process that happens spontaneously and depends on an integration of the previous levels of imaginary engagement. As described in the chapter on psychodrama a large ball is used spontaneously by a client as a container for the physical expression of her rage. As a symbol it has associations for her with the therapy group as container. She can also project onto it the objects of her rage. It is put in a composite role that includes aspects of herself and of those people who frustrate her. At the same time it is important that it is

seen as a ball, an inanimate object that cannot be damaged by her rage. The imaginary and the concrete levels are used in conjunction with each other in the service of her therapeutic process.

Focus on Improvisation

Improvisation is a core process in the development stage of sessions with those groups able to tackle it. The degree of engagement in improvisation is dependent upon the expressive skills of each group member, and the level of trust and interpersonal communication in the group. In this sense, improvisation is life in microcosm, and the skills learnt in improvisation are of value in the wider social context outside the group.

A group improvisation is a shared creative act. A balance must be found between each person's individual contribution and the needs of the whole. An imbalance in this area will be revealed within the forum of the improvisation, for instance when one group member dominates and undermines the contributions of others. The group challenge is then to work with what is, and to try and move on in a way that is acceptable. The dominant member may be challenged from within role, for example by capturing, taking hostage, or otherwise containing him or her, not as themselves, which would be very confrontational, but in whatever role they have put themselves in within the improvisation, e.g. tyrant, criminal, trickster. Another approach to the challenge thrown up by a dominant group member might be to divert the story away from him or her. The other group members might create a change of direction within the narrative, so that a sub-plot for example becomes the main plot.

Intertwined with the narrative level of improvisation there are usually interesting dynamics between group members. This interpersonal level is often expressed more vividly in improvisation than in direct conventional communication within the group, which may be quite stereotyped. The apparent disguise of the imaginary world paradoxically permits a more truthful expression of the here and now dynamics in the group.

In one improvisational structure each person was invited in turn to take on the role of a sculptor or a painter and to make a sculpture or picture of their choice by positioning the other group members and any objects in the studio. The combination of clear guidelines and scope for free expression provides a productive framework for improvisation. One of the core dynamics in this group was competition and hostility between two clients, Richard and Jim. Physically, they were opposites. Richard was tall, overweight and ambulant, but chaotic and uncontained in his movements. Jim was small, physically cautious, fragile, and dependent on his electronic wheelchair, which he operated himself despite limitations in arm and hand movements. Both men were articulate. Jim talked mostly about concrete things in his life, such as his wheelchair and stereo system and liked to see himself as compliant, while Richard expressed himself verbally through an aggressive sense of humour and a strong imagination. He saw himself more as an uncontainable rebel. Richard seemed at first to look down on Jim in the group because of his physical limitations and there was a danger that he could bully Jim by taking control of his chair by force. Jim's way of dealing with the situation was primarily through words. He allied himself with the therapeutic team and adopted a teasing tone in relation to Richard, whom he addressed as 'Trouble'. This was quite an effective strategy and coping mechanism, but did not do credit to the depth of Jim's feelings.

Within the sculptor improvisation Jim used Richard as the central figure in his sculpture. He instructed Richard to lie sprawling on the floor and placed two other group members at his sides, one reaching out to him, the other touching him. His title for the piece was 'the accident' and he described the situation as Richard having had a bad accident and the people around him were trying to help. It was a strong image. At one level it was perhaps an expression of Jim's anger and vengeful fantasies. He was not in a position to lay Richard flat in a fight, but perhaps other things being equal this is what he would have liked to do. At another level it was a way of showing Richard what it feels like to be in the vulnerable position of physical dependency. This could be seen as a statement of 'This is how it is for me.' At a further level I felt it to be an expression of Jim's desire to reach out to Richard and to recognise his vulnerability. Jim was perhaps more able to see and accept the vulnerable side of Richard than Richard was himself.

Improvisation can give expression to whole group concerns as well as specific interpersonal dynamics. In the last session of a dramatherapy group that had gone on for two years and had made extensive use of improvisation, the group chose to locate their last improvisation at Glastonbury Tor. The group perception of this setting was a church and garden on a hill, which we created by using play shapes and a real tree on wheels, one of the permanent props within the studio. Monks were tending the gardens and showing visitors around. There was no predetermined content to the scene. What emerged spontaneously as an expression of the group concern was a funeral. All were called together to attend a funeral. Everyone participated in this ritual with solemnity and a particular quality of energy that emerges in a group when an adequate form is found to express the current group issue.

The image of the funeral marked the ending or death of the group. I was also interested in the idea of the funeral as a rite of passage, as a way of marking the transition from one state into another. At the end of the funeral scene I asked the group whether we had finished or what might happen next. There was a discussion about what happened after death. No-one knew for sure, but there was a common interest in the concept of heaven. We moved into a metaphysical scene expressing the group's view of heaven. This was embodied in movement, with each person turning and orbiting in role as stars or planets. The improvisation was accompanied by an evocative tape of instrumental music, in response to which different moments were declared 'night' or 'day'. The suggestion of cyclical and cosmic processes set the idea of ending in the wider context of continuity.

Starting points for improvisation
The spontaneous elements of improvisation can be stimulated and contained by a variety of structures suited to work with this client group.

(1) **Defined activity.** The creation of a sculpt as described above can be the starting point for a scene. The completed tableau can be brought to life by a sound cue, or a touch from the sculptor or therapist. At this point the actors relate to each other according to their sense of the roles and relationships embodied in the sculpt. The scene can be brought to an end in a similar way. Either the dramatherapist or preferably the sculptor as director can freeze the action by giving a verbal instruction or striking a gong. At this moment actors hold their position and a closing tableau is created.

The creation of an imaginary photograph follows similar principles to the sculpt. The creator positions other group members for a group photograph. This might be a fantasy family portrait, or just a fleeting moment of everyday life caught by a passing photographer. The creator can put him- or herself in the photograph at the end and join in the improvisation which begins at the moment the imaginary photograph is taken.

A further variation involves using an actual photograph or picture as the starting point. The group might choose one from a selection on offer, and explore together how they can translate the picture into three dimensional reality. The starting point is someone else's creation, but there is still scope for personal and group contributions to the exercise. The preference to explore one picture rather than another has significance, as do the roles chosen, and the interpretation of the picture by the group. The negotiations and interactions in the process of transferring the picture onto the stage area often have a drama of their own, which is further developed through the imaginary world once the picture is brought to life.

(2) **Character.** Character and role can be a useful impetus for improvisation work. Broadly sketched character types are usually more easily accessible than subtle roles. Clients often draw on a shared cultural experience based in myth, story, television and well known figures from current affairs.

Character can be created from the starting point of movement. Different kinds of movement and gesture can be repeated and exaggerated, revealing characteristics that are used as the basis for a role. This is an interesting process, but one that requires a high degree of autonomy in the group, particularly if the different characters are truly emerging from each client's movement pattern.

A more easily accessible approach to character is for group members to select a hat from a collection of hats available. The hat is an external device for defining the role. Some hats indicate a particular social function, such as policeman, traffic warden, builder, nurse. Some, such as the top hat or the deerstalker imply a certain status. Others such as the sun hat, or the fancy hat with flowers suggest particular situations such as holidays and weddings. Once the range of characters is established a possible setting can be agreed upon and created in the studio, and the improvisation can unfold without further preparation.

(3) **Place.** A location can be the starting point for improvisation. Settings may be imaginary or places known in real life. Once the context is established character and action follow with relative ease. If, for example, the setting is given as a spaceship then it is likely that the characters will be astronauts or beings from outer space, and the situation will be one involving travelling to new and strange places.

The dramatherapist may choose such a location in advance of the session with a sense that this framework would meet the needs of a particular group at a particular time. The advantage of choosing a location beforehand is that useful pictures, props and music can be made ready. The disadvantage is that this degree of planning may make the therapist neglect to follow up more immediate clues as to the current group concern.

It can be preferable to approach the session without preconceived ideas, but this requires an act of trust in the process and a willingness on the part of the therapist to enter into the spirit of improvisation. Props, costume and music can be found in response to the moment. The setting for an improvisation might emerge out of the arrival and warm-up phases of the session as group members interact. Or the group can be given responsibility for choosing a location for improvisation together. The therapist can facilitate this by offering a variety of pictures to choose from, or by setting out a choice of three possibilities and inviting the group to vote.

Once a setting is agreed upon the whole group can participate in the shared task of transforming the space and accessing the relevant props. This acts as an organic warm-up to inhabiting the space in role. I sometimes suggest the further discipline that only two or three group members enter the imaginary space at first, to set the improvisation in motion and establish a context to which others can relate. Other group members follow at intervals. Those with less skill in taking on a role often find their way into the improvisation by relating directly to the setting, props, and to those group members who are in role.

The idea of a journey is a favourite device for getting an improvisation off the ground. The initial choice made by the group may simply be a mode of transport: spaceship, plane, train, ship, bus, horseback, or on foot. Once the method of travelling is established, ideas for a destination usually come to mind quite readily. Groups have travelled in this way to Kenya, India, Brighton, London, a desert island, and into outer space. The metaphorical journey into improvisation is facilitated by the enacted journeying together to the chosen destination. The de-roling process and return to the here and now is similarly facilitated by the return journey from the destination. After the improvisation and as part of the closure reflections can be elicited by inviting each person to show the group an imaginary snapshot of the trip. In this way particular moments of impact can be recollected and shared.

(4) **Props.** Props are a safe starting point for improvisation. It is fun to handle different textures, and to explore the potential of an object. This may be less threatening than relating directly to another person. Such an exploration can provide the impulse for relating to other group members via the medium of the prop.

A selection of large pieces of stretchy cloths in boldly contrasting colours can be used to inspire movement. The initial choice of cloth is made on the basis of the colour. Once the cloth has been chosen the client can explore different ways of moving with it, or of wrapping it around the body so as to suggest a particular character or the embodiment of a particular mood. If more than one person chooses the same cloth they can find ways of wearing or using it together, and a collective role may emerge. Having established the basic roles, the next stage is to find out what happens when, for example, 'flowing blue' meets 'fiery red'. The kind of improvisation that emerges can be quite abstract, focusing on the interaction of fire and water, or more human characters might emerge which embody the same characteristics as the abstract elements. There might perhaps be an encounter between Count Dracula and the Snow Queen.

Props can also be used to structure the narrative of an improvisation. A variety of objects can be laid out and group members are invited to examine them, then to choose one that is of interest. The group task is then to incorporate each of the objects into a story. Location and character are chosen in response to the props and the need to create a narrative where the props come into play. This approach to improvisation makes use of the group's ingenuity and demands a high level of cooperation and spontaneity.

(5) **Theme**. It is often the case that group concerns, intrapersonal and interpersonal issues, come to light through the process of improvisation. The particular way the narrative develops or how different characters interact can be seen as an indirect expression of what is going on in the group beneath the surface and an indication of significant themes.

It is also possible, where the issues are already apparent, to work in the opposite direction: to set up an improvisation consciously to address the group concern. A succinct way of doing this is for the dramatherapist to propose a title for a story or improvisation. In a group suffering from poor attendance, for example, or which someone has left, it could be useful to work on an improvisation inspired by the title 'Loss', or 'On shaky ground'.

There may be a particular feeling tone in the group at a certain time. The feeling can be named explicitly, acknowledged and perhaps discussed in the group. It can also be explored creatively through movement or by means of a sculpt. The group can devise an improvisation that acknowledges the current mood or feeling as a starting point, but nonetheless works at an imaginary or fictional level. The dramatherapist can invite ideas from the group to create a situation and characters that might also feel sad/angry/disappointed/lost. The fictional context can be liberating and feel less personally exposing to more vulnerable clients.

Focus on Skills

In the work described above, improvisation is the main focus of the sessions, a process for which the warm-up prepares the group, and from which de-roling and closure activities help the group to disengage. Where this is the approach creativity is a central goal, and is implicitly valued as healing. Improvisation as a process straddles both the conscious and unconscious worlds. The interplay between the two is fertile and creative ground.

The emphasis of dramatherapy can also be on building useful skills. A sequence of sessions may be designed with the specific goal of increasing participants' relaxation skills. Group members are introduced to breath, movement and physical awareness exercises. Many of these stem from acting training systems, others have their origin in the preparation for meditation. The exercises are practised on a weekly basis within sessions until they become familiar. In so far as the session is a rehearsal for life, clients can be encouraged to practise between sessions and integrate the skills into everyday life.

Although the emphasis is not so strongly on the creative process when working on a skills level, there is a place for exercising the imagination within the session. Exercises can come to life by associating different movements with visual images, e.g. 'let your hands circle around your head like clouds swirling around the top of a mountain.' At the end of a session, once the participants are well grounded in their bodies, they are invited to lie on a mat, close their eyes, notice their breathing and listen to soothing music. The dramatherapist can use guided imagery during these periods to enrich the experience of relaxation and to encourage a deeper letting go of tension.

Language and communication is an appropriate focus for skills based sessions. The dramatherapy perspective can contribute to the work of speech and language therapists. I participated in a one week intensive speech and language/dramatherapy project. The goal of the week from the speech and language therapy perspective was that the group of eight clients who lived together should learn and practise their makaton signing skills, so that makaton would become more integrated into their home culture.

Ways in which the vocabulary was practised included games based on the use of picture cards, and actual snacks eaten at table, during which all requests were to be made using makaton. The contribution of the dramatherapy approach was threefold.

First, greeting and dramatherapy warm-up exercises were used to create a sense of group identity and cohesion. This helped with the motivation to learn and communicate together in a spirit of fun. Second, particular strategies were developed to tackle individual problems within the group. Rob had a good knowledge of makaton, and the ability to speak, but the volume of his spoken word was such that no one could hear him. We worked each day on throwing our voices by means of creating a circle, and throwing a large inflatable ball to each other, whilst calling out a name. The scale of the physical movement helped the group to access the idea of a 'big voice' that has to carry across the space. Rob made some progress but seemed to lack the necessary confidence to really enter into the exercise. I sensed that he was afraid of the impact his true voice would make in the silence, so I 'doubled' him, standing with him and calling together with him quite loudly. He could increase the volume of his own voice without his voice being exposed individually. I then stopped using my own voice, but still stayed with Rob and shared the physical build-up to calling. It worked, and he was delighted to find that he could make a loud noise, and be praised for it. I wondered about the origin of his reluctance to be heard or to make a noise, but this was beyond the remit of a skills focused project.

The third contribution was in terms of follow-up. The project had given the opportunity for communication between the two therapeutic disciplines. This meant that I was aware of the areas of ongoing work for the clients involved and could easily incorporate some makaton into informal contacts with the clients. Whenever I saw Rob we called out to each other, so I was able to support his integrating his new found voice beyond the context of the workshop.

Some of the makaton group members were also members of an ongoing dramatherapy group. After a trip to Mexico I arrived in this group with a collection of interesting artefacts I had brought back with me. One object that caught the group's imagination was a carved and painted wooden lizard. This was named 'Happy' by the group and given the appropriate makaton sign. Over the following few sessions we created a story together in the group about Happy. Each element in the story was accompanied by makaton signs where possible, and jointly created movement symbols where there was no sign available. As the story developed over the weeks we recited and signed it together. The imaginary world created by the group gave an unusual context to the makaton, which is otherwise often used in a purely functional way.

Focus on Performance

One of the preconceptions about dramatherapy is that it is for people with dramatic talent, and that it is about putting on plays for an audience. This is a long way from the true nature of the method, which is usually conducted in a private context, and in response to need rather than talent.

There can be value, however, in working with performance. It can be an important personal step in self-esteem for a client to stand up and be seen. For the group as a whole performance involves taking a big risk, but taking it together, and being applauded for the achievement. In terms of this client group I only consider performance work for clients who understand what it means to perform and who actively consent to do so. In both the performance projects described below the final performance was held in the dramatherapy studio and to an invited audience. The location ensures that the performance is seen within the overall context of therapy, and that it constitutes one moment in an ongoing dramatherapy process. The audience is invited by the clients and the therapeutic team, so that there is more control on who is present, and to ensure that the group feels supported by the audience.

I have followed two different models of performance work with this client group: a five day intensive workshop culminating in a performance entitled 'The Magic Music Tree'; and a three-month improvisation based project prepared within the context of ongoing weekly dramatherapy sessions. This led to the creation of a piece called 'Waiting'.

Intensive workshop approach

The central idea for the performance was predetermined by myself. As a child, I was influenced by an enchanting German television series called The Singing Ringing Tree. As we were building up the dramatherapy studio I found the image of this tree on my mind, and decided we needed a real but mobile tree in the studio as a permanent prop. (The image of the tree used in Chapter 1 bears witness to my personal resonance with the symbol. See also Jennings and Minde 1993 p.30 for further reflections on the image of the tree in dramatherapy.) I could imagine it being a useful prop for scene setting, or for hanging things on, and an appropriate symbol of growth for a space devoted to creativity and therapy. Two hospital workers from the gardening and works department were inspired by the idea and together created this tree. It stands about six feet tall, and is made of the top of a tree from the hospital grounds that was pruned and set in a base made out a polished piece of tree trunk on castors.

The project would culminate in the inauguration of this prop, but the details of how we would get to that point were decided as we began to work. The performance group comprised eight clients with experience of dramatherapy and with varying levels of communication and dramatic skill. They were invited to attend the studio each morning and afternoon for five days. The last session was to be the performance.

Mornings were devoted to rehearsal, whilst afternoons were used for creation and exploration of props. These included leaves to hang on the bare branches of the tree, nests created out of wicker and lined with moss, and a large rain stick made out of a piece of plastic piping, sealed at each end and partially filled with plastic beads. When held at an angle the beads would fall and create the sounds of rain.

One afternoon session was put aside for a research trip to visit an ancient hollow tree in a country churchyard. The group was receptive to the powerful atmosphere of this tree, and responded to its magic by circling it, entering its hollow trunk and creating a musical improvisation using bells and other hand held instruments.

The group worked best as a whole group, with everyone involved on stage continuously. Within this format, those who were able to had moments of special responsibility. After the first session the therapeutic team wrote a basic outline for the piece, which became the framework for the future sessions. The enactment dealt with the passing of winter and the coming of spring, focusing on the disappearance and return of a flock of birds, and the nature of the winter weather they leave behind. It was a piece in three scenes.

Scene 1: A giant nest was created out of a pile of bean bags. The group snuggled and draped themselves in this as a family of birds. The first two lines of the scene, 'winter is coming, winter is come' were shared between the two most confident members of the group, who had the responsibility for opening the piece. Their announcement was followed by a single strike on a gong. There was an improvised conversation in the nest about the weather getting colder and one bird would suggest moving off to warmer climes such as Africa. The scene concluded with an exit out of one door of the studio as a flock of birds making their way south. Anyone who was reluctant to leave the nest (as happened to one performer during the performance) was cajoled by the other birds and quickly included in the flock.

Scene 2: The group re-entered the studio by another door, no longer in role as birds but as themselves creating sound and movement images of winter. The timing of each phase of the scene was coordinated by myself as narrator. This device helped to make sense of the scene to the audience and gave vital cues to the performers. The scene took place with the group standing in a circle. Movement and voice were used to portray the effects of the cold. Each person took a gardening cane and used them to either blow into to create the sound of the wind, or to tap rapidly on the floor to suggest the sound of the rain. Individual contributions were made using various other props. One person played the rain stick made by the group, turning it gradually so that the beads tumbled down inside it. Another group member had mastered the art of blowing across a glass bottle to create the sounds of the wind. We had all tried this in the group, with varying degrees of success. He had taken to it and tenaciously practised his new skill at every spare moment. Another group member played a metallic thunder sheet, to create a storm, accompanied by another performer on the drum and another pouring water from a jug into a bowl. The scene concluded with an interpretation in movement of the end of winter, the first warm touch of sun, and the beginning of new growth.

Scene 3: The group left the studio. The tree, bedecked with painted leaves and instruments, was wheeled onto centre stage, and the bean bags placed around it in a circle. The return of the birds was announced and the group re-entered the space in role as the flock of birds from the door out of which they had exited at the end of the first scene. Each person selected their chosen instrument from the tree and took it to their place in the circle. There were chime bars, maracas, a sliding whoopee whistle, drums, tambourine, and Tibetan bells. These were used in a structured musical improvisation on the sounds of spring. A particular sequence of sounds was used to begin and end the piece, while the central part of the improvisation was free.

Devising and performing a play was a new experience for all the clients. On the day of the performance, as the audience came in, one client, Vince, recognised his key worker and decided to sit with him in the audience rather than take his place on the acting area. Vince was the only entirely non-verbal client in the group. He had a tendency to get easily excited and upset by situations, which he would express both by masturbating and by hitting himself. His level of self-containment and ability to focus was considerably higher in the context of dramatherapy than in other situations, which is why he had been invited to take part in the performance project. The other group members had been noticeably supportive and tolerant of him. It seemed when it came to the most anxious moment, the performance itself, that he would be unable to join in the group's journey from within the play. We assured him that he was welcome to watch the play with his key worker if he wanted to, but that it would be good if he felt able to join in. At the last moment he moved from audience to performer, and was able to stay with the process from that position until the end.

The period of applause was in itself both a theatrical and a therapeutic moment. It represented the appreciation of and recognition by the audience of the achievement of the group at an artistic and personal level.

Weekly sessions approach: a devised performance
In the first performance project the therapeutic team devised the framework for the piece. Creative ideas of the group were incorporated into each scene, but the explicit content and the overall form of the piece was a product of the therapeutic team. In the second project the group was able to take more

responsibility for the content and form of their performance piece. The creative process and therapeutic context were quite different. The work took place both at branch and leaf level.

I was in no hurry to engage in another performance project with this client group. Although I could recognise the therapeutic value of the music tree project I had found it personally stressful to open out the work that normally happens in a private context to the scrutiny of outside eyes, however selected the audience. It was also clear from the outset that there would be a high degree of uncertainty as to what would happen on the day of performance, and indeed we had nearly had to adapt to one performer becoming an audience member at the last moment. Two factors changed my mind in opening myself to the idea of performance work again. First, some of the actors from the first project remembered it and valued it years after the event. It had been meaningful, not only at the time, but also in some way beyond the event itself. Some aspects of the process were internalised and carried with the group members as a valued part of their identity. This impressed me.

Second, I was about to start work with a new group of six clients. They all had mental health problems as well as learning disabilities. While the individual pathologies and histories varied considerably, there were some common characteristics and challenges to be met.

- Problems with boundaries. These were expressed in a number of ways. At a physical level several group members tended to stand too close to others, to touch inappropriately, or to have problems about being touched. (At least one man had a history of sexual abuse that made him invasive in all communication initiated by himself, and uncomfortable with any touch initiated by others.) At a verbal level, there was a tendency for most group members to 'swamp' others, to use words in a way that overwhelms and neglects to listen. Boundary problems also tended to be expressed in relation to the time boundaries of sessions, and the basic issue of attendance.

- A strong and conflicted need to communicate, to be heard and seen. The powerful need to communicate tended to be expressed in unskilful ways, so that others were alienated rather than drawn into rapport. The frustration around this coloured the clients' attempts to communicate, and so a vicious circle was in operation.

My sense was that both these factors could be addressed and contained through a performance model of working with this particular group. Performance work is sophisticated team work, requiring discipline and an awareness of self in the context of the wider whole of the group. This discipline highlights boundary problems and gives a context to working on them. The end product is a moment of communication through a defined and practised form. I felt it would be satisfying for the group to achieve such a moment, in the presence of significant people in their lives, who would be present to witness, listen and watch.

The role of theatre director allows for a different kind of intervention and relationship with the group than that of the therapist. As therapist I may be more facilitative, less structuring and directive. The tight discipline required by performance-oriented work makes demands on the director and on the actors alike. We all follow the form, which is given a greater importance than individual wishes. There is a rehearsal schedule to be observed, and each group member has particular responsibilities at different moments, which need to be practised. As theatre director I may be able to make demands on attention and behaviour that would be difficult and inappropriate in other contexts. The demands may be accepted as impersonal, necessary for the sake of the show.

Bearing this in mind I decided that some kind of performance project could be useful on this occasion. I was also influenced by my assessments and knowledge of the individual clients in the group

Ben: Having worked with him before and having discussed his patterns with the multi-disciplinary team I was aware of how difficult Ben found it to see any project through to the end. His life was full of projects started and left unfinished. On the day to day level he avoided staying with processes that either failed to meet his immediate wishes, or challenged him in some way. He escaped such moments by going to the toilet excessively, or walking out. My aim was to take him through a project from start to finish, and to encourage him to stay with it. If he could achieve this in a short term and highly rewarding project such as the performance, he might be more committed to staying with processes in other areas of his life. His dreams of a more independent life in the community would be closer to becoming a reality.

Doreen (see also Chapter 8 on fairy tales): She had a hunger for performance and for being praised/liked. At the same time her tendency to paranoia and aggression got in the way of her building the friendships she longed for. My hope was that the project would be a useful container, would help her remain grounded in a shared reality, and promote her self-esteem.

Mandy (see also Chapter 8 on fairy tales): She was beginning to come out of a long period of depression and psychosis. Mandy had taken part in several dramatherapy groups with me over the years. We had attempted individual dramatherapy together during her period of illness, but she had found this too intense. She was offered a place in the project on the basis of how she had valued the music tree project and other group dramatherapy. Within these contexts she had been able to function easefully at a sophisticated and sensitive level.

Cindy: Last time Cindy had been in a dramatherapy group she was unable to stay with what was happening in the group at all. She refused to participate, sabotaged the work and finally spat at another group member. She was more stable at this point, but still had problems with finding a comfortable relationship between her own egocentric needs and the discipline of belonging to a group. Perhaps a short term performance project would provide a focus for her to experience the positive side of contributing as an individual to a creative group process.

Pete: Pete had never worked in dramatherapy before. He brought with him a reputation for being sexually invasive with his peer group, and had become something of a scapegoat in the hospital community. He had a history of sexual abuse, and his boundaries were clearly confused. He was desperate to be liked and to be helpful, and was unable to stay within the boundaries of the sessions. He would come into my office space at other times during the week, and was clearly very needy. His speaking style was overwhelming and hard to understand, and he found it difficult to stop long enough to listen to any reply. Both he and I would need clear boundaries if we were to be able to work together. The performance project could perhaps provide the necessary form and discipline.

Julie: Julie too was new to dramatherapy. She had a history of institutional abuse, and suffered from low self-esteem with paranoid and hysterical tendencies. She was articulate and very motivated to tell her story.

The work process fell into five stages.

(1) **Assessment.** Assessment for the two newcomers to dramatherapy was through two or three individual sessions. For Ben, Doreen and Mandy whom we knew well, assessment for the group was through recent multi-disciplinary case conferences which I had attended, and through which particular goals were highlighted. Cindy was a last minute addition to the group, and

her place was based entirely on the written referral and verbal consultation with her key worker.

(2) **Establishing the group.** This took place over three sessions, during which time we came to an agreement to work towards performance. The theme of waiting grew out of my reflections on the group process during this stage. Beginnings of sessions were difficult. By the time everyone managed to get to the session someone would leave the room to go the toilet. By the time they came back someone else wanted to go. For those who had arrived early or punctually the process of arrivals seemed to be endless, and there was impatience and frustration on the part of the clients and members of the therapeutic team alike. We had an opening greeting and introduction ritual in which each person in turn stood and introduced themselves by name, 'My name is X', then turned to the next person in the circle and asked 'What's your name?' Every time there was a gap in the circle where a group member had not arrived or had left the room there was a break in the ritual. Eventually Cindy incorporated it into the structure by pointing at the empty chair and saying accusingly 'Not there.'

On one occasion the group started to sing 'Why are we waiting?' I reflected 'I guess that waiting is something we all know something about in this group.' There were nods and sounds of agreement. I asked if each person could think of other situations where they had had to wait. Everyone described a situation they thought of in turn, and it occurred to me that this could be the foundation for a devised piece of theatre. I mentioned how one of the century's most famous plays, *Waiting for Godot* by Samuel Beckett, was about this very theme.

The group was enthusiastic about making their own piece of theatre and we drew up a rehearsal schedule. They decided on a ten week period of rehearsal, which we drew up on a flip chart and we fixed a date for performance. I pointed out that we would need to be able to rely on each other to be present and punctual for this schedule if the play was to be possible. Each person signed their name on the flip chart. We had a contract, and I thought it would be interesting to see how well the group members would be able to honour it.

(3) **Devising and rehearsing.** Two scenes were created through improvisation based on the ideas of Ben and Julie. They were representative of the range of ideas expressed by the group in response to the theme of waiting. Ben's scene was about experiences of waiting in the outside community, at a bus stop, whilst Julie's was about waiting as part of the institutional way

of life. Her scene was initially about waiting to be allowed to get up in the morning, but developed into waiting to get to sleep and then having to get up. In both versions of her scene time is seen as belonging to and structured by the institution rather than the individual.

A third scene arose not from the initial brainstorming, but as a spontaneous and rather bizarre game during the rehearsal process. Doreen introduced the game of 'ether' and was adamant that it should be included in the play. The structure was quite simple. She would approach another group member with her hands open and outstretched towards their face, perhaps like an old-fashioned dentist's gas mask. As she approached she would say 'ether', and they were expected to fall asleep immediately, standing on the spot, as if under her spell. As the scene developed she would then re-awaken them and they would come back to life.

I found the scene fascinating both from the point of view of Doreen's individual characteristics, and as an existential image. For Doreen the structure gave her complete control over everyone in the group. She had the power of consciousness, life and death. She had a strong aggressive tendency that would usually be expressed in verbal attacks and criticisms. Here she had a structure that allowed her to kill people off at will, but only temporarily, until she chose to allow them to exist again. She was omnipotent! She loved it, and could hardly contain her excitement each time she performed it. At the same time she realised that she could be heavy handed, and would check out anxiously that she had not actually hurt any one during the scene.

At an existential level the image was evocative. We never talked about what it might be about in the group, but for me it suggested a concern with the nature of life and death reminiscent of Beckett. There was also a sense of it being a reflection on the condition of having learning disabilities in particular. There is an investment in staying unconscious and anaesthetised to the pain.

The rehearsal process allowed clients to experience and re-experience each scene. Group members could work on and refine particular moments of performance in ways for which opportunities seldom occur in real life. The experience of mastery of a particular exercise or form is a therapeutic factor in many ritualised and repeated dramatherapy structures used with this client group. It is at the heart of performance-oriented therapy.

(4) **Performance.** By the time the piece was performed it had developed into a series of six scenes. These had been rehearsed and refined but still maintained an element of improvisation. Doreen's mental state had deteriorated and she was unable to take part over the last few sessions. Her scene

was still included in the show, however. There was an important lesson learnt in the group about dealing with the unforeseen. Whenever someone was unable to take part, either because of an absence or a short term inability to cope, the group covered for them, adapted to the new situation, and the show was not compromised. This was a reflection of the mature working roles adopted by the group as a whole. In Doreen's case I played her role in her special scene, and she was present in the audience to witness it and to hear her contribution acknowledged.

The content of the scenes was quite simple. The first scene was entitled 'Introduction' and was a ritualised development of the first 'hello' exercise we had done as a group. As a structure it allowed each person to be introduced individually, to speak alone and then to take part in a group shout. The second scene, 'Mirror Images', also grew out of an early warm-up exercise that was practised each week. Performers faced each other in pairs, focusing on each others' movement and trying to move as if a reflection of each other to the accompaniment of dreamy music. The third scene was Ben's 'Waiting for the Bus', in which different characters wait in a queue for a bus that eventually drives straight past them. The fourth scene was 'Waiting for Ether' as described above. The fifth scene was Julie's 'Waiting for Sleep', in which group members embodied the passing of the hours of the night, whilst Julie tried unsuccessfully to get to sleep. She eventually dropped off at six o'clock, only to be awakened by the nurses on the seven o'clock shift. The sixth scene was 'The Finale', in which the cast stood in line, and counted down individually with numbers and movements to a final group shout of 'The End!' and a bow to the audience.

Therapeutic value

The content of the scenes had therapeutic significance for different individuals at different levels, that were not necessarily obvious to the audience, or to the group as a whole. The fact that Ben and Pete were able to work sensitively and creatively together in the mirroring scene was enormously important for both of them. Their relationship with each other over the previous couple of years had been a difficult one, at times intimate, at other times hostile. It had been characterised by unclear boundaries, and a lack of mutuality. At the outset of the group I had serious reservations about their ability to work together. Within this scene, however, and within the rehearsal process as a whole, they were able to observe the appropriate space between them, and to adapt in a spirit of respectful give and take to each others' suggestions and responses. In microcosm it was a mature and healthy relationship in action.

The bus stop scene had therapeutic significance for Ben that I only appreciated when discussing his therapy with two colleagues who had been working with him in individual therapy. His work with them had revealed a strong desire to live a 'normal' life in the community. One of his images of this was using the public transport system. Every time he was given the opportunity to spend more time in the community, however, he sabotaged his own attempts, by walking out of difficult situations and failing to commit his energy to what he was doing. His self-image was very low indeed, and this was reflected in a sense of sexual inadequacy that led him to expose himself to women. Although he aspired to a traditional sexual and emotional relationship with a woman, his sexual fantasies centred around being punished and spanked. He said he hated himself and that he could not imagine ever achieving the lifestyle he wanted.

The scene he contributed to the performance piece allowed him to enact the affirming experience of using the public transport system each week during the rehearsal period. The character he developed in this scene was that of a kind and courteous boyfriend, taking his girlfriend to have a meal out, followed by a trip to the theatre to see a Shakespeare play. It was an image of the normality he aspired to, and within the drama he was quite capable of fulfilling the role. His 'girlfriend' in the scene was an older member of the therapeutic team, safely out of bounds as a real possibility for romantic liaison, on the grounds both of her professional status, and their relative ages.

The content of the scene then clearly related to his aspirations, and fed his self-esteem. There was, moreover, therapeutic value in the process of rehearsal. In many areas of his life Ben used going to the toilet as a way of leaving situations that were hard to deal with, or that did not meet his immediate wishes. Any time he had been questioned about this behaviour he would deny that it had any significance and would walk out angrily. He was consequently rarely challenged about this pattern and in some early rehearsals he was in and out of the studio many times, leaving the group to wait or cope without him.

In my role as director I felt I had to address the situation. At the beginning of one rehearsal session I spoke to Ben in the group. I acknowledged that he needed to go to the toilet a lot and asked him if he felt he would be able to get through a scene without disappearing when we did the actual performance in front of an audience. He reacted by glaring at me angrily, then leaving the session altogether. We carried on the rehearsal, unsure if Ben would return at all. Perhaps this would become yet another unfinished project for him. However, he returned the following week and made a brief statement to the group acknowledging that he had walked out the previous week, but was now back in the group. The visits to the toilet became less frequent and during the performance he stayed with the process from beginning to end without needing to retreat. Most important, the goal of performance had given him the incentive to work through difficulties and to follow a commitment through to its end point.

The presence of an audience had therapeutic value. They were witnesses to the creativity of the group, to its desire to express something personal, and to the achievement of its goal. Cindy and Julie gave their best performances on the day, the presence of an audience helping them to access something more authentic in the roles they were playing. The audience was small, composed exclusively of people we had invited. There were family members and members of the hospital staff. The consultant psychiatrist who specialised in people with learning disabilities and superimposed mental illness was present. She knew the group as patients and was able to appreciate their achievements and see a wider view of them. Also present was a member of the senior management team. He was moved by what he saw, particularly by the sense of the inner world of the actors expressed in the roles they were playing. He was touched by the subjectivity of the patients as people. So often in large institutions senior management operates at a distance from the service users, and both sides lose out from this situation. The therapeutic value here was as much for the manager as witness as for the performers. In a small but significant way theatre provided a forum for transcending the institutionalised communication problems.

CHAPTER 8

The Use of Fairy Tales in Group Dramatherapy

A Dramatherapy and Music Therapy Collaboration

Fairy tales offer a rich resource for dramatherapy work with both children and adults. Specialists in fairy tales have written extensively on the power of the fairy tale and the reasons for its enduring popularity (Bettelheim 1976, Roheim 1992), whilst psychotherapists of Freudian and Jungian orientations have attempted to interpret its hidden meanings. The dramatherapist can learn from these perspectives and also directly from the stories themselves.

Fairy tales are well known. Many exist with modifications in different countries worldwide. They are part of a cultural heritage that is shared by children and adults from a multitude of backgrounds. They are familiar, part of a common language that affirms our connection with each other. They are non-exclusive and accessible to many people with learning disabilities.

There is evidence that there are variations of traditional fairy tales in different parts of the world and at different times in history. These variations bring out a particular aspect of the story that needs to be heard at that time and place and by that person or group of people. The stories are flexible enough to hold many meanings. As the common property of all people they are living parts of the culture, capable of growth and change. If they are seen only as a fixed entity, incapable of change – what Moreno called a 'cultural conserve' (Fox 1987) – some of their potential is lost. The dramatherapist and dramatherapy group may usefully adapt the stories to meet the needs of the micro-culture of the group.

Fairy tales convey different meanings according to the developmental stage of the child or adult. The same child may hear a particular story at different ages and respond to a different subtext as she grows up, or as new concerns preoccupy her. She may at one point identify with one character, at another point with another. Different moments of the story become significant at different times.

The Cinderella Project

The story of Cinderella as written by the brothers Grimm (1984) was used as part of a short term, eight month group I ran with music therapist Isabel Oman and dramatherapy assistant Pat McCulloch. The group comprised eight women, four from one residential unit, and four from another a couple of miles away. These two units were soon to merge under common management, and we set up the group initially as a 'friendship' group, an opportunity to make links and develop relationships. Since Isabel and I were also based at different sites the themes of friendship and relationship extended also to the challenge of finding helpful ways to combine dramatherapy and music therapy in the context of a weekly women's group. The story of Cinderella provided a framework within which both therapeutic methods could be used, and through which group concerns could be expressed.

The location for the group alternated every four weeks between the dramatherapy studio on one site and the music therapy room on the other site. This allowed each sub-group the opportunity both to visit and to be hosts. At the end of the project we worked each day in the dramatherapy studio on an intensive week long workshop. The work incorporated the full spectrum of dramatherapy process, from root to leaf; the use of story and enactment giving a particular emphasis to branch level work (see Chapter 1).

Group members were in their thirties to sixties, and had been in care for many years. They were all verbal to some extent. One, Charlotte, was particularly difficult to understand and quite quiet in her speech; another, Harriet was very talkative and had a tendency to dominate by talking without listening. All but one participant, Lyn, were ambulant at the outset; she was able to move herself in a wheelchair. Half way through the course of the group, another participant, Sally ended up in a wheelchair temporarily, due to an accident.

There were four phases of work.

(1) November and December: we searched for a way to be together. Our group solution was the creation of a nativity play.

(2) January to March: the Cinderella story served as a doorway through which the group began to explore loss. Emotional catharsis was achieved through a combination of role work and music.

(3) April: this was a period of fragmentation and difficulty.

(4) May: we met for a one week intensive workshop to conclude the Cinderella story, and to address issues of marriage, birth, dreams and endings.

Before exploring these individual phases of work, the challenges they presented and some of the solutions we discovered, I should like to consider the *Leitmotiv* of the whole project. This *Leitmotiv* was the theme of life cycle, expressed through images of birth, death and marriage.

The central mystery of the life cycle was relevant at a number of different levels. A therapy group has a life cycle; within the four phases defined above the group formed, discovered its nature to some extent, grew with struggles towards completion and had some kind of death in closure.

At the same time, each individual within the group was at a certain point within her own biological life cycle, from early thirties to mid-sixties. Some were biologically capable of becoming mothers, others were post-menopausal. They were all at a stage in life where they were having to face the death of people who were close to them. Two or three were actively dealing with the death of one or both parents, another was acutely aware of the death of a close friend. The music therapist, by contrast, was pregnant, and carried an increasingly evident twelfth member of the group into the sessions, a reminder of fertility, newness and birth. There was a poignant coming together of different moments of transition within the life cycle.

There is more to age as a factor in identity than the counting of biological life years. In recent times there has been an increasing awareness of the need to relate in an 'age appropriate' manner to people with learning disabilities. This is not a one dimensional task however. Each adult in the women's group contained and expressed within the group a multiplicity of identities, a complex collection of psychological roles of different ages. The same woman might express herself as a child mourning for her parents, a sibling fighting for space, and a post-menopausal woman seeing the signs of ageing and the inevitability of death in herself. These are all aspects of the adult, whether or not the adult has learning disabilities.

The absence or death of a parent, the task of getting our needs met in the face of competition, and seeing the signs of our own mortality: these are challenging issues for most people. There tend to be further difficulties for those with learning disabilities. The hospital or institutional setting in particular tends to perpetuate the role of the dependant child in need of protection from the realities of the life cycle. Even for those who are in a sexual relationship there is the likely reality that they will not live out the role of wife or mother. So, however carefully we try to validate the adult roles in our clients, we cannot avoid the fact that many will not get to express their idea of maturity and adulthood in the way they would wish.

The institution itself participates in a life cycle. The time of this group was one of transformation and uncertainty. Two separate sites were being encouraged to consider themselves as one. Was this perhaps an arranged marriage? One of the two sites would eventually be earmarked for closure, as the unit retracted onto one site. Was this a death? There was a great deal of anxiety among staff. Uncertainty about the future meant that many staff were choosing to move on, looking for security and promotion elsewhere. The attitude to the residents was protective – 'don't worry them until we are certain what will happen. They might have to move, they might not.' There was a sense of institutional dissolution and death accompanied by an atmosphere of taboo in the face of disturbing realities.

The working methods in this group had their foundations in the creative arts, in particular drama and music. The creative process itself has a life cycle. At first there is the impulse to give expression to a feeling or perception. There follows the struggle to find a suitable form, a way of expressing what needs to be expressed. This raw material may be refined and developed, its potential exploited. The initial impulse is fulfilled and dies away. There may be a period of waiting and eventually a new moment brings with it a new need and another impulse towards creation. The process is continuous, cyclical.

These different perspectives of the life cycle theme were all part of the context of the women's group, existing both at an external level and also as part of the inner lives of the clients and the therapists. The spontaneous responses of the clients to the working structures offered revealed a concern with the life cycle to be at the heart of the group matrix.

Phase One: The Search for a Way to be Together

The initial sessions were dedicated to finding some common languages. Isabel and I hoped that these would form the basis for future exploration, and would indicate to us common themes and issues in this particular group. We introduced various working structures in a spirit of both warm-up and assessment. These structures focused on three areas: talking/sharing; making music; and movement/drama work.

Talking activity

From the outset it was clear that the group had energy for talking, but lacked skill in terms of listening, verbal sharing and discussion. On arrival at either work space, before even entering the room, two or three group members would habitually bombard Isabel and myself with words. We were being talked at rather than talked to. The interaction was overwhelming at two levels. First, in terms of physical proximity we were literally given no space. Second, the content itself seemed overwhelming. It usually consisted of fragments of news delivered without either introduction or explanation, as when a young child seeks a parents' attention. It was hard to understand, and there was an implicit role demand for us to investigate or follow up what was being said there and then at the expense of our own agenda, which was that the group as a whole should come together.

This pattern of communication is not uncommon when running groups with this client group. The subtext is perhaps: 'Hear me, understand me, feed me, NOW! Never mind them, what about ME.' Clearly this is an expression of neediness without much social disguise. To some extent it may be explicable in terms of developmental levels relating to the learning disabilities of the clients. However this explanation does not take into account the social realities of institutional life. Habitual communication patterns within the institution reinforce habitual roles. Staff are seen as the only legitimate and valid source of relationship; in relating to these provider figures clients tend to present as needy children, in competition with an enormous brood of other children for parental attention. Staff reciprocate from a parental role and make few demands on clients to change. The therapy group can be seen to some extent as a microcosm of the wider institutional world, and so the communication patterns are revealed as if under a microscope.

As a therapeutic team we recognised the sense of neediness in the group. Was it possible to address the theme of 'friendship' in such an atmosphere of demand and need? We reflected on how non-learning disabled people manage the inevitable compromise between immediate personal need and building meaningful relationships. We decided that the process depended on some personal ability to contain ourselves, to use our listening skills, and our empathic awareness of others. We wondered whether the group would be capable of some of this discipline; in other words, whether they would be able to learn and apply new life roles. We felt that this group probably were able to work towards change. With this in mind we decided to work with the group initially at a skill-building level, whilst allowing space to express feelings within appropriate structures.

Since there was interest and a need to talk on coming together as a group, we encouraged group members to sit down in a circle first before engaging in conversation. This was a challenge to participants to contain the desire for immediate attention and wait a few moments so that we were all in a position to listen. Once seated, we began a simple turn-taking go-round in which each group member was invited to share any news from the week. The other group members were encouraged to listen actively. When two or more people were speaking at once about different things we would stop the discussion, point out the situation, the impossibility of listening to several people at once, and ask who we should listen to first. The responsibility to decide this was with the group, and they were able to make a decision. Their habitual way of sharing was still to direct statements and gaze at Isabel and myself. Over time we encouraged group members to address the whole group and not just the therapeutic team. This proposal was more acceptable to some than to others.

Musical activity

Musical improvisation was another group activity that encouraged a combination of personal creative expression and listening. In one structure each person chose a hand-held instrument, and we took it in turns to play briefly and listen. When we had heard all the instruments we improvised together freely, having been given permission to play for either some or all of the time, until the piece came to an organic end. The emotional content and the quality of listening varied from week to week, and the exercise acted as a sounding board for the group. Sometimes we focused more specifically on turn-taking, by insisting that each person joined in the improvisation one at a time around the circle until everyone was playing.

We used 'bongo conversations' as a structure to encourage creative dialogue and interaction in pairs, whilst the rest of the group listened and were invited to comment. This structure has great dramatic as well as musical potential. Two people play a pair of bongos, one on each half of the instrument. The interaction may be playful, aggressive, cautious or joyful and the rhythmic expression is often accompanied by good eye contact, facial interplay and words. The bongos provide a form and an incentive to engage with another person without the restrictions of verbal ability. Sometimes the same patterns of communication seem to be revealed through the bongo conversations as in verbal dialogue. Someone who dare not speak may be afraid of making a sound on the bongos, or someone who talks without pausing or listening to the other may play in a similar way. For some people, however, the form may facilitate the expression of feelings that would be difficult to express in words, or allow flexibility and experimentation in relating to another person. It was a structure that I have since used in a variety of dramatherapy groups.

Music was an important part of the group ritual marking the beginning and the end of the group. We created a song based on a North American Indian chant. The song celebrated friendship, connection, and individuality within the context of the whole:

> We are a circle,
> We are friends,
> We are a circle,
> We are friends,
> Holding hands together
> With our friends
> Holding hands together
> With our friends
> Hello/Goodbye Annie, hello/goodbye Mandy etc.
> Hello/Goodbye everyone.

By creating a song about the circle we were intuitively working with the underlying theme of cycles and life cycles. The words were simple enough for everyone to remember, and different group members were able to put themselves forward to initiate the singing of the group song.

Towards drama

Half the group had previous experience of dramatherapy, the other half were new to drama. The talking part of the session and the musical warm-ups described above took place sitting in a circle. We used movement warm-ups to get participants up and out of their seats and into exploring the room. Initially there was a lack of spontaneity in movement, particularly among those new to dramatherapy. I decided to work with the support of Gabrielle Roth's music for movement, which inspires movement of various kinds. We explored simple movements using different parts of the body to create a dance. I called out different body parts and we explored the kind of movements we could make with that body part in response to the music. The decision as to what part of the body to move was decided by me, and this allowed the clients to put their energy and focus into the movements rather than the questions of whether to move and how to move. Spontaneity grows by stages. Where there is a lack of spontaneity it is supportive to give guidelines until the confidence grows and suggestions begin to come more organically from the group.

A further structure for movement involved working in pairs using the image of a mirror to encourage observation, the equivalent of listening at a movement level. Initially group members were reluctant to choose partners, predictably wanting to partner one of the therapeutic team rather than their peer group. We dealt with this by changing partners frequently so that clients had the experience of working with both staff and other clients. Participants began to take more risks and to be more open to each other. The change occurred gradually over several weeks, and required patience and tenacity on the part of the therapists.

The nativity

The first moment of power and even grace in the group came when they first branched out into role play. This was initiated by the clients. Christmas was approaching, and they talked of doing a nativity play and singing Christmas carols. Harriet, the most talkative and dominant group member said that she had a doll that she would bring the following week. We were not sure if she would remember, but her intention was clearly strong enough to last the week and she arrived at the next session with the doll that was to represent the baby Jesus.

We passed the doll around the circle as a warm-up to creating the dramatic scene. I wanted the scene to represent the group's perception of the nativity rather than falling into my own assumptions about what they were likely to have in mind. I began by asking where the scene should be set: 'A stable'. I invited the group to set up the stable using play shapes. They created walls, a chair and a bed. Our location was ready and we now had to people it with the relevant characters. I asked who was present at the stable. Doreen replied without hesitation 'God'. I invited her to take on this role, which she did by choosing herself some material to drape around her shoulders. She then entered the scene, costumed, in role and with dignity. She chose her position, standing just behind the stable where she could oversee the proceedings. From this moment it was clear that this nativity would transcend cliché for the participants.

The process of taking on roles continued in this manner. Each role was self-selected and each time elements of costume and prop enabled the participants to enter the scene with an adequate sense of their role. Two women put themselves forward to play Mary, and so we ended up with two Marys. Harriet, who had brought the doll, was Mary the mother, holding her 'baby', whilst Lyn in her wheelchair took her own place as Mary the wife. She sat statuesque and proud next to her husband, Joseph, a role taken by Charlotte. Sally, who was quite shy in the group, accepted the role of the star, followed by the three wise men who were Mandy, Jill and Annie. Isabel and Pat as members of the therapeutic team were cast as angels at the group's request, whilst I stayed outside of the drama and had the role of director, narrator and photographer.

The piece consisted mostly of tableaux, as would have happened in the medieval mystery plays. There was some movement as the star led the three wise men to the stable, and they offered up their gifts. There was little dialogue. The silence and stillness gave a sense of awed celebration, the simplicity and naiveté gave power. For the first time, the group was sharing an imaginary world, one which had meaning for each participant and for the group as a whole. There was a shared need to enact and a shared commitment to the whole group creation. I took photographs of different moments within the drama as a record for the group. After the enactment we sang carols from within the scene and included some instrumental accompaniment. This provided an outlet for the energy raised in the enactment and was at the same time a return to a more familiar way of being together.

The themes of birth, marriage and the mysteries of the life cycle, present in this enactment, were to recur during the life of the group with other moments of power. This first birth was at one level the mystery of stepping together into another reality. It also prefigured the announcement of Isabel's real life pregnancy in the new year.

Phase Two: The Cinderella Story as a Doorway to Explore Difficult Feelings

Lyn's weekly contribution to the verbal sharing at the beginning of the first few groups was to bring in sections of fairy stories she had attempted to copy type during the week. This contributed to the idea of working with a fairy tale. I was drawn to the story of Cinderella and we began work on this in the new year.

I introduced the story at the end of one session, by reading the first paragraph of the Grimm's version to the group and asking if they would be interested in exploring the story. They were keen and we began the enactment the following week.

The deathbed scene

The Cinderella story begins powerfully with the death of Cinderella's mother, and this was the first scene we enacted.

Harriet had been talking of her profound feelings of loss at the death of her friend. She spoke of not wanting to live any more. It was Mandy, however, who was keen to play the part of Cinderella. Mandy is a woman in her forties, very able and articulate much of the time, but who lapses periodically into phases of depression and psychosis. At these times she exhibits 'challenging behaviours' in terms of violence towards herself and others. Her parents had died several years before this group got together. She had not yet accepted the fact of their death or her associated feelings. She had had difficulty addressing this material through talking therapies. During her phases of depression she appeared confused about the passage of time and would talk about her parents as if they were still alive.

Having heard the beginning of the story, Mandy immediately volunteered to take the role of the only daughter at the deathbed scene. Whilst she often had difficulty in talking about the reality of her losses, she had an 'act hunger' for this role. The fairy tale as fictional story provided a safe distance which paradoxically enabled her to explore her own life role as bereaved daughter.

Doreen, also in her forties, had a similar act hunger for the role of sick and dying mother. She had lost her own mother some years earlier; and several months later, during the course of the group, was to lose her father unexpectedly. Her attraction to the role of mother in the deathbed scene seemed to be based partly on the enjoyment of being a 'patient' who needed to be made comfortable and who was fussed over. She also enjoyed the sheer drama and emotional intensity of the scene. Her role in the nativity play had been God – both were strong, powerful and dramatic roles, central to the scenes they inhabited.

There was a further role. Cinderella's mother is also a wife, married to a wealthy merchant. The role of the husband was shared between Harriet and Charlotte. They did little in the scene, and were largely in the background. Nonetheless, simply being in role can have a personal impact. For Harriet it was enough just to hold the role of the bereaved partner. This was as close as she was able to come at this point to working with her feelings of loss, in relation to her friend who had died, and perhaps in relation to other earlier losses.

Although the scene required only three characters, the whole group involved itself in setting the scene and as audience. We had to build a bed for the mother, improvising a pillow and blanket from things that were to hand. Cinderella knelt by her mother's bedside and the scene unfolded with a combination of spontaneous dialogue and prompts from myself based on the story. In the scene it was acknowledged that the mother was dying; both characters expressed their sadness and their love for each other; and the mother gave her daughter advice that would help her in her future life. She told her to 'be good' and to remember her mother. In this way the 'good mother' could be internalised and guide the daughter even after the external mother had died.

The physical enactment of a scene, even a short vignette such as this, faces the group with issues and feelings in a powerful and immediate way. It is important that the therapist planning such a session allows time for personal comment and de-roling at the end of the session before the group disbands. Of course, there is no such thing as an absolute end. There is a continuity of process at a psychological level that links one session to the next. This is particularly the case when working within the framework of a story or dramatic text. Nonetheless, it is important to pay attention to adequate containment by structuring the ending of each session. In the case of the deathbed scene the group commentary occurred first non-verbally through a group musical expression of feelings, and then verbally as actors and audience were invited to talk about the story and connections with their own experience. This double process was an attempt to address the need for 'digesting' the work at both emotional and cognitive levels.

The ritual of transformation

The next scene in the story involves the daughter visiting her mother's grave every day and weeping over it. Time passes and the seasons change. Winter comes, followed by spring, at which point her father remarries. The trans-formation of the seasons in this way is a reminder of the cycle of death and rebirth as it manifests in nature. In the story this process is set in the context of Cinderella's mourning at the graveside.

In the next session we returned to the beginning of the story, repeating the first scene before moving into the enactment at the graveside. The group chose to maintain the same roles. We added an extra dimension to the now familiar scene by inviting those who were not acting to make a musical commentary on the action. Annie took up this suggestion and made a musical contribution reflecting the mood of the scene. Throughout the project we often found it useful to recap in action. This is partly to serve as a reminder of the story so far, and partly so that something new can be explored through a familiar form.

In the second scene, Mandy knelt alone at the graveside, and covered her face with her hands to show her grief. The gesture was stylised, allowing Mandy to evoke the relevant feelings whilst ensuring a certain personal distance. She was not simply Mandy crying at the loss of her mother; she was Everyman or 'Everydaughter' representing something communal that touches us all. The stylisation continued as the passage of the seasons was depicted. Lyn volunteered to cover the grave with a layer of snow, a piece of white fabric. The group accompanied this with sad and bleak music. Winter had come. As spring came in turn the group created the mood of sunshine and hope through musical improvisation – the snow was melting, Lyn's cue to sweep back the fabric from the grave. Life, hope, fertility were reborn.

The third scene of this session involved a return to the father/husband figure. As the desolation of winter passes he remarries. We touched on this briefly, by making a tableau as if for a wedding photograph. The stepmother role was taken quite readily by Sally but there was a noticeable reluctance in the group to take on the role of the ugly sisters. There was energy in this reluctance, and on reflection after the session the therapeutic team decided that we would guide the group towards focusing on these sisters and the family relationships in the story.

The sisters

The next paragraph in the story describes the sisters. They are not ugly as in the pantomime stereotype. They are beautiful on the outside but wicked inside. Their appearance and their true nature are at odds. They are duplicitous and complex. We decided to focus on this aspect of the sisters rather than their appalling abuse of Cinderella, whom they bullied from morning till night. There were many occasions whilst working with the story when we made a choice as therapists to emphasise one aspect of the story over another. The therapeutic journey could have been quite different if we had chosen other points of emphasis. Our thinking at this point was that it could feel unsafe to explore the bullying theme, that it would be particularly burdensome to whoever played Cinderella, and that it could be too destructive for the group as a whole. The concept of discrepancy between outer presentation and inner motives, on the other hand, seemed to hold some useful therapeutic lessons for the group. We could affirm that everyone has inner thoughts and feelings that are not always expressed and are often selfish or negative, but that can be recognised in the context of a therapy group. We might be able to challenge the prevalent conditioning that 'patients' should appear to be patient, compliant and nice. This 'good girl, good boy' mentality inhibits people with learning disabilities from owning and exploring the fuller range of their feelings, and from maturing. We might also be able to address the sibling rivalry that was expressed continuously but indirectly in the group.

We began the session with some verbal sharing, and the group song. We brought the focus on to inner feelings as Isabel invited each person in turn to express how they were feeling at that moment on an instrument. On this occasion they mostly kept to positive and happy feelings in the music, although Jill seemed not to be interested in the exercise at all. She began to talk about being upset that she had been told off on her ward, apparently for needing to go to the toilet. At a surface level she did not seem to be in touch with the exercise. In fact she was in touch with her feelings and had found her own way to share these with the group. We encouraged the group to reflect on what she was saying, and asked them how she must be feeling. We ended up all stamping our feet as an expression of solidarity with her anger and frustration, an appropriate beginning to looking at the theme of feelings beneath the surface.

We moved on to a movement warm-up without music, and this developed into 'movement conversations' in which group members were invited to pair up and work with movement, responding to whatever their partner did. The group was responsive to this and so began to work on the theme of relationship, cooperation and competition.

I read the paragraph about the sisters in the Cinderella story and we talked about how someone can present a nice mask to the world but be full of greedy, nasty or angry feelings. We invited the group to take on the roles of the nice face or the feelings underneath. The group was happy to take on the role of 'niceness'. Doreen and Harriet played these roles, but no one was prepared to explore the other side of the sisters from role. It was perhaps too exposing. In the end Pat and I as members of the therapeutic team took on the roles ourselves and gave ourselves permission to wallow in nastiness and enjoy the roles. We were modelling the fact that it is acceptable to explore the shadow side of the personality in the group, and also showing that the nasty roles can be satisfying and enjoyable to play. The group participated from a distance, from the role of audience or witness. There was energy in the roles, an element of forbidden fruit, and the group responded to this with interest. After Pat and I de-roled there was a group discussion. The group members were able to talk about the fact that there is more than one side to each person and that they too had 'nasty' thoughts from time to time. This was an important insight and revelation, particularly for those with a tendency to see themselves in a one dimensional light and who had an overriding need to please others.

Cinderella becomes assertive

Over time we kept returning to the beginning of the story and recapped the work so far. On the whole, group members maintained their original roles in this, and the therapeutic team was able to change the emphasis and highlight various themes according to our perception of the needs of the group at that moment. On one such occasion we returned to the paragraph

about the sisters and their bullying. We set up the scene in a styl
using musical instruments with two main intentions in mind:

- to encourage the quieter and more passive group members to assert
  themselves and get themselves heard in the face of competition from
  the more dominant group members – this could be seen as role
  training for other life situations where they needed to be more
  assertive
- to give an outlet for the expression of anger and other strong feelings
  that seemed hard to bring to the group.

The structure involved the two 'sisters' standing together at some drums and
expressing in music their power, dominance and spiteful feelings. These
'nasty' roles were no longer taboo in the group, and two group members
volunteered. Mandy, who was keen to take the Cinderella role again, was
given the task of interrupting her sisters and making herself heard once they
were into role and expressing themselves loudly. Cinderella was learning to
be assertive! Like the sisters, Cinderella was to use drums and cymbals. It was
not easy and at first Mandy/Cinderella gave up. The two others were making
too much noise together for her to make herself heard: she needed some
help. At this point I brought in the element of movement. The idea of the
exercise was that Cinderella should grow metaphorically in stature and
power. I put myself in role concretely as her power. I began curled up and
small, crouching on the floor, and the more assertively Mandy played, the
taller and bigger I grew. If she lapsed I began to shrink again. It worked for
her to have this immediate visual feedback of her efforts and her eventual
victory. The group as a whole was energised by the challenge and confrontation. For Isabel and me it was a satisfying combination of the use of story,
role, music and movement.

It was often easier to address painful areas through the medium of the
story rather than directly. Shortly after this occasion Mandy (the group
Cinderella) was uncharacteristically absent. She had apparently become
confused and wandered off. At the same session, Doreen arrived in some
distress with the news that her father had died unexpectedly. It was poignant
that this should have happened to the person who had played the dying
parent several times in our group. The group had great difficulty staying with
Doreen's news. They almost seemed not to hear it. Instead they expressed
their concern that 'Cinderella had gone missing.' They knew Mandy's name
but expressed their loss and concern in terms of her role and the story which
had become a vital part of the group's language.

Later in the session we moved on again to the scene in which Cinderella stands up to the sisters, as described above. Doreen had put herself in role as one of the sisters on a number of occasions. It was a satisfying role for her, and one which reflected her jealous relationship with her own sister. In this session she had been understandably withdrawn, concerned with the news of her father's death. Towards the end of the session she decided suddenly and clearly that she wanted to play a different role, Cinderella standing up to the sisters. It was like a storm breaking. She found her energy and anger and was able to channel it into the drumming. She was heard not only by the sisters in role, but by the whole group in the here and now drama of the group process. She was standing up to her 'sisters' in the group.

There was further distress and loss in the group at this time. Sally broke her ankle and spent a week in hospital before returning to the group in a wheelchair. The other women were able to express their concern and sympathy when they found out what had happened to her and decided together to send her a card from the group. They had an awareness of their group identity and the therapeutic team welcomed the suggestion of a group card, which we made together in the session. Doreen, who would be going to visit her in hospital, was given the task of delivering the card.

It is ironic that the group had been unable to give Doreen the support and sympathy she needed directly when her father died, yet here she was as representative of the group's concern for Sally. There were some familiar features in this for Doreen. She had an intensely jealous relationship with her real-life sister, and often ended up in familiar situations of rivalry with her female friends. She tended to be the needy one in these relationships, bending over backwards to please them, whilst suffering intense feelings of jealousy and anger inside. It is not surprising that she was often drawn to the role of one of the sisters in the Cinderella story, where she could acknowledge and give vent to some of those feelings that were hard to deal with in real life.

The father's journey

As the story continues the father goes on a journey to the fair, and asks each of his daughters what he should bring them back. The two stepsisters ask for clothes and jewellery while Cinderella asks that he bring her back the first branch that knocks against his hat. When he returns he gives each of the girls what she has wished for. Cinderella plants the branch at her mother's grave and waters it with her tears. It grows into a magic tree inhabited by a white bird that grants her wishes.

This short piece of the story is rich in themes to be explored: journeys, shopping, wishes, loyalty, presents, clothes, magic, grief and transformation. The first time we approached it we looked at wishes. The group members were invited to share something they wished for. All responses were about food, the most basic desire for nourishment and sensual enjoyment.

The following session we enacted the piece. Harriet chose the role of father. She enjoyed playing a man, carefully choosing a man's hat with a feather in it for her role. She continued to choose male roles whenever possible for the rest of the group process. Doreen and Lyn continued to play the stepsisters, whilst Mandy carried on as Cinderella. The four of them improvised the conversation before father leaves for the fair. Lyn's wish in role was for tights – a luxury item for her in her wheelchair; I had never seen her wearing tights. Doreen asked for jewellery, whilst Mandy requested the branch, as dictated by the text. By this stage in the work these group members were developing confidence in role play and in characterisation. They stayed in role and had a sense of their own and others' parts in the whole.

Harriet decided that her journey to the fair would be by horse and sustained a solo as she rode off with the orders for shopping from the stepdaughters. Those without a role were invited to make sound effects on the temple blocks or vocally. At the fair Annie volunteered to be a shopkeeper and to sell the father the tights he needed to buy. Jill also wanted to play a shopkeeper but felt unable to do it alone, so she and I shared the role. This technique of role sharing is valuable for those who feel unwilling to take the risk of playing a role alone. Jill usually presented as a shy little girl in the group despite her advanced years. She was delighted to have me to herself in sharing the role and felt proud of having managed to play the part with support. She was subsequently able to move on to more and more autonomy in the group, finally taking over the role of Cinderella. This was an important first step for her in this process.

On the way back from the fair a branch from a tree was to brush against the father's hat. Pat took on the role of branch and later of the magic tree that grows from it at the grave when Cinderella plants it and waters it with her tears. Gradually she uncurled and grew, rather as I had done to mirror Cinderella's assertiveness in earlier sessions. Annie volunteered eagerly to be the white bird and 'flew' around the studio enthusiastically, whilst other group members played some appropriately light and tinkling music. The role of the bird had personal significance for Annie. Three years on I worked with her again in a different group (see Chapter 10 on psychodrama) and she often used the action of 'flapping' and taking off as her movement warm-up to the sessions. The movement and its energy had stayed with her. It seemed to be a role that put her in touch with a sense of joy, freedom, laughter and light – in contrast to one of her dominant habitual life roles of rageful self injurer.

Phase Three: Fragmentation and Difficulty

The group seemed to be going well, but 'progress' was not smooth or continuous. We came to an uncomfortable and chaotic time. We had survived a number of difficulties, deaths and injuries. We were approaching the end of the period of weekly sessions. The group had agreed enthusiastically to the proposed one week intensive, but there was an awareness that the end was in sight. Not only would the group end, but Isabel would be going off to have her baby.

From the perspective of the therapists the group was feeling demanding and hard to handle. The sense of overwhelming need that had been apparent at the start of the process returned. Half the group seemed bursting to talk, others were withdrawn but upset. Journeys between sites in the minibus were a struggle. There were absences and illnesses. Therapists and clients alike were stuck in the mud, and the effort to extract ourselves from it felt almost too much.

It is not unusual to come across sticky times in ongoing group therapy. The members of the therapeutic team reflected on our feelings and roles. We felt exhausted, like mothers incapable of meeting the demands of our children. We decided on three strategies that might help and were at least worth trying.

(1) **Staying on the boundary of the group.** Leave the group alone together for a few minutes at the start of the session to settle/talk/arrive while we took a moment together to collect ourselves before the session, especially after the journey between sites. The thinking behind this was that the clients would have to take responsibility for their interaction themselves and begin to relate directly to each other rather than attempting to relate always to and through the therapeutic team. They would access their adult roles. At the same time the therapists would be taking care of their own needs in preparation for the group.

(2) **Giving appropriate warm-up to the session.** Use musical improvisation to discharge the emotional 'static' at the start of the session. This gives a structured form to channel and contain the feelings, and perhaps help the group to come together and focus.

(3) **Structuring a discussion** in which the group could talk about what they were bringing with them to the group and about what was going on in the group at this time.

Each of these strategies proved to have some value in the situation, enabling the group to continue a little further with the Cinderella work. One outcome of leaving the group together briefly at the start of the sessions was that the women began to take care of each other. Charlotte arrived upset one week, and when Isabel, Pat and I walked in she was being comforted competently by Harriet.

We decided to set some guidelines for the musical improvisation. Group members were invited to choose a partner to play with, and their instruments. We were in the well equipped music therapy room at this point so there was plenty of choice. They were asked to approach their improvisation with an awareness of the need to give space to the other and to listen. As each pair played it was clear when they were both aware of each other. Mostly there was one dominant player together with a partner who listened and responded sensitively. In this way the exercise was diagnostic of the current dyadic relationships in the group, whilst also serving the function of allowing the expression of the feelings of the moment.

The third strategy, based on verbal discussion was the most difficult for the group, involving a great deal of patience for some, and too much direct disclosure for others. Again the story provided some outlet for the expression of group feelings and the development of group themes.

There were two drama-based pieces of work during this phase. The first was a variation on the scene where Cinderella stands up to her sisters, but with each role being a multiple one, held by two or more group members. Not everyone was able to take part in this. Those who did managed to work through their feelings to some extent, ending the session in a very different emotional state from the one in which they had started it. Some felt unable to take on a role or to take part in the musical encounter, and they remained subdued throughout the session. The combination of role play and musical improvisation was indeed transformative – but the group was split into those who could use this form and those who could not.

The other dramatic exercise was based on the next stage of the story, and was accessible to all the women in the group. In the story the king announces a ball at which his son the prince is to choose his bride. The idea of a stately ball was used as a way of working on adult roles, dignity and a sense of womanhood. We talked about these qualities in the group and each woman chose a fan from a collection I brought to the session, and we set up the session as a preparation for the ball. No one was in a conspicuous role from the story. We were all in role as courtiers preparing for the big night. We worked together in a spirit of rehearsal or role training on the kind of posture and movements that would be compatible with fan dancing and a formal ball of this kind at a palace. Having rehearsed for a while I put on a tape of Pachelbel's *Canon*, a slow and dignified piece of music. The whole group danced to this music using their fans and changing partners gracefully in a spontaneous way. The simple and dignified role of courtier without particular individual traits was enough to inspire a different way of being and working in the group. There was a sense of containment and a possibility of moving on.

Phase Four: The One Week Intensive Workshop

The group met each morning for five days. Sessions were two hours long, which was longer than previously. We worked in the dramatherapy studio, where there were plenty of props to hand and more space than in the music therapy room at the other site. The therapists devoted up to a further two hours a day to reflection, processing and preparation.

Behind the scenes

Isabel and I spent time before the week considering our goals. We wanted to come to the end of the Cinderella story or to a point where the group found its own conclusion with it. We also wanted to continue with the idea of friendship and relationships within the here and now of the group, and to find a way of ending.

In addition to our plans for the whole group we considered what personal value each woman might gain from the week. At a general level we were open to seeing what themes emerged from the story and to considering how the emergent themes could be useful for the group. At a more specific level we had worked with the group for long enough to have some ideas about the particular characteristics and patterns of each woman. We clarified these thoughts before the intensive. This helped us in our co-therapy partnership during the week, giving us some broad shared guidelines through which we might address individual needs within the context of a group process.

Aims for individuals

Harriet: We saw her as assertive, articulate and enthusiastic in the group, but very dominant and often lacking awareness of others. The idea came up that she might take on a dramatic role which satisfied her desire to be important while at the same time requiring her to step back a little from centre stage and work at paying attention to others. The ideal role would be the fairy godmother. There is no such figure in the Grimm's version of the tale, but the group would be familiar with the pantomime versions of the story and it would not be difficult to include the character in our story. She could help all the courtiers prepare for the ball in our first session. We could give her the task of finding out size, length and colour of costume desired by each courtier for the ball and helping to prepare them. The role would require her to use her listening skills.

Jill: Her perception of herself seemed to be a shy little girl of about five. In fact she was in her sixties. She tended to smile and talk in a confiding whisper to gain intimacy. We recognised an element of flirtatiousness in this, but of a disconcertingly childlike kind. Perhaps the role of courtier could help her to develop a more adult version of the flirt role, and through this a sense of herself as a woman. We did not know if she was too set in her ways to find this new role. Her enjoyment of the preparatory work we had done with the fans gave us hope. We decided to give her every encouragement to find an adult woman/flirt role.

Annie: Annie had been using the group well. She was very responsive to both music and drama. Her habitual role was quite loud and aggressive. We were struck by how different she was when she chose the role of the bird for herself. It seemed to bring out a more joyful, gentle and nurturing side. On one occasion she had consoled Cinderella tenderly from this role. We decided to keep an awareness of this potential in her, but not to do anything particularly directive about it.

Charlotte: Charlotte had a speech impediment, which led to feelings of frustration when others could not understand her. She enjoyed being in the group, and had brought her feelings of sadness and upset on more than one occasion. Her main characteristic was a profound lack of confidence. We had a sense that we needed to be very gentle with her and to take every opportunity to build her confidence.

Mandy: Mandy had entered one of her periodic phases of depression. At such times her level of functioning was radically lower than when she was on form. She had not been able to take on any dramatic roles recently, nor contribute as actively in discussion and sharing as she would otherwise. We acknowledged our feelings of sadness at seeing her in this condition. It was particularly disappointing in the light of the work she had been able to start in the group on her core issues of loss and bereavement. Any aims we had for Mandy this week would have to take her current condition as the starting point. We felt she needed plenty of reassurance that she was okay – there were some elements of paranoia in her current state. We should also provide opportunities for her to channel and express her feelings, probably in company with the whole group rather than in the spotlight of solo work.

Sally: Like Charlotte, Sally's main problem was a lack of confidence. She was still having problems walking after her leg injury and so was experiencing more limitations than otherwise. She liked to make her own decisions about when to join in and when to sit out and did not respond well to direct encouragement or pressure to join in. When she did participate it was always on her own terms and she would enjoy it, but her mood could swing rapidly. What she had enjoyed most in the past was movement work, and this was now less accessible to her. We decided to have the general intention of confidence building for Sally, but realised that we would have to be oblique and subtle about any demands we made.

Lyn: Lyn was isolated in the group. She was the only person habitually in a wheelchair but this was not the only reason for her isolation. She was articulate and able to engage sensitively in musical improvisation and enactment. The problem was a difficulty or reluctance in reaching out to others. She had some typical characteristics of an only child. She seemed to resent others in the group, but disguised any raw feelings under a polite middle class mask and a desire to please those in authority. She had significantly chosen to play one of the duplicitous sisters in the story. Our main aim with Lyn was that she should make contact with others in the group, and if possible that she might begin to be more authentic in her interactions in the group. We were tentative about this – it may only be within the drama that she could express her less acceptable feelings. The mask of niceness could perhaps only be dropped from behind the mask of role.

Doreen: Doreen was enthusiastic in the group. She enjoyed being a centre stage performer and had a strong sense of the dramatic, through which she was already expressing her own feelings and issues around loss and jealousy. We considered how the work this week might give her opportunities for self-expression and leadership, a chance to stretch herself and meet her need for the dramatic in a way that everyday life did not. We would look out for roles that would challenge her. Initially, perhaps, she could host the ball.

The Sessions

Monday. We had planned to approach the scene of the palace ball through working with Harriet as fairy godmother. She was, however, absent from the session, and so we set up the scene without that role. The focus was on the grace of the occasion, and the issue of being chosen or not chosen by the prince to dance.

Two core themes emerged in this session: bereavement/loss and jealousy/competition. In the initial sharing that was part of the arrival and warm-up process for the group Doreen was very sad and tearful. She had just learnt that a nurse she was close to was leaving. This loss touched on her feelings about the recent death of her father. She reached a hand across to Isabel for comfort and perhaps in acknowledgement that Isabel too would be leaving, and that the group as a whole was coming to an end. It seemed an appropriate beginning to the week, relevant at a personal level to Doreen, and at a group level pertinent to all of us. The end was implicit in the beginning – we were dealing here with a life cycle.

The theme of jealousy and competition was expressed through the enactment phase of the session, which took some surprising turns. We prepared for this stage initially with a physical warm-up, that generated energy and concentration. Fans and cloths were chosen and the group danced together using the ideas and skills we had already worked on in a previous session. There was dramatic power in this, a real journey into another world and a sense of taking off, shared by the group.

Even Sally, who was sitting out, was to some degree in role. She chose to sit on a stately wooden throne-like chair and spontaneously took on a role that included elements of the prince and of the court gossip. Lyn had volunteered for the prince role and positioned herself enthroned in her wheelchair in the centre of the room whilst other group members paid court to her as prince, whom they tried to impress with their dancing. Annie entered into the spirit of the improvisation freely. She flirted with the prince and expressed her sense of competition by making bitchy and witty comments about the other courtiers.

Sally, watching from the outside, joined in the gossip. It was a scandal, she said, the prince should marry Isabel, but she was pregnant already, and by another man! Sally had brought the reality situation, an important part of the current group dynamic, into the Cinderella improvisation. Isabel's pregnancy was perceived at a primitive level as proof of her infidelity to the group. She was involved with someone else, an outsider, and it was shocking. The group incorporated Sally's contribution into the story and Isabel was somehow cast by group consent as a pregnant Cinderella, the chosen one, who danced with the prince. The Cinderella story provided a form through which the group could express their awareness of and feelings about Isabel's situation. There was also perhaps a sense that Isabel, as someone from the real world of marriage and children was the most appropriate recipient of the prince's attentions.

The enactment was followed by two musical improvisations in role. First, Lyn and Isabel played their feelings about being 'the happy couple'. Then the whole group was invited to put themselves collectively in the position of those who had not been chosen by the prince, and to express their feelings about this in music. This was the most cathartic and uninhibited piece of playing they had done. Jealousy and anger came in noisy waves. One explosive passage followed another as group members picked up on each other's energy and passion. There was no sense of being led by the therapeutic team. The piece went on for about a quarter of an hour, whether or not the therapists were playing. Group members were playing for themselves and really enjoying it. As people with learning disabilities they must have been drawing on many experiences of feeling unlucky, unsuccessful in competition, abandoned and not chosen.

As part of the de-roling process we asked people how they had felt during different parts of the work. We refrained from asking group members to make specific connections with their own life. The story had provided a necessary dramatic distance, enabling them to contact deep feelings. With this group at this time it may have felt too confrontational to remove the veil of the story and demand direct ownership of their feelings.

The session had been a particularly interesting one for Jill in terms of our aims for her to take on more adult roles. At the start of the session in the verbal sharing she followed her usual childlike pattern of whispering confidences to me. Mindful of our aims for her this week I refused to be drawn by her role demand. I reminded her that this was a time to share with the whole group, and asked her to tell all of us her news. My not colluding with her habitual communication style pushed her into something new.

Later, as we approached the ballroom improvisation, she showed interest in the tape recorder I was about to use. I invited her to turn it on for the group. She was shy and unsure at first, saying that she did not know how to do it, but she took the risk and managed it. She was proud of her achievement and gained the confidence to throw herself into the role of stately flirtatious courtier with commitment.

The most interesting moment happened on the boundaries of the group. She left the studio to go to the toilet, which meant walking through a large hall where a couple of young workmen were working. On her way back she stopped to chat to them. She told them what we were doing in the group without whispering, losing her presence or falling into the little girl role. This was a new role in action! When she came back she told us with pride and excitement that she had been talking with the men.

Tuesday. Our next planned stopping point in the story was to be the moment of midnight, when the prince seems to lose his new found love and when Cinderella makes her sudden exit from the ball. Our intention was to recreate the ball scene and to carry it on beyond the moment when she leaves. We could explore the aftermath of her leaving through musical improvisation and dialogue. How does the prince feel? What can his courtiers say to him? Perhaps we could create some music to heal his sense of loss. Or we could focus on the feelings of Cinderella. What is it like to be the one who leaves?

On arrival, the group was already in touch with issues of loss. In the verbal sharing Doreen was distressed about the nurse who was leaving, and Charlotte shared that she too was upset about a different member of staff who was about to leave. Sally, who was also close to the nurse Doreen was talking about, began to cry. It was clearly a group concern.

I made a spontaneous decision to offer them the opportunity to use the psychodramatic technique of the empty chair to work on this issue. I placed an empty bean bag chair in the circle and explained that if they wished to they could imagine the nurse or staff member was sitting there. They could say whatever they were feeling or would like to say to that person. The technique is different from any of the ways we had previously worked in the group. It lacks the dramatic distance that the story work utilises. I was inviting them to explore their feelings without disguise and I had an open mind as to whether the structure would be tolerable.

Doreen went first. She addressed the empty chair and said how much she liked the nurse, that she did not want her to go, and that she would miss her. It would not be the same without her after all the years they had known each other. I invited her to role reverse with the nurse, to sit on the empty chair and be her for a short while. I invited her from the role of the nurse to say something back to Doreen. It was not easy for her to stay in role as the other, but with support and reminders she said from the nurse's role that she would miss Doreen too, but that it was time for her to move on. I asked her if she would forget Doreen and from role she answered 'No.' I asked Doreen to reverse back into her own role and gave her the opportunity to say more if she wanted to. She did not. It was enough.

The group had not only been listening attentively but also making suggestions as to what Doreen should say. To my surprise, Charlotte, who was characteristically reticent in the group, wanted to try the empty chair work herself and address the member of staff she was going to miss. She sat silently looking at the chair for some time and had difficulty finding the words. I used the technique of the empathic double, sitting with her and saying the things she might be wanting to say. I asked her to repeat anything that was right, and not to say anything that was not true to her feelings. As a matter of principle I try to be cautious and to avoid putting words into the mouth of people with limited expressive ability. On this occasion I was reassured that Charlotte discriminated between what she repeated and what she ignored. When something I doubled hit the mark she was able to add to it spontaneously in her own words. The group also helped by making suggestions. They could all identify with her feelings. Between us we facilitated Charlotte in expressing herself and being heard in the group. I did not attempt to use any role reversal. It was enough for her to say what needed to be said from her own role and in the presence of the group.

The psychodramatic work facilitated a discussion about other losses, the end of the group and particularly Isabel's going on maternity leave. Perhaps it was easier to approach this loss via other losses outside the group.

We moved on to the enactment and musical improvisations as planned. There were some interesting choices of role. Doreen and Lyn returned to the roles of the stepsisters, and Harriet took on the role of the prince. Most striking was Jill's choice of role as Cinderella. Mandy had no interest in Cinderella the courtier. Her interest had been more in Cinderella the bereaved daughter and Cinderella reclaiming her power. As for Jill, we had seen her growing in confidence and stature the day before. She had finally made her way to the starring role! Something in her self-image had shifted. She had come a long way since the days when she could only take on a role if she could share the responsibility with me.

Although Jill was officially in role as Cinderella, Harriet as prince chose to dance with Isabel. Harriet had not been with us the previous session but intuitively picked up the group identification of Isabel with the role of Cinderella. She was the one who would be leaving, not at the stroke of midnight but at a precise moment determined by her special condition, her pregnancy. She was also the chosen one, married, fertile, magically endowed with the promise of future life. Group members frequently asked when the baby would arrive, whether it would be a boy or girl, and whether they could hold it. Perhaps by dancing with Isabel there was a sense of sharing in the mystery.

The feelings of loss in the group found expression through identification with the prince. This was where there was most energy. Once Cinderella disappeared the whole group came together in the collective role of the prince who has lost something precious. They played with passion in a piece that began painfully with Harriet thrashing the cymbals. The feelings of pain, loss and anger that were being expressed through the pretext of the role and the story had many sources in the lives of the group members.

Wednesday. We had plans for Wednesday based on the next part of the Cinderella story. The idea was to explore the theme of searching for what has been lost, using the structure of looking for a particular pair of hands or eyes in the group. We would then enact the trial by shoe. In the Grimm's story the sisters mutilate their feet to make them fit the shoe. We would focus on the theme of social conformity – fitting in or not fitting in. We had a pair of silver shoes that the prince could invite everyone to try on. Who would they fit?

The session did not go well. Both themes were painful ones and the group did not have much commitment to go into them. The structures were not in tune with the current concerns of the group. During the 'searching scene' there was a lack of energy, no focus, little eye contact. Sally sat out for most of the session. There was little excitement in the shoe scene and the musical improvisation, although loud, seemed to lack any real feeling.

The real group energy was in talking about the end of the story and the end of the group. The story must end with a wedding and the couple would have to live happily ever after. We asked what 'happy ever after' meant for the group. Marriage, babies, dancing. As for the end of the group, the request was that we should have a party on Friday.

Isabel and I had some interesting discussions that afternoon. Should we go with the wishes of the group or take responsibility for setting an agenda from our own perspective as therapists? Isabel's concern was that the group had unrealistic ideas about the nature of marriage, relationships and motherhood. Surely we should challenge the fantasy notion of 'happy ever after' in favour of a reality principle. The clients were idealising other peoples' lives in the belief that others had perfect and unproblematic lives whilst their own were failures. Surely we had a responsibility to help them find a more balanced and mature perspective.

On the other hand, we had clearly missed the target that morning. I put the argument that the women had a great deal of energy and commitment for enacting their group fantasy of a happy ending. They may not be able to try out marriage in a real life situation, but maybe a group enactment of the collective wish could in itself be healing. There seemed to be a group 'act hunger' for this, and on the whole I felt we should go with the group and with the fantasy. Isabel agreed that it was worth a try and we made some preparations accordingly.

Thursday – The Wedding. Sally rang the group to let us know that she was ill and would not be coming. Often on the periphery of the group, it was a pity that she missed this session, which was a particularly meaningful one for the group and a culmination of the work.

Jill seemed to be growing from strength to strength. She told us she had asserted herself on her ward, insisting that she had to wear a dress today. Harriet in turn had made sure she was dressed in trousers, having already decided that she was going to play the bridegroom. She brought the doll with her, as she had done for the nativity play six months before. There was a sense of coming full circle, and that the image of the baby was a necessary part of this cycle.

We began with our familiar ritual warm-ups. During the physical warm-up each person took it in turns to lead the group in a particular movement. Everyone was able to contribute on this occasion and take centre stage for a moment. At the end Jill was able to perform each person's movement in sequence from memory. She would never have been able to put herself under this kind of pressure in the earlier stages of the group process.

Preparation for the enactment: as in real life weddings, there were preparations to be made for our enactment. First, roles were chosen: Jill was to be Cinderella the bride, Harriet the prince bridegroom. Lyn moved from being the sister to taking on the role of Cinderella's father, the one who would give her away. In this enactment it seemed there was no place for the sisters and their jealousy. Everyone wanted to be in a role where they could truly celebrate without bitterness. Doreen chose to be the vicar and conduct the marriage ceremony. Charlotte and Annie chose to be bridesmaids, whilst Mandy was happy to be a courtier/guest along with the therapists.

We knew which roles we would be playing. The next stage of preparation was to define the space. We placed play shapes around the studio to indicate the dimensions and boundaries of the large room/church within the palace where the marriage would take place. Everyone took part in decorating this space with fresh flowers and greenery, each person choosing where to place their contribution to best effect. We were making the place special in honour of the special occasion.

The final preparation was the dressing up. We left the set and each person chose her own costume, selecting various coloured cloths to drape and tie, a hat and a buttonhole to pin onto the costume. The bride wore a long white veil and a head-dress of yellow flowers reminiscent of the 1920s. The groom wore a crown and a cape.

The careful preparations added to the group's sense of anticipation. We were ready.

The enactment: one by one the characters entered the space. The guests arrived first, followed by the vicar, and then the prince. A tape of the wedding march began to play and Cinderella came in with her father and the bridesmaids. As the music stopped, there was a moment of silence and then Doreen as priest began the ceremony with great authority. With very little prompting from Harriet as the bridegroom and myself she conducted the proceedings more or less in the conventional manner. The bride and groom took their vows, signed the register and had their photographs taken. As the happy couple left the space we cheered and threw confetti over them. The quality of attention in the group was extraordinary. There was a vibrant mixture of solemnity and joy as the group's act hunger for a fantasy fairy tale wedding was met. It felt as important, and as intense as a real wedding.

The ceremony over, we left the special space for a moment and then returned to it for a celebratory dance. This was a circle dance using Pachelbel's *Canon* that we had worked with previously. The bride and groom danced together as a couple within the circle of the group. The rest of us danced around them and whenever we caught their eye we bowed or curtseyed, and they acknowledged us graciously. It was a poignant moment. The marriage was happening within and on behalf of the group, symbolised by the fantasy wedding couple within the circle of the group. We were all involved, sharing in the mystery.

There are a number of reasons this enactment was so powerful. The culmination of the fairy tale story we had been working on contrasted powerfully with the reality of the clients' lives, but coincided with their unfulfilled dreams of happiness. There was little chance that the dream of marriage would become a reality for these women. It was possible, however, to embody the group fantasy concretely and collectively. At a symbolic level the marriage represented wholeness, health and normality; the ability to share in the rituals and *rites de passage* of the wider community. The poignancy arose out of the underlying sense of loss.

After the enactment: after such a vivid experience of ritual drama it was important to allow some time to digest the experience and to de-role. The process of distancing from a role can be instantaneous. On this occasion the process needed to be gradual. We removed our pieces of costume as a symbolic first act of de-roling and sat in a circle. We asked the group to reflect on the idea of 'happy ever after' and what that might mean, deliberately leaving it open for group members to stay within the story or talk about their own lives. Harriet's response was immediate and within the context of the story. First there should be a honeymoon and then there had to be a baby. She brought the doll into the circle for us to pass around and sing to.

There was an interesting interchange at this point. Annie reminded Harriet brusquely, 'The doll is not a real baby.' Harriet replied 'It's a real doll though'. Annie may have resented Harriet's insistence on remaining at the centre of the story as one of a happy and fruitful fairy tale couple even after we had left the enactment. She certainly had a need to re-establish some clear boundaries between what is real and what is make-believe. She needed to break through the poignant atmosphere around the make-believe baby in our midst and perhaps, by implication, the reality of Isabel's pregnancy. She wanted Harriet and the group to come back down to earth. Harriet's response was, I feel, also a statement about the whole enactment. The doll may only be a doll, a story is only a story, and a piece of drama is only a piece of drama, but each holds a reality that is not to be dismissed lightly. Something real and meaningful had happened in the group that session.

We discussed the end of the story, and I asked the group if they thought the fate of the stepsisters smitten with blindness was just or too cruel. We had a vote, and the majority decision was that it served them right. We gradually found our way out of the story and were able to focus as a group on how we would say goodbye the next day. The fantasy of 'happy endings' led to requests for a celebration, a chance to dress up for a party. There should be music and most importantly food, an endless supply of chocolate mousse...

Friday. The plan for this last session was in five stages:

(1) to begin with our familiar rituals, coffee, circle song, sharing

(2) to acknowledge this is the final session, and to focus on feelings around saying goodbye to each other

(3) to continue the de-roling or distancing process from the story work by recollecting the different roles each person had played and if possible reflecting on how these roles were similar or different from the life roles of the player

(4) to celebrate in the way the group had requested, with food, drink and music

(5) to finish with a musical structure chosen by the group.

The emotional tone of the session was needy, sad and anxious. The
in marked contrast to the fantasy celebration of the day before.
dealing now with a more mundane level of experience. The therap.
brought in various snacks and drinks, and it was our intention that the
members would take responsibility for acting as host for each other, offe
refreshment in a spirit of friendship: all very adult. The reality was different.
The clients' idea behind the party was actually that the therapists should take
on the nurturing roles, provide an enormous feast for the hungry group
members. There was clearly a symbolic aspect to this; a statement of need
on the part of the clients and a partial regression to a mother–baby dynamic
at a time of anxiety and distress. The clients wanted more food, literally in
terms of what was on the table, and symbolically in terms of the many levels
of nourishment provided by the therapy group over time.

Endings are often difficult. The dramatherapy experience offers access to
a rich shared world and it is difficult for the client to re-create this experience
outside of the context of the group. The hope is that elements of the
experience may be internalised and brought in a transformative way into
other life situations. In the case of the Cinderella group, we had worked
together for eight months, and the timing of the ending was perhaps
premature, dictated largely by the timing of Isabel's maternity leave. Given
the recurrent theme of the life cycle in this group it may be that we would
have benefited from a further month of weekly sessions to work towards the
ending. This would have made a nine month process in all to come full term.

Retrospective View of the Use of the Fairy Tale

As mentioned above, the story of Cinderella could provide a framework for
a variety of different therapeutic journeys. Our own journey with this story
grew partly out of the group's intuitive response to it, and partly out of
choices made consciously by the therapists. In effect, we analysed the
thematic therapeutic potential for each part of the story and chose to exploit
some potentials at the expense of others that we considered less relevant at
that moment. There follows a table of analysis of Cinderella. A summary of
each phase of the story is followed by an analysis of the possible themes,
and a note of the themes chosen as a focus. The method could be applied to
other fairy tales.

Table of Analysis of Cinderella

Summary	Possible themes	Themes actually chosen
Man's wife falls ill. She says goodbye to her daughter, gives her advice and dies.	illness, death, loss, marital relationship, parent child relationship	illness, death, goodbyes, mother daughter relationship
The girl weeps at the grave all winter.	keeping memories alive, grief, the passage of time, graves	graves, grief, seasons
The father remarries.	remarriage, change, family loyalty, stepfamilies, jealousy, celebration, fears	remarriage, change
The stepmother has two daughters who look good but are wicked.	good and bad mothers, jealousy, outer form and inner essence	jealousy, duplicity
They treat the girl badly, dress her in rags and overwork her	abuse, bullying, clothes, self-image, image in the eyes of others, victimisation, odd one out	assertiveness in adverse circumstances
They call her Cinderella.	names, name calling, labels	none
Father goes to the fair. He asks all three what they would like. The stepsisters ask for dresses and jewellery, Cinderella for the first branch that knocks his hat.	going shopping, journeys, choices, presents, greed, vanity, instinctual/magic knowledge, father daughter relationship	journey, choices
He gives each of them what they have asked for.	giving and receiving gifts	gifts
Cinderella plants the branch on the mother's grave and weeps over it. It grows and becomes a tree, host to a white bird that grants wishes	grief, sadness, growth, transformation, magic, wish fulfilment	grief and magic transformation

Summary	Possible themes	Themes actually chosen
The king throws a party to find a bride for the prince.	Father son relationship, celebration, courtship, finding a partner, celebration, dancing, choosing and being chosen	celebration, adult courtly behaviour, wanting to be chosen, finding a partner
Cinderella has to help her sisters and is not allowed to go the ball in her own right.	disappointment, inclusion, exclusion, missing out, not getting what you want	none
Stepmother sets an impossible task, sorting out good and bad beans in a tub. Cinderella completes it with the help of the bird.	facing difficulty, asking for/accepting help, differentiating good from bad, secret strengths	none
The prince looks for the one whose foot will fit the slipper.	looking for someone, recognition, disappointment and continuing to try.	looking for someone, loss, being chosen, feelings of disappointment
The older sister tries it on and when it does not fit her mother tells er to cut off her toe, which she does.	mutilation, pain, injury, bad advice, right and wrong, ambition, desire to fit in	none
The prince is taken in by the deception and rides off with her, but the dove in the magic tree tell him she is not the right one. He is deceived again by the second stepsister, and the bird corrects him again.	mistakes, learning, deception, forces of good, justice, happy endings	none
He returns, Cinderella tries on the shoe. He recognises her and takes her away to be married, with the blessing of the birds.	recognition, happy endings	happy endings, fantasies

Summary	Possible themes	Themes actually chosen
There is a big wedding.	marriage, celebration, sex, babies	marriage, parties, babies, happy endings, future fantasy
The sisters are smitten with blindness for their wickedness.	justice, punishment, revenge	punishment, revenge

CHAPTER 9

Psychodrama and Learning Disabilities

Psychodrama is not synonymous with dramatherapy. As I have explored elsewhere (Chesner 1994b) there are obvious similarities between the two disciplines. They are both based in dramatic and theatrical processes, but whilst dramatherapy draws freely on the full range of dramatic methods, classical psychodrama follows a more clearly defined pattern. As I have shown elsewhere (Chapter 7 and Chapter 8) dramatherapy uses largely fictional, metaphorical, story-based material through which individual and group issues can be explored indirectly. In classical psychodrama, by contrast, the main therapeutic focus tends to be on one group member per session. This person is chosen as protagonist and it is his or her perception and issue that is enacted and worked through in the psychodrama. The group as a whole acts in support of the protagonist both as witness/audience to their drama and as auxiliary egos playing the roles of the protagonist's significant others. These roles are usually assigned by the protagonist according to his or her perception of each group member's affinity with or capacity to play a certain role. This is different from dramatherapy, where roles are often self-assigned, and where the perception that is explored in the session is that of the group as a whole.

Psychodrama is a rich, powerful and creative method for focusing on and working through therapeutic material. Under the direction of a trained psychodrama psychotherapist it helps in challenging dysfunctional belief systems and habitual patterns of behaviour and thought. By working on and with the subjective world of the client, psychodrama often involves accessing and expressing deeply felt emotions. How relevant is it as a method for working with people with learning disabilities?

Many people with severe and profound learning disabilities would not be able to cope with the cognitive and expressive demands of the method. Clients need to have some basic level of personal insight, preferably some verbal or expressive facility, and the ability to concentrate on their own and other peoples' processes in order for psychodrama to be an appropriate therapeutic form. Group members need to be able to take on roles for each other, at another person's request, and to cope with the fundamental technique of role reversal. At the simplest level the protagonist, P, enroles group member, G, as a significant person in P's life (eg. P's parent) or a significant aspect of P's self-perception (eg. P's anger). G portrays this role according to the cues given by P and according to G's intuitive sense of the role. Role reversal involves P taking G's place as the other and speaking/moving/communicating in that role, whilst G holds P's role. The roles are then swapped and G repeats the gist of P's portrayal of the role of the other. This gives P the opportunity to respond and interact with the role of the other according to P's own perception of that role.

The technique is more easily demonstrated in action than described in words, and the role reversal is facilitated by the spatial move between roles. Even so this is not a simple process and both P and G need sufficient self-definition to know the difference between the two roles and sufficient self-confidence to hold the role of another person. They need, with the help of the director or psychodramatist, to be able to keep track of who is who at what moment. Those members of the group who are not required as actors, or auxiliaries, at any time watch the process that is unfolding on stage as audience, ready to take on a role within the drama if required. This assumes the ability to watch with interest, to follow the action and to empathise, whilst containing their own need to participate spontaneously on their own terms.

In terms of the spectrum of dramatherapy approaches and the metaphor of the tree (see Chapter 1), I place psychodrama amongst the branches and leaves, in the arena of thought, insight, and transformation. The risk factor is relatively high as there is an invitation to overt personal disclosure. A grounding of trust (root level) is a prerequisite, as is the ability to deal with the rules, discipline and form of the method (trunk level). The ability to reach out and connect internally with the imagination and externally with other group members (branch level) is part of the challenge, and ultimately there is the possibility of shedding light on personal real-life issues (leaf level) and working towards change at the interface with the external world.

Setting up a Psychodrama Group

I had occasionally used some psychodramatic techniques within ongoing dramatherapy groups (see Chapter 8 on fairy tales). On completion of the practical part of my psychodrama training I set up a new weekly therapy group to work specifically through psychodrama. From the outset I intended to explore the relevance of the method to this client group, and to consider how the method might usefully be adapted to take into account their special needs. I invited Isabel Oman, my music therapist colleague, to join me on this project, our first experience of working together since the Cinderella group. My thinking was that the verbal communication difficulties of this client group called out for the use of other expressive modalities to give form to the emotional material that would arise.

The selection process for the group was rigorous. Therapists, nursing staff and consultant psychiatrists were invited to make referrals of clients who had some verbal skills, the potential for insight into their own and others' behaviour, and who might benefit from an ongoing action based psychotherapy group. The initial commitment would be for ten months, with the possibility of continuation beyond that date. I stated explicitly that attendance would need to be regular and that carers would need to be aware that the work could have an impact on the emotional state of clients between sessions.

I met with each referred client, and places were offered on the basis of these meetings. I gave a step by step description of what I was offering. This began with an exploration of the word 'drama', then the idea of a weekly group commitment in which drama would be used to explore the hopes and fears and memories and dreams of group members. We discussed how they might explore their own history and feelings, and considered what the issues might be. I also inquired about how they would feel about helping someone else explore their hopes and fears and memories and dreams. I introduced the idea of taking on roles, and demonstrated role reversal using anything from salt and pepper cellars to empty chairs. We talked about music and about how music might be used as well as drama to express feelings in the group.

Invitations to join the group were sent to those clients who seemed able to understand the basic concepts described and for whom the description of the work evoked enthusiasm. The selection process differed from my usual style in that clients were asked from the outset to conceptualise and to reflect on potentially difficult areas of their life. The method would be conceptually and emotionally more demanding than some of the dramatherapy approaches I use, so it was appropriate to make the assessment interviews similarly demanding.

The final composition of the group was five men and three women, living in three different long stay residential institutions. They embodied a variety of diagnoses and life issues.

The clients

Annie: in her mid thirties, Annie was adopted as a baby, comes from a close-knit family and has a younger brother. Her learning disabilities became apparent at school. She became aggressive at home as an adolescent and was admitted into residential care when her family could no longer cope. Her parents keep contact. She lives in a single sex environment. She has long standing behavioural problems involving self-inflicted bleeding on her hands and within her vagina.

Hal: in his early forties, Hal came into care later in his life, at about thirty. His family of origin were ashamed of him and he was neglected as a child. When his father remarried there were difficulties with his stepmother, who led him to believe that he was the product of a curse. There was violence at home and he ended up sleeping rough before being taken into care. His parents subsequently died. His only family is a stepbrother, with whom there is infrequent contact. Hal has verbal skills but is very withdrawn and shy. He has spent a lot of money over the years on pornography.

Trudy: in her forties, Trudy came into care as an adolescent. She is the oldest of three children from a middle class family. She has a diagnosis of schizophrenia as well as learning disabilities caused by brain damage at birth. Her mother also has a history of mental illness. Trudy presents as shy and smiling, at times withdrawn, at other times expansive. She still has contact with her family and has an intensely jealous relationship with her sister.

Nick: in his forties, Nick is the oldest of five siblings in an Anglo-European family. His father died a year before he joined the psychodrama group. He continues to be close to his family, particularly his mother, who is described as protective. Nick's learning disabilities are very mild but he has a diagnosis of personality disorder, presents as lacking in emotion and wanting to please. He has a long history of offending, particularly through arson, often preceded by drinking and gambling. He has been in and out of a variety of institutions.

Sam: in his thirties, Sam came into hospital care as a teenager, when his parents divorced. He has a genetic syndrome which has left him with very poor eyesight, but he does not wear glasses, as he breaks them. He is classified as having severe challenging behaviours and has a reputation for being very destructive towards his own room, other residents and sometimes staff. He maintains contact with his father, but not his mother. He presented to me as verbally and emotionally articulate, communicative and creative.

Derek: in his forties, Derek came into hospital care in his twenties. He has a diagnosis of schizophrenia and epilepsy as well as learning disabilities related to a genetic syndrome. He has severe speech problems and presents as unkempt. He has a history of violence towards his own possessions and towards other residents. He maintains contact with his parents. His mother is physically disabled. He was in a relationship with a female resident who was not part of the psychodrama group.

Tom: in his twenties, Tom comes from a middle class background and presents in a rather caricatured way as someone three times his age. He has difficulty with anger, and was admitted to residential care as a result of aggressive outbursts at home. He has a history of depression with suicide attempts.

The backgrounds and diagnoses are varied but there are a number of issues that are common. Each group member had difficulty in appropriate expression of feeling and a tendency towards destructive and self-destructive outbursts. There were issues of loss, attachment and rejection in relation to the family and the ongoing question of how to deal with living in a special institutional setting.

Adaptations to the Method

We incorporated some extra devices into the method in view of the particular needs of the client group.

The mandala

I had described the psychodrama group when I met clients for assessment as 'a place to explore your hopes, fears, memories and dreams'. In order to keep this thought in mind and remind us of the focus for being together, Isabel and I created a three dimensional mandala, that could be placed in the centre of the group. This would form part of our opening ritual and warm-up to the work. A cardboard disc was drawn up, divided into four sections representing the four categories of focus. This was stuck onto a painted tyre on wheels that could be easily spun at the centre of the group so that the word 'hopes', 'fears', 'memories' or 'dreams' could be turned to face in any direction.

The mandala created a concrete, visible focus for centring ourselves. It is easier to look at an object like this than to focus on the spoken word. Even for those who could not read the written words, the mandala came to represent the words that were written on it. At times when the group was in danger of losing its focus we could re-introduce the mandala and reflect on it together in the group. During our first long break group members wrote their names on it as a symbolic gesture of being 'held' by the group over the break.

The closure song

In classical psychodrama, sessions end with the process of sharing. Group members are invited to share verbally how they identify or connect with the protagonist's psychodrama. The focus and heat moves from the protagonist to the group as a whole. In working psychodramatically with people with learning disabilities it seemed appropriate to include a further phase in the session for distancing from the psychodramatic action, reconnecting with the group as a whole, and preparing to move out from the special therapeutic space into the larger hospital environment. The method we chose to ritualise this process was a group song, accompanied by guitar. Everyone was invited to sit together in a circle for the song and to sing. Each group member was named individually within the song. This helped us to re-connect as a group after individual work in order to say goodbye from a position of togetherness.

The words of the song link up with the words of the mandala, so that there is a sense of cycle and completion between the beginning and end of the session:

> Together we are here
> A place where we can share
> Our hopes and fears
> And memories and dreams.
> And now the session's over
> And it's time to say goodbye
> Until we meet again next Monday morning.
> Goodbye X, Goodbye Y etc...
> Goodbye everyone, goodbye.

The use of music

Music was used as a container for material that may be highly charged emotionally and for which verbal expression might be difficult to access. It was used as a further string to the expressive bow of the group, a way of warming up to feelings and a way of giving them form.

Some people become especially articulate when emotionally fired up. By contrast, many people with learning disabilities lose some of their verbal facility when overwhelmed with feeling. Each client in the psychodrama group had problems with appropriate expression of feeling in their lives, resorting to self-injury, destruction of objects and physical attack on others. It was important as a matter of containment that there should be adequate ways to express powerful and difficult feelings within the context of psychodramatic work. A protagonist warmed up to his or her pain is in a vulnerable position and dependent on the therapist to give appropriate guidance. Isabel and I agreed to create a culture within the group whereby these feelings could be channelled into percussion work as well as physical and verbal expression when possible.

In order to create this culture of expression through music we included a regular invitation to group members to express their feelings through a solo musical improvisation as part of the warm-up. Clients chose from a selection of snare drum, bongos, cymbal, xylophone, metallophone, and chime bars. We increased the number of instruments to choose from gradually over time, so that the group could get used to the different possibilities and techniques gradually. The music based warm-up allowed clients to access and share their feelings with the group, then to reflect on how they had played and what feelings they brought with them. Those who chose not to play were given the possibility of expressing their feelings through movement.

Within the context of a psychodrama scene musical instruments could then be introduced and a protagonist or auxiliary ego could express the emotional subtext of the scene through this medium.

Care with roles

Psychodrama allows participants to develop and expand their role repertoire. It can be as enlightening and as therapeutic to play a variety of auxiliary roles for other group members as it is to work from the position of protagonist on personal material. In a resilient group with good ego-strength the process can unfold spontaneously. In a more vulnerable group such as this I took on the added responsibility of monitoring the auxiliary roles. I wanted to make sure that no one took on inappropriate roles from which they might have inadequate ability to separate, and which might lead at worst to a form of self-abuse.

In practice, the group was able to take responsibility for themselves and each other to a greater extent than I had anticipated. Whenever someone was chosen for an auxiliary role I simply investigated whether they were comfortable with playing that role for the protagonist. Reluctance and refusal were respected as valid choices on the basis that the auxiliary is able to sense the nature of the role and whether he or she is drawn to exploring it at that moment. On some occasions Isabel was invited by the protagonist to hold a role which other client group members might have found disturbing. As director I was unable to take on auxiliary roles.

Once a scene is under way the protagonist might need to express hostility and aggression towards a negatively perceived significant other. With a robust group the auxiliary would usually deal with such an attack from within the role. If I sensed that there was a need for this kind of expression on the part of the protagonist I followed a strategy of reminding the auxiliary that they were playing a role (ie. underlining the distance between them and the role played). If appropriate, they could vacate the position, leaving the protagonist to address an empty chair or cushion to represent the auxiliary role. This strategy slows the action and takes some of the spontaneity and heat out of it in the interests of safety and containment. In some groups this could act as an inhibiting factor, but in this group protagonists seemed to need and appreciate the slower pace.

Approaches to sharing

The sharing phase of a psychodrama session is important both for the protagonist and for the group as a whole. The protagonist needs to know that he or she is not alone, that others can understand and connect with the material and feelings that have been exposed on the group stage. For the other participants, those who have played an auxiliary role and those who have watched as audience this is the time in the session when they can focus on themselves and how the work relates to their personal experiences. The process is one of reflection, integration and connexion.

Cognitively this process is quite demanding, depending heavily on thought and verbal response. People with learning disabilities often have difficulty with generalising, and so with relating what is seen out there in someone else's work with personal experience. Clients may relate it appropriately at an intuitive or emotional level, but still might have difficulty in expressing what they sense both to themselves and to the group. So with this client group the therapist needs to take a more active role during this stage of the session. Questions can be asked to help keep the focus on the psychodrama work and on the process of sharing. It has been useful to ask specific questions about feeling responses to different moments in the work. eg.

- 'How do you think the protagonist felt when…?'
- 'Are there situations where you have felt sad/angry/confused?'
- 'How do you react when you feel rejected/hurt/disappointed?'
- 'What moment in this drama did you find most interesting/enjoyable/difficult? Why might that be?'

Length of individual psychodramas

A classical psychodrama can last for two or more hours, during which time the action may move between several remembered or imaginary locations. Interactions may be explored with different groups of significant others in the protagonist's inner and outer world, past, present and future. The process is a complex journey from the present to the past and back again with a view to integrating change into the future.

The concentration and emotional robustness required for such a journey would often be too much for this client group. Shorter pieces of work, such as a one scene vignette or a small series of two or three short scenes offer a more appropriate structure. The psychodrama method is sufficiently flexible to accommodate to the needs of the individual and the group in this way. Even a short psychodramatic exploration has a big impact on the protagonist whose world it explores. The culture of personal disclosure and emotional acceptance that is part of the psychodrama ethos is an important aspect of the therapy and one that is not dependant on the length of an individual piece of work.

Type of participation

When a protagonist is chosen and begins a personal piece of work, attention must be paid to the participation of other group members. Clients with learning disabilities may find it difficult to watch another group member work as 'the chosen one', to keep involved with the drama and to be ready to take on an auxiliary role if required. In terms of the transference, group members may feel overlooked and neglected by the therapist/mother whose attention is primarily with the protagonist. This kind of dynamic can arise with other client groups but is perhaps more acute with a group of people with learning disabilities. There is often a lack of skill in competing overtly for attention. In a psychodrama group this would mean putting oneself forward to be chosen as protagonist in competition with other needy group members, and risking the disappointment of not being chosen to work. It may be an easier choice to cut off from the feelings of need and jealousy and to withdraw attention from the psychodrama.

There are two strategies which have helped in this situation. The first is that the psychodrama director remembers to keep the psychodrama theatrically interesting and to include as many auxiliary roles on set as possible. Auxiliaries can be enroled in all sorts of creative and expressionistic ways so that they are part of the scene. Even in a scene where the protagonist is alone or with one significant other the other group members can be invited to help flesh out the setting, taking on the role of a mood or an object in the space. The director can invite these auxiliaries to contribute from the role from time to time and in this way support the sense of connexion with the protagonist and group as a whole.

The second strategy is to avoid focus on one individual as protagonist. The group as a whole can explore a particular shared issue from individual perspectives. This approach is closer to sociodrama than classical psychodrama and has the definite advantage of encouraging full participation in the group. This kind of focus is similar to conventional dramatherapy where there is often a whole group exploration. The issue being explored may be more overtly stated in sociodrama than in dramatherapy, where the theme of the work is often embedded in fiction or metaphor.

Moments of Practice

Each person's journey in the group was composed of fragments of personal work, like small shafts of light gradually illuminating a personal picture. Insight and change came not necessarily through protagonist work, but through the ongoing group process, including warm-up work, musical improvisation, personal psychodramas, and sharing. The individual processes within the group highlighted both benefits and difficulties with the psychodrama method. I shall look at some key moments of interest in the journeys of different group members.

Derek

The first introduction to role play was an invitation individually and one at a time to take on the role of 'someone you know, who knows you and likes you.' Each person was invited to view themselves from the positive perception of a friend or loved one, then to choose someone in the group to play that person, to role reverse and hear that positive perception from their own role. They then had the chance to say something to their chosen other and, if appropriate, to carry on role reversing until the short interchange was complete. The way each person engaged with this exercise was personal and revealing.

Derek chose to bring his girlfriend, and was able to see himself positively from her role and to describe himself as 'Handsome, good looking, charming.' This was perhaps unrealistic considering how unkempt he looked in terms of hair style, shaving, and clothing and how disjointed he was in his speech and movements. There may have been an element of wishful thinking and an over-idealistic view of himself, or maybe this was indeed an accurate representation of Mary's favourable perception of him. Once he moved into his own role he asked urgently 'Will you marry me?' and the response he gave to this question from her role was 'Yes.' Whatever the real relationship may have been like, he had expressed in the context of the group the importance of being in the relationship and of his desire to marry in the future. In the here and now of the group he had chosen Annie to play the role of Mary.

On his fortieth birthday I suggested Derek might explore a dream of the future as he looked forward into a new era of his life. The group supported him in this and set up a wedding scene in which he imagined himself marrying Mary by the time he was forty-five. Again he asked Annie to play the role of Mary. At first she refused and Isabel played the role, but as the drama progressed she changed her mind and ended up taking the role herself and dancing with Derek.

The following week Derek arrived at the session stating that it was all over with Mary and that Annie was his new girlfriend. I asked him how he felt about his relationship with Mary being over. He replied, smiling, that he was 'devastated', but without any emotion in his voice. It seemed that the transference relationship with Annie, which had informed his choice of her as auxiliary ego in his dramas, was stronger and more attractive to him than the real life ups and downs of his relationship with Mary. He had not taken account of Annie's wishes, who was initially ambivalent about her relationship with Derek, torn between getting involved with him romantically outside the group or continuing with her own ongoing relationship with another man. It was some weeks before the relationship settled enough for both group members to focus on their own work in the therapy group without a self-conscious investment in the other person. Derek informed us that he had re-established contact with Mary and when he asked Annie if he should come and visit her she was able to reply nonchalantly 'That's up to you Derek.'

The power of the psychodramatic work and its impact on Derek and Annie had an effect on other group members. The fact that these two seemed to have a social or romantic agenda in the group while the given reason for the group was therapeutic caused some unease and confusion and could have undermined the group culture. The mandala was useful at this point as a device to remind each person that they were there for their own therapeutic exploration. The discomfort was brought into the open and made explicit, which was a relief to several group members and helped Derek and Annie to resolve the situation.

The incident served as a reminder of the importance of de-roling not only from auxiliary roles but also from the group process. There was a need to make a clear distinction between the therapy group as special place with special rules, and the task of dealing with real life. When life is tough and frustrating it is tempting to invest in the therapy group as a substitute.

Derek's idealised perception of himself in the first role play and his apparent lack of concern in relation to splitting up with his girlfriend are examples of his general style of self-presentation in the group. This could be summarised as a difficulty in accessing, acknowledging and expressing uncomfortable or painful feelings and states of mind. He tended to detract from serious moments in the group and in his musical playing he was rather like a clown. He habitually used a comical sounding rhythm and would look up grinning at the group as if waiting for applause and approval. He occasionally talked about his speech defect being a problem and wanting help with it, but the feelings associated with this were not expressed.

As this musical pattern became apparent, Isabel made a directive intervention to help Derek bypass a mode of playing that had become mechanical and cut off from feeling. She asked him when playing a solo at the start of a session to close his eyes, to forget his rhythm and just play, letting whatever sounds would come out come. It was an effective intervention, allowing a more spontaneous, and seemingly more authentic role to emerge. By closing his eyes Derek was able to let go momentarily of the habitual role of anxious performer seeking approval through clowning. This is not an uncommon life role for people with learning disabilities, a jolly disguise for a real need for recognition, approval and love.

This role was also touched on through psychodramatic work. On one occasion Derek put himself forward to work as protagonist. The warm-up had addressed the theme of need and not having needs met. His ensuing vignette could be entitled Derek's Dummy. The moment of disappointment

sharing. Eventually they were expressed not towards the parental figures in the drama, nor towards the symbolic audience Derek was trying to please, but as hostility towards the protagonist. Sam turned to Derek, laughed, and said 'You're a dummy.' Through this rather attacking pun Sam acknowledged that he understood Derek had been dealing both with his speech difficulties and his learning disabilities in this psychodrama.

Hal

Hal presented as quiet, colourless and withdrawn, his chest hollow and head dropped. He exuded an atmosphere of sadness. When given the opportunity to take on the role of a person who liked him, he chose his one surviving relative, a stepbrother, Bob. I interviewed him in this role.

DIRECTOR: Can you say a few words about your half brother Hal?

HAL *in role as Bob:* All right, he's all right.

It was impossible for him to say anything more committed or more positive about himself. Indeed the noncommital word 'all right' was his stock reply whenever asked how he was feeling. Eventually I asked the group for suggestions of other ways of describing what Bob might like about Hal. They suggested 'sensitive', 'hard working' and 'good fun'. Hal chose Annie to play the auxiliary role and smiled with shy pleasure to hear himself spoken about positively. I was left with the feeling that Hal found it very difficult to make a stand for himself and to give himself love and appreciation. He seemed hungry for validation and recognition, while being almost resigned to hopelessness and to not getting his needs met. His history of neglect had had a predictable effect on his self-image and expectations of the world. Asked why he was so tired in the sessions he replied that he had been up late into the night watching sex films. His experience of real intimacy in the family had been very limited and painful. It was presumably safer to avoid real relationships and vulnerability, and this led him to withdraw frequently in the sessions.

Some time later Hal put himself forward as protagonist to explore his relationship with Bob further. The warm-up discussion had focused on feelings of hurt and anger. The starting point for Hal's drama was the fact that Bob visited him only for fifteen minutes a year. I asked him to show us such a visit, starting from before Bob arrived. Hal set up the scene to show us himself working in the hospital kitchens washing dishes. He was not expecting a visit until a nurse came in to announce that he had a visitor. I asked Hal to role reverse with Bob a few moments before arriving for the visit. From this role he revealed that he had come because of a sense of duty, and that he had brought sweets with him to give to Hal.

Annie was again chosen to play the role of Bob, which she was able to do competently. We played the scene in which Hal and Bob met twice. First, Hal played his stepbrother Bob; then we replayed the scene with him in his own role. The action involved them greeting, Bob giving him the sweets, and Hal preparing a cup of tea and a piece of cake which they ate in the kitchen, Hal's workplace. Hal's style of communication with his stepbrother was apologetic and compliant. He spoke quickly and quietly, checking both with Bob and with me as director if he was doing 'all right'. My analysis of his role was that in the context of meeting with his only relative Hal was compliant, undemanding, and committed to hiding the depth of his feelings. Maybe he was afraid that asking for what he really wanted would drive his brother away and he would be left with nothing.

I acknowledged his having shown us how it is when his brother comes, and invited him within the drama to say what he was feeling and what he really wanted. He found this difficult and was helped by group members doubling 'I want you to stay longer' and 'I wish you would come more often.' He agreed with these doubling statements but when it came to putting them in his own words he asked instead for more sweets and a video film. I decided to check out what his real priorities were.

DIRECTOR: Hal, you have asked for more sweets and a video from Bob. Can I check with you which is more important for you – these presents, or Bob's visit?

HAL: It's the visits, isn't it?

DIRECTOR: I don't know, is it?

HAL: Yes it's the visits.

Isabel suggested Hal use the cymbals, drum and bongos to play his feelings in this scene. He followed this suggestion for a while and stopped. I felt he had not yet expressed his feelings and that he was capable of more, so I made a further suggestion:

DIRECTOR: I would like you to look Bob in the eyes, to say what you want from him, and to use the instruments to support this.

Hal was very receptive to this idea. He came right up to Bob, took his time looking him hard in the eye, and said:

HAL: I want you to come more often… come more often.

DIRECTOR: Anything else?

HAL: An hour, come for an hour. Yes I want you to come for an hour, not fifteen minutes.

Hal took the energy from this assertive request and began to play on the percussion instruments. Isabel played with him, supporting the passion in his playing, and afterwards letting him know that she had picked up the feelings of hurt and anger in the playing. The combination of psychodramatic role work and musical improvisation came into its own druing this intervention.

I asked how we might finish the psychodrama, and suggestions came from the group that Bob should take Hal out in his car. I checked with Hal how that would be and he was pleased with the idea. He wanted to be taken to McDonalds. The scene ended in an upbeat and hopeful mood with the two of them in the car on the way out for a Big Mac. This was a 'surplus reality' scene, one that had not happened in real life, but gave the protagonist a taster of a wished for experience, or one that he he might actually try to create for himself (Moreno in Fox 1987).

In a longer piece of work it would have been appropriate to find out more about Bob's unwillingness or inability to meet Hal's needs. Ultimately it might be useful for Hal to understand his brother's perspective and to find a way of coming to terms with reality. In this psychodrama, however, I was aware of how much of a risk Hal was taking just in daring to acknowledge his needs and feelings. I chose not to follow each potential for investigation as might be possible in a more complex piece of work, but to focus on one major challenge without complicating the issue. This approach is an important adaptation of the method to the needs of the client group. Hal was given the experience of validation by Isabel, myself and the group for having feelings and needs and for beginning to do something very new – express them.

A related issue for Hal was the death of his parents. The tenth anniversary of his father's death was approaching and revealed itself as a significant concern for Hal through a warm-up activity. That session I was aware of it being Derek's fortieth birthday and so was trying to find a warm-up that could lead into exploring hopes and dreams for the future. I have sometimes used a large transparent inflatable ball as a crystal ball to look into. On this occasion I tried a variation on this idea. I introduced an antique pair of binoculars to the group, and invited everyone in turn to hold them, look through them and wait until a dream of their future revealed itself to them, which they could then describe to the group. Devices such as this work differently for different people. Hal was attracted to the magic of the exercise and held the binoculars to his eyes with a real expectation that his dream would be revealed. Hal's usual difficulty with verbal expression was temporarily suspended as he saw a clear image of his personal hope for the future. What he saw was his father's grave, and himself bringing flowers to it in a gesture of remembrance. He remembered that the tenth anniversary of the death was approaching and that it had been several years since he had visited the grave.

He made a request that I help him organise a trip there, which raised an interesting dilemma. Should I encourage him to make the trip at a psychodramatic level only and as part of his therapy? Should the therapeutic work focus on preparing him to ask assertively enough that he be taken to the grave? Or should I help arrange the trip for him as someone with a voice who recognised its importance for him?

I compromised. I recognised the potential value of his going to the grave psychodramatically, but I felt he also had the right to make the trip in reality. We discussed in the group who he would need to ask in order to make the trip a reality and what he would need to say. He agreed to try and do this during the week. By the following session he had not managed to make the request and again asked me for help as the date of the anniversary was approaching. I spoke to the appropriate person and the trip took place.

This had implications in terms of our relationship. I had to some extent provided a magical solution to his desires, at the expense of his finding within himself the appropriate roles to get his needs met in the real world. In terms of the transference that was part of our relationship I was the all-providing mother, the one he had not had in his own life but was still seeking desparately. However I was neither willing nor able to fulfill such a role on a permanent basis. He asked me to set up another visit for him. When I made it clear that I would support him in making it happen but that he would have to do the work himself he withdrew into himself. I had now become the withholding and denying one. His response was an unbearable anger that he could only express passively, by sleeping in sessions, describing himself consistently as 'all right' and contributing very little to the group process. He was doing in the group what he had done in his life. We were stuck.

The eventual shift came through the technique of doubling, both verbal and musical. It was at the start of a session, and everyone else had played their feelings in a solo. Hal was offered the chance to play and for the third week in a row declined, saying 'I'm all right' whilst looking lifeless and withdrawn. I approached him and crouched beside his chair. I asked him if I could double what he might be feeling and reminded him that he could correct me and reject anything that was not quite right. He agreed.

DOUBLE: I say I'm all right but that's because I don't want to say what I'm really feeling. It's not very pleasant.

HAL: Yes, that's right.

DOUBLE: I'm all hunched up with my arms folded, and I'm looking down. It's safer that way. But inside it's painful.

HAL: Yes, it is. I have got feelings.

ANNA/DIRECTOR: Can you tell us about these feelings? Do they have a colour?

HAL: Yes, they're red, aren't they.

I brought over a large red cloth and asked Hal if he could wear it, as an expression of how he was feeling. He put it on and sat down again. I asked if he could play that redness on the instruments. He declined. Isabel asked the group if they knew what red feelings felt like. They did and agreed to play red for Hal. Nick, who had problems owning his own feelings said that he had no red feelings of his own but that he could act them. He went to fetch a mask, and put on a red hat with a stuffed shark sticking out of the front. He was in role, a place where he could safely access strong feelings, and the group was ready. The sound that emerged was loud and full of energy in stark contrast to the way Hal had been in the preceding weeks. He looked up and smiled as he listened. When we finished playing I asked him how he found it. He replied 'all right' and laughed. I asked him if the music expressed the way he felt, and he said that it did. I felt it was important that he make some small expression of that feeling himself, so invited him to stand up in his red cloak, to stand tall and to raise his head. This was a challenge to Hal to begin to inhabit and own the red role himself. He was able to do this briefly, helped by my having doubled him verbally, and the group having doubled him musically.

Annie

Hal was by no means the only member of the group who had difficulty with anger. Nick's destructive impulses had led to his committing arson on many occasions, but he had great difficulty in recognising any of his own feelings as anything other than 'happy'. Sam's room bore testimony to his uncontrolled outbursts. Tom's body had suffered self-inflicted fractures, Derek destroyed radios on a regular basis and got into fights with other residents, while Annie had a history of cutting herself.

It was Annie who first chose to work directly on this theme after the group had been working together for six months. She had shared with us both directly and indirectly that she experienced her feelings as unmanage-able. At an indirect level she communicated this problem for the first few weeks via her relationship with the coffee break at the end of each session. She would ask how many cups of coffee she would be allowed to drink. When the time came for the break, whether we limited the number of cups or not it was never enough. She became tense, excited and verbally abusive. She had been able to use the main part of the sessions very well with an adult approach to the therapeutic space and the structures offered. At the end of the session however she showed us a much younger, less contained and more needy role. She talked in a confused way about getting an injection to calm her down. I checked with her whether that was something she wanted and to my surprise she said that it was. I addressed myself in a quiet and matter of fact voice to her inner adult role and suggested that if what she wanted was an injection she should simply ask the nursing staff for one directly, when she got back to her ward and save herself all the distress she was going through. This seemed to be a helpful intervention for her, reminding her that she had some control over herself. She started to talk to herself in a calming way. The issue of the coffee lost its loadedness for her from this time. The incident, at the periphery of the session, served to let the therapists and the group know how overwhelming her anxiety and anger could be and that she had a problem containing herself at times of distress. As therapists it was important for us to notice the ongoing life roles of group members in the here and now of the group. Role analysis was as relevant here as in the formal psychodramas.

There were some occasions when Annie declined to use the opportunity to play her feelings musically at the beginning of the session. She suggested that it would be too destructive or overwhelming. When given assurance that the instruments could take her anger and would not be hurt, she was sometimes able to play. One session she allowed herself to play but expressed some concern that there might be too much anger to keep the focus on the instruments. I brought over the large solid foam ball that I use for trust work and placed it by her side instructing her to pummel it with her fists and use her voice if she felt unable to keep hold of her musical beaters. She was reassured by this added safety net and used both instruments and ball to share her angry feelings with the group.

The day of Annie's first piece of work as protagonist she arrived at the session early, holding out her hand as she entered the studio to show me a fresh line of stitches across her wrist where she had cut herself two days before with the glass from a broken picture. She asked me 'What are we going to do about it? What can I do?' I suggested she might use the group to explore why she had done this to herself.

On arrival of the rest of the group the first warm-up involved passing a small ball around the circle as a device for focusing on each person in turn. When each person held the ball they were invited to share with the group one feeling state they had experienced at some point during the week. Annie's word was 'anger'. Those who wished to followed this warm-up with musical solos and some reflections on how they had played. Anger was a common theme at this time. When it came to Annie's turn to play she stood up and began to play explosively, then stopped abruptly, pointing out that she must not damage her stitches. She asked how her playing had sounded. I said 'Like a start'. Isabel suggested the whole group could play Annie's feelings for her from what we had sensed so far. Annie sat down, and we all took up beaters, faced her, and played with passion. The matching of our playing with her feelings was moving. She beat time with clenched fists at first, in encouragement, then stopped and seemed to just listen to the sounds as they resonated with her own feelings. She was tearful.

When the playing stopped I moved over to her and rested a hand on her back.

DIRECTOR: There seems to be a lot of sadness in there too.

ANNIE: Yes, what can we do?

DIRECTOR: Tell the group what happened. Not everyone knows.

ANNIE: I got so angry I broke a picture and cut myself.

DIRECTOR: Would you like to hear how people in the group feel about that?

ANNIE: Yes.

(Each person is given time to reflect, and shares a response, ranging from anger, disapproval, horror to sadness)

DIRECTOR: Can you each come over and be close to Annie, support her with your different responses.

(The whole group moves over physically to join Annie, expressing support through closeness and the willingness to move for her.)

I checked with Annie if she wanted to use the group to explore why she had done what she had done. She was keen to, and the group agreed to support the work. We moved across to the action area of the room, and I turned on the red lights.

Annie set up a scene to show us what led up to her cutting herself. I asked her to choose someone to play the part of her arm. We needed to separate out the two roles of aggressor and victim that she had given expression to within the arena of her own body. The person she chose to play her wounded arm was Tom, a man who had done himself great injury on one occasion. She intuitively knew that he would understand the role. In role reversal with the arm she acknowledged the pain she was feeling.

Two other group members were put in role as nurses and we began to explore the incident that had led to her self-injury.

NURSES: You can't have any pudding. You can't have what you want.

Hearing these lines put Annie in touch with the feelings prior to her cutting herself. She asked for the big foam ball to be brought into the scene. Its symbolic and concrete association for her as a safe place to put her aggression was well established by now.

As the nurses repeated their message to Annie she became angry and agitated and mimed how she channeled those feelings into cutting herself. I asked her to put the feelings into the ball instead. Three group members joined her, hammering with their fists on the ball. I asked her to find the words within the actions.

ANNIE: Give me a banana. Give me pudding. Give me what I want. I hate not getting what I want. I'm so furious. I'm frustrated. I don't know what to do. I could kill myself. I don't know what to do.

DIRECTOR: Is there someone who would know what to do, who could advise you here?

ANNIE: Yes, Lyn, another nurse.

DIRECTOR: Be her. What do you want to say to Annie here?

ANNIE as Lyn: These are bad nurses. I'm very cross with them.

I was unsure whether the nurses had really denied Annie her pudding, or whether there was a similar dynamic as she had created in our group around the coffee. If the energy of the psychodrama went simply into blaming the nurses for not meeting her every need this would be an avoidance of her tackling her difficulty in tolerating any disappointment.

DIRECTOR: That may be, but what do you think of Annie cutting herself when she can't get what she wants?

ANNIE as Lyn (angrily towards the auxiliary holding Annie's role): Very bad, that's very bad. You mustn't. You must be good.

We were in danger of getting lost in the need to be the conforming good girl, or patient patient. This would encourage the very repression that can contribute to overwhelming outbursts of aggression. The role of Lyn the advisor seemed to to consist of three parts: blaming the other nurses from the same perspective as Annie but with more authority; appropriate anger with Annie's self-destructive actions; and a repressive request for her to be good. I asked Annie to return to her own role.

DIRECTOR *to the three nurses:* Tell me, do you always get your own way?

NURSES: No, not at all.

DIRECTOR: And do you attack yourself in this way like Annie?

NURSES: No.

DIRECTOR: What do you think of Annie doing that?

NURSE 1 *(Sam, in touch with real fury walks away from the scene. He is asked to return and bring his feelings into the drama. He goes up to the ball and beats it passionately, then sits down in role as the nurse.)*

ANNIE *(having witnessed the incident):* I'm sorry. Once I nearly killed myself with it, nearly went up there and didn't come back. That's terrible.

DIRECTOR: Do you want to do that again?

ANNIE: No.

DIRECTOR: Well, you have a choice. What could you do instead?

ANNIE: Put it in the ball.

DIRECTOR: Yes, you can bring your feelings to a safe place, to therapy. Good, what else?

ANNIE: Say what I'm feeling.

NURSE 2: You could go to your room when you're angry and sit down.

ANNIE: I could try. And I'll bring it to the ball and say what I'm feeling.

As director I was satisfied with this for the moment. It might be tempting in a longer psychodrama to investigate the history and origins of Annie's behaviour. For now I was pleased she had seen the connexion between her self-injury and her anger and that we had identified the context as situations where she does not get fed in the way she wants. She had recognised therapy as a safe place for her anger, and the ball as a more appropriate object to get the brunt of her rage. I felt we needed to round the piece of work up, and that to do this she would need to reconnect with her arm.

DIRECTOR: Good, that's better than putting your life at risk for the sake of a banana. What's more important, your pudding or your life?

ANNIE: My life.

DIRECTOR: Yes. Now look at your wounded arm here *(indicating the auxiliary Tom)*. Before we finish I would like you to say something kind to this arm.

ANNIE: *(reaching across to Tom, and looking at him, tenderly)* Precious arm... please be healed... bless you.

DIRECTOR: Reverse roles and hear this. *(Annie needed to hear this message from the role of the injured arm, the wounded one as well as the aggressor. It would also be useful for Tom to say these words in the light of his own history of self-injury.)*

In the sharing Sam, who had become so angry in the drama, showed the group his own scarred wrist and recollected the day he broke all the windows in his workplace with an outburst of destructive anger. Others in the group were less able to share how they connected with Annie's work, but over the following sessions links were made and it was clear that her psychodrama had not only been relevant to the group as a whole but had also enabled a shift within the group. Hal, for example, whose work I have described above, made a small but significant change in the group the following session. First, he volunteered enthusiastically to play his own feelings in a solo. Some minutes later, when Annie asked the group to help her play the sheer volume of her anger he stood up to join in, took a red beater from my hand and played with energy and enjoyment. This was a new role for Hal. My sense is that he was able to inhabit this role partly because of his own personal work, but also through having witnessed the group as an adequate container for Annie's work the previous week. The psychodramatic method is sometimes seen as giving one-off therapy experiences through a piece of work. With this client group the therapeutic value stems at least equally from the ongoing group process within the culture of psychodrama.

The Coming Together of Music and Drama in Moments of Musical Psychodrama

Tom

Tom began to access a new life role quite early on in the group process when he realised that he could give expression to his feelings musically. He presented habitually as a caricature of a rigid country gentleman, with a stiff upper lip and very firm beliefs about not talking about certain things, especially relating to sexuality and feelings. He was given encouragement to allow his feelings expression both through the drama and through musical expression. In both modes he was allowed some distance from the feelings, which could be expressed via role and metaphor in the case of drama, and via a musical instrument in the case of music. When he first touched on powerful feelings through musical solos he stopped abruptly and retreated. With guidance from Isabel he gradually learned that it felt better, and was safe to stay with the feelings until a moment of natural completion in the music.

After several months he reached a new level in his playing. He arrived at the session talking about colleagues of his having teased him during the week, in particular about the senseitive subject of sex. He was offended and had asked to move to a different workplace on a different site. When he played his solo there was a clear sense of anger, which was directed precisely at a cymbal, a drum and a pair of bongos. He struck these with deliberate and considered aggression, and with a single strong blow, almost as if he were saying, 'Take that!' After his playing Isabel asked about the feelings he had been playing.

ISABEL: How did that feel?

TOM: Happy.

ISABEL: Happy? It seemed very strong, and you hit those instruments very precisely.

TOM: Yes, I was happy.

Tom was having some difficulty finding words to describe the feeling he was playing. He may have felt happy about playing, but the feelings evoked by his music and his appearance whilst playing suggested that something other than 'happiness' was being expressed. At this point I remembered what Tom had been talking about on arrival at the session. I decided to take the plunge of regarding the instruments as roles or characters in his life. I stood up and pointed to each of the instruments he had hit with such sharp precision, asking 'If this were a person who would it be?' He responded without hesitation with the names of the colleagues who had been teasing him. The 'happy' feeling he had mentioned was the happiness of leaving his work placement with them, and a positive feeling of triumph in being able to find work elsewhere. The exchange highlights a characteristic difficulty with the client group in identifying the right words to express feelings. 'Happy' is a word that usually brings a positive response from others, and so becomes the word of choice when asked 'How do you feel?'

That session continued with Annie's work on self-injuring, in which Tom played her wounded arm. As someone who had harmed himself this role touched on issues of his own, and I was interested to see what impact the work would have on him. The following session he arrived early, limping and talking about having knocked some jars onto his foot accidentally. He said he was in pain. His entrance seemed to be making a clear subtextual statement about his own capacity to self-injure: 'Look, see my wound too, see what I do to myself.'

His playing was, like the previous week's, full of powerful aggression, and I asked again who the different instruments could represent. This time he responded 'Me, they are all me. I'm angry with myself.' He was sitting next to Annie, and, remembering his difficulty in sharing after her work the previous week, I reminded him of her psychodrama. She too gets angry with herself and hurts herself. I asked them if they had something in common there, and both agreed that they did. This process of making connexions and identifications in psychodrama is usually part of the sharing. With this client group there is sometimes a reluctance to identify with the problems of others and acknowledge similarities. The process of sharing can take several sessions and occur indirectly and outside of the designated moment for sharing. The therapist may need to help build the bridges and find the appropriate moment to bring the connexions into consciousness.

Trudy

Trudy's participation in the group was a challenge. She had great difficulty in staying with the more powerful moments. She seemed to value the sessions, but was often unable to give to others. She wanted attention for herself, but the only way she seemed to know how to get it was by withholding or withdrawing. She had several ways of doing this. During a piece of psychodramatic work she often retreated away from the action to the back of the studio. Here she might curl up in front of a heater, or go to sleep at a table, with her back to the action and the group. When playing instrumental solos she chose to play only the xylophone week after week, and that in a hypnotic way that served to cut herself off from the group rather than contact them. Isabel often had to break her trance in order to get her to stop playing and remember the other people present.

The problem was tackled in several ways. Initially the group tried to encourage her to join in. At first this seemed to work, then she needed more and more encouragement, and still preferred to withhold. We tried inviting her to join in when she was ready and not make a fuss if she chose to sit out. Again this had some success, but inconsistently. Eventually some group members expressed irritation with her to the therapists, but not to her directly. They felt she did not deserve a drink after the session, or that she should perhaps be excluded from the goodbye song.

On one occasion I joined her at her table where she had been sitting with her back to the group and her head on the table. I followed a strategy of making minimal and manageable demands that she could meet rather than requesting full participation. I asked her first, if she could hear me; then if she could raise her head from the table; then if she were prepared to listen to me. She managed to assent to all of these. Having got her attention I asked her if she could find a way of joining in with what was happening in the group. She replied that she did not want to. I reminded her that the group was about looking at our hopes and fears and memories and dreams, assured her that I realised that this was difficult and painful for her, but asked her if she would at least think about staying with what we were doing. She consented to think about it, and found her way into role work the following week.

She was able to take on positive roles, such as a mother stuffing a turkey, or a little girl playing with a snowman. On this occasion she decided, half way through a scene, that she wanted to be the snowman rather than the little girl. I decided not to meet this child-like and omnipotent request, which would have meant taking the role away from the auxiliary already in role. Instead I suggested that the little girl was envious of the snowman and could play at being a snowman. She agreed that the little girl was indeed envious. She was able to own this feeling from within the drama, at some distance from the actual dynamics of the group, where she was also manifestly deeply envious and jealous.

It was through a combination of the music and dramatic imagery, however, that the problem was tackled most successfully. Month after month the group had witnessed her playing hypnotically on the xylophone. One session whilst I watched her play an image came to mind of Trudy isolated and unreachable on an island. I knew she was familiar with Cornwall, and so I told her and the group that I could see her standing on St Michael's Mount, surrounded by the sea, and cut off from the rest of us. She knew the place and liked the image, agreeing that it expressed how she felt too. I told her that when I experienced her as cut off I wanted to wave at her and shout across to her, 'Trudy, we're here.' I demonstrated with energy what I meant, my own feelings of frustration being quite strong by now. The group shared the same feelings, and joined in. She stood in the middle with her xylophone, surrounded by the whole group calling to her, waving at her. She waved back, made eye contact, and smiled.

The image and action became a device for the group to contact Trudy, either when she was playing hypnotically, or at other times when she seemed to enter her own world. Initially she could not both play and keep connexion with others. She would play until called, and would then look up and stop. Gradually she learnt to play and keep eye contact with me. She was slowly becoming more present in the group.

On one occasion I took a further risk. She had maintained eye contact and awareness of the group whilst playing, but still refused to touch any instrument other than the xylophone, which on this occasion she played with more energy. I had a beater in my hand and reached across to tap the cymbal whilst she was playing. She looked up at me, stopped playing and sat down. Isabel asked her how she felt in the playing and she said 'Miserable, because I had to stop.' My one beat on the cymbal had had the power to make her stop. Isabel invited her to try again and not to let me stop her. She doubled her in the playing, giving her musical support in holding her ground. Every time I beat the cymbal she answered back, not only on the xylophone but also on the bongos, drums, and cymbal. She was beaming with pride. At one point Sam came up and started to play the bongos noisily. Trudy managed to stand up to him too. The group as a whole applauded her at the end, aware of how major a shift she had made. I felt we had reached the climax of an ongoing psychodrama that had been going on for many months in the group process.

In classical psychodrama, when a new role has been learnt and old patterns have been confronted the protagonist is encouraged to strengthen the new role through role training. This often takes the form of returning to a scene where the protagonist has experienced difficulty, and where he or she applies the new role. In the case of Trudy's piece of work Sam called the whole group to attention at the end of the session. He insisted on total silence, then asked Trudy to agree in future to not cut herself off from the group and not restrict herself to the xylophone in her playing. She contracted to do this, and significantly the therapeutic agent in this case was a fellow group member.

Conclusion

I have described some of the adaptatations to the psychodramatic method, and given some instances of work in action. The use of psychodrama with this client group is not without problems. However, the work was valued by the clients, perhaps even because it is challenging. As a psychodramatist I felt that the method gave much needed opportunities for direct therapeutic work, and I was sometimes surprised at the positive way the group was able to use their weekly sessions. It was paramount for the therapeutic team to remain flexible in terms of the method, allowing the focus to shift between individual and group, between drama, music and talking with fluidity and patience.

References

Bettleheim, B. (1976) *The Uses of Enchantment; The Meaning and Importance of Fairy Tales.* Harmonsdworth: Penguin.

Blatner, M. D., with Blatner, A. (1988) *Foundations of Psychodrama, History, Theory and Practice.* New York: Springer Publishing Company.

Chesner, A. (1994a) An integrated model of dramatherapy and its application with adults with learning disabilities. In S. Jennings *et al. The Handbook of Dramatherapy.* London: Routledge.

Chesner, A. (1994b) Dramatherapy and psychodrama: similarities and differences. In S. Jennings *et al. The Handbook of Dramatherapy.* London: Routledge.

Clegg, J.A. (1993) Putting people first: A social constructionist approach to learning disability. *British Journal of Clinical Psychology, 32,* 389–406.

Estés, C.P. (1992) *Women who Run with the Wolves; Contacting the Power of the Wild Woman.* London: Rider.

Fox, J. (ed) (1987) *The Essential Moreno; Writings on Psychodrama, Group Method, and Spontaneity by J.L. Moreno.* New York: Springer Publishing Company.

Grimm (1984) *The Complete Illustrated Stories of The Brothers Grimm.* London: Chancellor Press.

Jennings, S. (1978) *Remedial Drama.* London: A.C. Black.

Jennings, S. (1986) *Creative Drama in Groupwork.* London: Winslow Press.

Jennings, S. (1987) Dramatherapy and groups. In S. Jennings (ed) *Dramatherapy Theory and Practice for Teachers and Clinicians.* London: Routledge.

Jennings, S. and Minde, Å. (1993) *Art Therapy and Dramatherapy: Masks of the Soul.* London: Jessica Kingsley Publishers.

Landy, R. (1986) *Drama Therapy Concepts and Practices.* Springfield Il.: Charles C. Thomas.

Opie, I. and Opie, P. (1974) *The Classic Fairy Tales.* Oxford: Oxford University Press.

Roheim, G. (1992) *Fire in the Dragon; and Other Psychoanalytic Essays on Folklore.* Princeton: Princeton University Press.

Sherborne, V. (1990) *Developmental Movement for Children: Mainstream, Special Needs and Pre-School.* Cambridge: Cambridge University Press.

Sinason, V. (1992) *Mental Handicap and The Human Condition, New Approaches from the Tavistock.* London: Free Association Books.

Shakespeare, W. (1993) *The Phoenix and The Turtle.* New York: Barnes and Noble Inc./Yale University Press.

Useful Addresses

For further information on professional training courses, contact:
British Association for Dramatherapists
5 Sunnydale Villas
Durlston Road
Swanage
Dorset
BH19 2HY

British Psychodrama Association
8 Rahere Road
Cowley
Oxford
OX4 3QG

'Soundbeam' is a registered trademark. Enquires to:
Unit 3
Highbury Villas
Kingsdown
Bristol
BS2 8BX

Subject Index